The Power of a PhD

"If you're a PhD struggling to get hired in industry, you absolutely need *The Power of a PhD*! In it, Isaiah demystifies the hiring process so that you can abandon the harmful misconceptions currently hampering your job search. Isaiah incisively breaks down the steps needed to develop and implement a highly effective strategy to land yourself a coveted role at a top company."

- Camillia Smith Barnes, PhD, Google

"*The Power of a PhD* addresses the pain experienced by PhDs all over the world when they start thinking about transitioning to industry jobs. Isaiah Hankel sets out to alleviate this pain by clearly laying out the rules of the game. *The Power of a PhD* is filled with rich insights into what employers are looking for and what PhDs must do to effectively distill their experience and bring out the most relevant aspects of their experience and interests in their job search. Isaiah effectively turns the whole job searching process on its head by working backwards from the employer's perspective rather than following a forward-looking plan from the perspective of a PhD scholar. Isaiah not only lays out a blueprint for what a PhD should do to make the job searching strategy a delightful endeavor, but also shows the reader what not to do in their own job-hunting process. Having personally followed its strategy, I can vouch for how successful its job hunting process was for me. I highly recommend reading this wonderful book to any PhD who wants to make their job-hunting process a systematic and well-oiled machine!

- Harshavardhan Sundar, PhD, Amazon

"*The Power of a PhD* is the no nonsense tough love kick up the backside that so many of us PhDs need as we navigate our way into a new and unfamiliar world. Dr. Isaiah Hankel draws from over a decade of experience supporting tens of thousands of PhDs in their transitions to successful industry careers. He distills the most essential key learnings into accessible bite sized digestible guidance that anyone with a PhD can leverage to boost their career development regardless of the specialty or direction. As a PhD in my fourth industry role, I found the take home messages are still relevant as I continue to adjust and adapt to diverse teams who have varying levels of experience working with PhDs and who may still need appropriate communication in order to understand our value. This work is a brilliant contribution to our community and one that will serve to lift up PhDs for years to come."

- Rebecca Sweet, PhD, Janssen Pharmaceuticals

"It's been said that success doesn't happen by accident. *The Power of a PhD* highlights the tough questions PhDs need to ask themselves before setting out on that journey towards becoming a successful industry professional. Isaiah stresses how this is not a trial-and-error experiment you would run in the lab. Instead, he goes step by step into the proper techniques for presenting yourself in your résumé all the way through negotiating a job offer. I wish I could have read *The Power of a PhD* a year before I graduated!"

- Brenton Ware, PhD, Medtronic

"Isaiah asks the relevant questions and forces you to define what you want in a career. Instead of chasing job titles as a job search strategy which Isaiah masterfully equates to taking rat poison, *The Power of a PhD* forces you to think about where you want to be on the spectrum of diverse roles and what truly will make you happy professionally. Isaiah successfully incorporates case studies to shine a clear light on the successes of being more strategic in valuing your PhD experiences. PhDs beware, after reading *The Power of a PhD*, there's no excuse for not taking proven steps to achieve the career you desire."

- Ralph Hazlewood, PhD, Regeneron

"I have known Isaiah for a while as a member of the Cheeky Scientist Association and I am grateful for what they taught me for my transition. Yet, *The Power of a PhD* has surprised me with a simple, didactic and organized framework, as well as groundbreaking real-life examples of success, providing food for thought for my next step. *The Power of a PhD* came to me during a turbulent time, and was fundamental to help me structure an objective and powerful plan towards safer and happier professional grounds. Thank you so much, Isaiah!"

- Elisa Maria Guimarães de Souza, PhD, Johnson & Johnson

"'*The Power of a PhD*'" is a MUST-read book for any PhD! It highlights the essential skills one would acquire during their academic journey and explains how they can be used to better an organization...If you want to learn how to land a highly-paid industry job in which you will bring forth your personal and academic strengths, you need *The Power of a PhD*. In fact, I would suggest using it as a syllabus book for the "What can I do with my PhD after I graduate" course that should be added to all PhD programs."

- Orly Levitan, PhD, Chief Scientist at HyGIeaCare Inc.

"Don't just be a creator of information. Instead, read *The Power of a PhD* to learn how to brilliantly communicate your PhD skills to get hired into an industry role and make progress throughout your professional career by leaving the academic mindset and developing revolutionary professional habits."

- Dignesh Shah, PhD, ThinkSono

"*The Power of a PhD* will help you target your fulfilling industry job and provide you with a plan for getting you there. The job search methodology taught in it has already placed thousands of PhDs into industry career positions. Many PhDs trapped in an academic mindset may think that luck is required to land a successful and fulfilling industry job. However, as Thomas Jefferson once said, "I'm a great believer in luck, and I find the harder I work, the more I have of it." *The Power of a PhD* gives you the steps required to work harder and more efficiently in your job search. In the competition to get a job, it is not the most qualified person who gets hired, it is the person who executes the job search most effectively. *The Power of a PhD* will help you execute your job search more effectively than your competition. Isaiah doesn't pull punches when correctly identifying moments where you stand in the way of your own success. *The Power of a PhD* is not merely a step-by-step guide to getting a job, it highlights negative habits and tendencies that are preventing you from achieving success on your job search and beyond."

- John Klecker, PhD, Cedilla Therapeutics

THE
POWER
of a PhD

*How Anyone
Can Use Their PhD to
Get Hired in Industry*

Dr. Isaiah Hankel
Founder of Cheeky Scientist

NEW YORK

LONDON • NASHVILLE • MELBOURNE • VANCOUVER

The Power of a PhD

How Anyone Can Use Their PhD to Get Hired in Industry

Published in New York, New York, by Morgan James Publishing. Morgan James is a trademark of Morgan James, LLC. www.MorganJamesPublishing.com

Proudly distributed by Ingram Publisher Services.

Morgan James BOGO™

A **FREE** ebook edition is available for you or a friend with the purchase of this print book.

CLEARLY SIGN YOUR NAME ABOVE

Instructions to claim your free ebook edition:
1. Visit MorganJamesBOGO.com
2. Sign your name CLEARLY in the space above
3. Complete the form and submit a photo of this entire page
4. You or your friend can download the ebook to your preferred device

ISBN 9781631958465 paperback
ISBN 9781631958472 ebook
Library of Congress Control Number:
2021951967

Cover Design by:
Chris Treccani
www.3dogcreative.net

Interior Design by:
Christopher Kirk
www.GFSstudio.com

Morgan James is a proud partner of Habitat for Humanity Peninsula and Greater Williamsburg. Partners in building since 2006.

Get involved today! Visit MorganJamesPublishing.com/giving-back

Table of Contents
· ·

Acknowledgments

· ·

This book is for every professor, teacher, mentor, family member, and friend who inspired me during the decades I spent in academia. My deepest thanks to those rare few who pushed me to achieve more than I ever thought possible and who never let their own ambitions or perspectives limit my potential.

To the science teachers who poured knowledge into me while letting me be myself as a young student, including Mr. Revis at Mountain View Middle School, Mr. Bartlett at East Valley High School, and Dr. Clara Moore at Franklin & Marshall College—thank you.

To my PhD thesis committee members who rigorously trained and encouraged me and who were kind to me, even during my darkest hours in graduate school, including Dr. Thomas Waldschmidt, Dr. Robert Cornell, and Dr. Paul Rothman—thank you.

To all the Cheeky Scientist Associates around the world, thank you for taking your careers and your lives into your own hands to achieve your biggest dreams. Your actions have inspired countless other PhDs to do the same. The world needs you now more than ever. Keep stretching yourselves. Keep adding value, and keep remembering how valuable you are as PhDs.

To everyone at Team Cheeky, thank you for making it possible to help PhDs around the world remember their value, get into their dream careers, and have a positive impact on the world.

To my wife, Laura, thank you for your love, guidance, and advice as I have navigated the challenges of growing a business, being a husband and a father, and writing this book. I could not have done any of these things without you. I love you.

To my daughters, Zara and Eve, thank you for making every day fun and for keeping my life in perspective. I love you both.

To my mom and dad, Karen and John Hankel, and my brother and sister, Noah and Jessica Hankel, thank you for your constant love and support.

To Morgan James Publishing for helping me bring this book into the world.

Foreword

· · · · · · · · · · · · · · · · · · · ·

W hen Isaiah asked me to write the foreword of his book, I found myself enveloped in effervescence. I truly was touched because Isaiah is a person who has inspired and impressed me since our very first meeting. It certainly helps that I feel he and I have true synergy in our life missions. We both enable people to look ahead, break free from their shackles, transform their lives, and realize their most sought-after goals.

Our paths intersected because he knew the power of LinkedIn® to conduct a successful job search. Isaiah reached out to me because my business specializes in LinkedIn®. My team and I empower professionals through career branding, by building success into their brands and aligning their stories to their goals. By optimizing clients' profiles, opportunity collides with them. I saw early on the professional opportunities available through LinkedIn® and how the platform leveled the playing field for every professional, regardless of title or background, in managing reputation, growing their brand, and positioning themselves for their career vision. As I worked with professionals, Isaiah was empowering PhDs to enter into the private sector. He knew LinkedIn® was the tool for them to find success.

Isaiah created a community of engaged PhDs, hungry to use their education, knowledge, and mental strength and persistence as a competitive edge in the professional world. It was after joining his Cheeky Scientist Association that I began to understand the true depth of what Isaiah was providing to his community. The Association was a family of PhDs who spent their lives studying and researching, felt stuck, unsupported, and alone. Isaiah gave them the confidence, motivation, and inspiration in addition to actual professional training. He provided the PhDs with impetus to change their lives and pivot in a more fruitful direction. These success stories of PhDs, who put his advice to use, changed their future vision, and found new, fulfilling, and well-paying careers outside of academia were inspiring and refreshing.

Even though I knew he was guiding and impacting his audience, I never truly understood what was driving his mission. It was during a podcast commercial break when I saw a video interview of Isaiah speaking of his own background as a PhD. He spoke of the hard work he had put into his career. Regardless of his dedication, there was an extreme lack of support in the academic world. The respect I had for him magnified, realizing that he once had been in his audience's shoes and now dedicates his life to empowering others so they would not have the negative experience he had, and they could find the right path in order to soar.

For you, your doctorate may have been your goal and vision. Know that there is more out there for you and it's time to pivot, to use all that you have acquired through years of dedication and research in a new way. This book is the tool that will help you take your strengths and abilities and create a new vision and ultimately a new future for yourself.

Most people do not understand that growth and success are forged because of sustained moments of discomfort, anxiety, and fear. Hopefully this book will trigger those feelings inside you, which will then lead to your growth and lead you outside your comfort zone and into that next chapter of your life. Keep your eye on the future you envision for yourself. Put your trust in Isaiah.

You have the power to determine your story and your future. The fact that you are reading this foreword should tell you that you are ready. It is your time right now to soar high and dream big! You too can live an inspired life! The instructions are right here, just keep reading.

Donna Serdula
Founder of Vision Board Media and LinkedIn®-Makeover.com
Author of *LinkedIn® Profile Optimization for Dummies*

Preface

Why I Now Feel Sorry for My Academic Advisor

· · · · · · · · · · · · · · · · · · · ·

"First principle: never to let one's self be beaten down by persons or by events."

— Marie Curie, PhD

"Answer me! I'm the boss!" my advisor yelled.

The whole lab fell quiet.

My advisor yelled again, "Answer me right now, or I'll write a letter to your department, and you'll never get your PhD!"

At that, the lab next to us fell quiet too. The professor managing the lab next door had closed his office door when my advisor started yelling. At the time I just thought this other professor didn't want to get involved, but now I see him as one more person scared and broken by the academic system.

I sat frozen, completely unable to compute what was happening. My professor stormed over to me, grabbed my arm, and shouted in my face one more time, "Do you understand me!?"

I meekly said, "Yes, okay."

He let go of my arm and walked away. Everyone acted like nothing had happened. I packed up my stuff and left the lab for the day. I went to the dean's office, but he only acted surprised by the incident and didn't seem to be able to offer much help.

A Common Problem

That incident with my professor was not isolated. The lack of accountability with no system for correcting poor management, let alone bullying, harassment, or other extreme cases of inappropriate behavior, was a common problem I ran into in academia repeatedly. A report by *Nature* defines this problem clearly:

> "The 'feudal' master-servant relationship existing between a PhD supervisor and his or her student has another facet seldom broached by academics. That is bullying. Employment legislation prohibits bullying at work, but, because PhDs are not salaried or contracted, they are not legally 'employees' and so are vulnerable to capricious supervisors."[1]

A report by *The Guardian* further explains why this problem has continued over the past fifteen years:

> "In other industries, the human resources departments are really strong on bullying, and if there is any accusation of bullying, it's taken seriously. But in academia, there's a culture that the line manager or head of department has absolute power. They can make or break your career, and people very rarely [get help]. I have spent several years working for a drug company and there the climate was much more professional. You were trained to look after the people in your group and to look out for any warning signs ... universities are 10 or 20 years behind."[2]

A few weeks after my advisor's outburst, I received an email from him informing me that a date had been set for my thesis defense and there was no need to come back to the lab. The entire downward spiral with my advisor happened because I wanted to get an industry job and I challenged my professor's authority. Like a lot of PhDs, I thought this was my fault. I thought I was alone. Later I found that what I experienced was extremely common, a result of an academic system that was systemically failing PhD students like me all around the world. And not only was the system failing me and other PhD students, but it was also failing PhDs across the entirety of academia, including postdoctoral researchers (postdocs) and professors like my advisor.

James Lane Allen, an American novelist from Transylvania University, once wrote, "Adversity does not build character, it reveals it." The adversity my advisor was facing exposed his poor character—nothing more or less. As PhDs, we all face moments of weakness in which the pressure of academia and the poverty-level compensation for our efforts break us temporarily.

What happened the day I left the lab wasn't entirely my advisor's fault. After all, he was older and was brought up in academia during a different time. In the 1970s, over 70 percent of professors would go on to get tenure, and 80 percent of faculty were full-time.[3] Considering that, he couldn't fathom why anyone would complete a PhD program only to leave academia. He told me I was a foolish failure for wanting to leave academia; therefore, I was not worth his time. He hadn't come to terms with how much the world had changed since he got his PhD. During my last year of graduate school, I remember reading a report by *The Royal Society* that found that only 0.45 percent of PhDs now become full-time professors.[4]

I thought: *What? How is this possible? Why am I here then? Am I chasing something that won't exist in a few years?*

The answer I arrived at was "yes" as the data I continued finding told a darker and darker story.

The Failure of Academia

The average graduate student across all fields now takes 8.2 years to get their PhD and is thirty-three years old by the time they defend.[5] Up to 80 percent of those PhDs end up unemployed or in low-paying postdoc and teaching assistant positions, which, according to the government, are training positions rather than real employment.[6] The average time spent in postdoc positions has swelled from just one year to anywhere from six to ten years—what is now referred to as "chasing postdocs."[7] Worse still is that universities have started to hide how many postdocs they have by labeling senior postdocs as "nonfaculty staff" or "research associates," even though the PhDs in these positions continue to get paid very poorly without access to any retirement benefits or, in some cases, healthcare. Full-time professorships have been replaced by poorly paid "professor in title only" part-time, adjunct, and contract professorships, which is why the *New York Times* recently dubbed academia as "Adjunctatopia."[8]

PhDs have gone from being revered experts the world relies on to invisible laborers trapped in a pyramid scheme supporting only a handful of full-time professors.

This is why there is, as *The Boston Globe* frames it, a "Glut of PhDs,"[9] which has resulted in, as *Policy Options Politiques* describes it, a "PhD employment crisis" that is "systemic" and can't be fixed.[10] It's also why so many PhDs dream of transitioning out of academia, even though they have no idea how to do so.

To my academic advisor, it was unimaginable that a PhD as deep into their academic career as I was would not want to be a professor. When he was in graduate school, professors were untouchable. They could do and say anything they wanted. They could call postdocs dumb, threaten to fire international PhDs and have them deported, and yell at graduate students with no repercussions. He withstood this behavior from his professors, and it was his turn to be on the other end of it. Most professors could get tenure when he was in graduate school, and it was a near impossibility to get fired for anything—ever. Things were different by the time I came through graduate school. My advisor didn't want to see it, but he knew what was happening. He knew academia was failing systemically and everything he had invested in was crumbling around him.

I Used to Want to be My Advisor

For the first two years of graduate school, I wanted to be just like my advisor. I started graduate school in 2006 with one of the largest entering classes of PhD students at the university. I quickly found a lab that was doing exciting research and started spending eighteen-hour days there—seriously, eighteen-hour days. I was so eager to impress my professor that I stayed in the lab until he went home. The second day I was in the lab, I got there at 8 a.m. and stayed until 2 a.m. the next morning. In retrospect, that was a horrible decision. After I did that, I was expected to work until at least 10 p.m. every night, but I didn't mind the work because it was all new and exciting. At the time, my advisor was happy. He had just gotten his first Research Project Grant (R01) funded a year earlier. He was running a new lab, and government funding was still relatively high. The future looked bright. My advisor was not only happy at the time, but his behavior was positive, logical, and alluring. He seemed to know everything. He had money and seemingly had power. He was buying new instruments left and right, and he let us buy whatever reagents we wanted. It was like he didn't have a care in the world. He would buy us at least six pizzas from the best pizza shop in town at every lab meeting, and we would talk about everyone's research and tell jokes. Everyone got along great. Who wouldn't want this life? That's when I knew I wanted to be just like my advisor. Of course, that changed after being exposed to who my advisor was under stress.

Fast-forward two years and everyone at our university was dealing with the financial crash of 2008. Labs throughout the university were shutting down, and grant funding was at an all-time low. Even tenured professors were getting pushed out of their positions because universities couldn't afford to pay them. My advisor's most recent $1.25-million R01 grant proposal had just been denied for the second time, he had invested in a project that was going nowhere, his lab was a mess by his own doing, and he was up for tenure in a matter of months. Things were grim. The scene was very similar to what occurred during and after the 2020 pandemic, and the same scene will play out repeatedly in academia in response to any and every economic fallout the world sees because higher education is built on a house of cards.

The house? Cheap PhD labor.

The cards? Poor PhDs.

PhDs are indentured servants, and universities are their masters. Don't believe me? Universities have banded together multiple times to fight governments against giving PhDs in postdoctoral positions overtime pay.[11] Think about that. The postdoc position did not exist fifty years ago. It was an experiment that was meant to provide one year—yes, just one year—of extra training for PhDs who wanted to run a lab. Likewise, teaching assistant (TA) positions have been completely abused. PhDs now commonly spend five to ten years in teaching assistant positions.

Academia failed my advisor, just like it failed me. His only hope was to squeeze every last drop of work out of me and the other PhDs working in his lab. Through lack of accountability, people management training, and support systems, academia had turned my advisor into a frantic, narrowly focused bully who couldn't control his emotions. I honestly believe I would have turned out the same way had I spent ten years in a postdoc position like he did. Fortunately, I transitioned into an industry career instead.

After transitioning into industry, I quickly became grateful that I didn't turn out like my advisor. In fact, I started to feel sorry for him. Not for who he was personally but for who he had allowed himself to become professionally—narrowly trained in a few niche areas and completely untrained in numerous crucial areas that could have made his career and the careers of those he mentored successful. His lack of management, leadership, and even financial training, as well as his complete lack of professional awareness at the time, became a cautionary tale for me—a tale that I want to pass on to you so you can reclaim control over your own professional career before it's too late.

Growing Industry Jobs versus the Decline of Academia

One of the reasons my advisor was so stressed after the 2008 financial crash was because he had blown a large percentage of his grant funding in 2006 and 2007. He wasn't tracking his spending well and was clueless when it came to simple financial concepts like how to read and react to a profit and loss statement. My advisor was a poor leader because neither he nor his academic institution cared about his ability to manage people or finances. He was brought up in a system that rewarded his technical skills and completely ignored his transferable skills—or lack thereof. Academia gave him titles like "academic advisor" and "mentor" without testing his ability to advise or mentor. Ultimately, my advisor believed that being able to end the careers of postdocs or graduate students fifteen years his junior made him powerful. He believed that making someone cry or calling someone dumb was winning. He also believed that he was being paid well for doing noble, cutting-edge work when, in fact, his salary was far less than the average PhD gets paid in industry, and his work wasn't noble or cutting-edge. There's nothing noble about being paid less than you're worth to do work that requires you to constantly beg for funding. There's nothing cutting-edge about piecing together just enough data to get the next grant funded and then using that grant funding to work on something other than what the grant was supposed to fund because you already know that the data you put in the proposal won't lead to any substantial or translational discoveries.

In today's world, the biggest discoveries are made—and the best salaries are paid—in industry. While academic postdocs, TAs, and overworked adjunct faculty continue to pile up and full-time faculty positions continue to decline, PhD salaries and opportunities in industry continue to climb. My advisor was part of a system that was—and is—slowly dying, and I don't envy the decline. I feel sorry for it—and motivated by it.

I'm motivated to help as many PhDs as possible know the truth about what's possible for their careers and lives outside of academia. I'm motivated to encourage PhDs (perhaps, like you) who have become disillusioned, isolated, or even abused by academia to know that they and their PhDs are incredibly valuable in industry.

My dream for this book is that it helps you remember your value as a PhD, shows you all the opportunities available to you in industry, and helps you seize the best opportunity for you.

Introduction

How PhDs Can Transition Out of Academia

· ·

"Do not let your fire go out, spark by irreplaceable spark in the hopeless swamps of the not-quite, the not-yet, and the not-at-all. Do not let the hero in your soul perish in lonely frustration for the life you deserved and have never been able to reach. The world you desire can be won. It exists ... it is real ... it is possible ... it's yours."

— Ayn Rand

In the Preface, I only scratched the surface of why PhDs want to transition out of academia. Many PhDs feel professionally unfulfilled in academic positions because they are overworked, work in uninspiring roles, and are paid marginal academic stipends, fellowships, and wages. Far too many PhDs are unable to find meaning or joy in their academic careers, which negatively impacts both their professional and personal lives. But most of these PhDs face a lack of training for how to get a job outside of academia. After all, most PhDs have spent decades—the entirety of their professional careers—in academia. They also face imposter syndrome. After spending their lives in academia, many PhDs think they can't be successful in industry. They falsely believe that their lack of post-PhD industry experience removes them from consideration for top industry roles.

But nothing could be further from the truth.

The Fourth Industrial Revolution

The *World Economic Forum* recently labeled today's industry landscape as the "Fourth Industrial Revolution." According to the *Forum*, the top three skills employers recruit for are complex problem-solving, critical thinking, and creativity.[12] In other words, employers need job candidates who can correctly identify problems, find the right problems to solve, and then solve those problems with creative solutions.

Guess what? PhDs like you excel in all three of those areas.

Never forget that, regardless of your PhD background, you are an expert researcher. You are highly trained in identifying problems and creating solutions to those problems. Think of all the hours, days, week, months, and years (even decades!) you've spent trying to find answers to the world's toughest questions. You know how to attack questions from every angle. You know how to follow a lead through fifteen academic journal articles, eight book references, and countless plots in obscure, barely readable figures published ten or more years ago just to (maybe) prove some minuscule aspect of your overall hypothesis. Employers deeply value this for any industry role. Make sure they know you have these skills.

Employers also value your ability to wrangle uncertainty. If you have a PhD or are getting a PhD, you've probably spent years of your life smack in the middle of uncertainty. You have no idea if your next grant is going to be funded. You have no idea if your paper is going to get past that third reviewer and be published. You have no idea when your committee is going to give you the green light to defend your thesis. You don't even know if the project you're working on has an answer at all! Everything you're doing—your life's work—could be proven untrue at any time. As a PhD, you're not just comfortable with uncertainty; you thrive on it.

You know that without uncertainty, discovery would be impossible. Innovation wouldn't exist. Most people don't understand the relationship between uncertainty and creation. You do. Most people want a sure thing and spend their entire lives choosing unhappiness over uncertainty. Use this to your advantage by leaning into your ability to work through uncertainty toward innovation. Make sure you communicate it to employers too.

One of my thesis committee members once told me the difference between leaving graduate school with a master's degree versus leaving with a PhD is that a master's degree is granted to those who have mastered a field while a PhD is granted to those who have added to a field. Less than 2 percent of the population has a PhD because adding to a field is hard.[13] Anyone can regurgitate information. That's easy. It's so much harder to create information, to bring new knowledge into existence for the very first time.

If you have a PhD, you are a creator of information. This is one of your most valuable and most transferable skills. Don't assume that everyone can create information. Most job candidates can't even write a book report. You, on the other hand, have spent years creating information and months putting it into a hundred-page story called a thesis just so five other people can read it. This kind of innovation and tenacity is uncommon and should be communicated to every employer you approach.

PhDs also learn faster than any other group of people. This is because PhDs are rigorously taught *how* to learn. After all, the acronym "PhD" stands for a Doctor of Philosophy, and philosophy stands for knowledge and the ability to ascertain knowledge, which makes PhDs quite literally *doctors of learning*. Your ability to learn quickly, especially on the job, is incredibly valuable to employers. It's also exceptionally rare. Just watch the average job candidate try to learn a new software program or standard operating procedure (SOP). Then watch a PhD learn that same software program or SOP. The speed at which the PhD learns, as well as the autonomous nature of their learning, is unmatched.

· ·

Speed of learning is a competitive advantage that frightens other job candidates. This fear is often expressed through misinformation like, "You're overqualified if you have a PhD" or "PhDs are lab rats and can't understand business" or "You can't get a job without industry experience." Don't believe those lies. Your ability to learn quickly should not only be communicated to employers but should also be leveraged to implement what you read in this book.

· ·

The ability of PhDs to learn quickly is, in large part, responsible for my success in helping hundreds of thousands of PhDs get hired into their dream industry careers. I've helped PhDs transition into all eleven sectors of business as defined by the S&P 500 index, including information technology, healthcare, communication services, consumer discretionary, financials, industrial, consumer staples, utilities, real estate, materials, and energy. Feeling blind in terms of your industry transition, feeling stuck in academia with no idea how to change your circumstances, or feeling as though you are begging to get hired or begging to get promoted to your next industry position does not have to be your professional experience. As a PhD, you have the value necessary to be sought after by industry employers throughout your career.

Your Guidebook to Success

Whether you want to be one of the highest-paid Chief Scientific Officers or Medical Directors in your field, or the most sought-after Data Scientist, Project Manager, Product Manager, Principal Scientist, Senior Engineer, User Experience Researcher, Application Scientist, Technical Sales Specialist, or Clinical Research Associate in your industry sector, the methods I've trained PhDs on over the past decade—the same ones in this book—will lead you to success.

The Power of a PhD is your guidebook for revealing your value as a PhD so that you will never have to feel blind, stuck, or disrespected in your career again. This guidebook is divided into eight core steps that cover:

1. Industry career options for PhDs
2. Communicating the right skills
3. Writing industry résumés
4. Mastering LinkedIn® profiles
5. Networking and job referrals
6. Generating informational interviews
7. Acing industry interviews
8. Negotiating your salary

These eight steps provide a consistent and proven methodology for transitioning into industry without suffering through the painful process of trial and error, uncertainty, and constant rejection. If you have a PhD or are on your way to having one, you can transition into industry. You can wake up excited for your career every day, knowing you will be respected by your peers and valued for your skills, training, and education. You can have the professional lifestyle you've always wanted. It's waiting for you. Let's begin.

STEP #1:

Understand That You Are Your Biggest Obstacle

"You are the only problem you will ever have and you are the only solution."

— Bob Proctor

Chapter 1

Academia Destroyed Your
Industry Job Search Strategy

. . . .

A n industry job search is maddening because PhDs are never rigorously trained how to do it properly during their academic careers. Most PhDs are never, ever trained how to execute a job search at all. You picked this book up for one simple reason: to transition out of academia and get hired into an industry job. Yet knowing—or not knowing—how to apply for a job is *the* limiting factor in determining how successful your industry job search and subsequent industry career will be. And how successful your career is will be a major determinant in your personal level of achievement and fulfillment, especially after spending decades in academia.

When it comes to executing an industry job search, most PhDs procrastinate, think about getting an industry job, procrastinate more, upload an academic résumé to hundreds of job sites, fail to get a response, and give up.

Does that sequence remind you of your own industry job search?

If you have a PhD or are about to get one, then probably. I have personally heard from tens of thousands of PhDs in over 150 countries that the above sequence encapsulates either their current industry job search strategy or the strategy they tried before reaching out to me. This particular job search strategy doesn't work because academia and your academic mindset have flipped it upside down. My job is to help you turn it right side up—starting now.

Every PhD starts their job search (after the procrastination period) by uploading résumés and hoping for the best. A small percentage of PhDs will look at interview questions and imagine answering them correctly. Only a handful will record their progress and connections during a job search. A select few, if any, will devise a networking strategy, build and reactivate their network, and seek job referrals. The problem is that everyone is executing their job search in the upside-down order that academia taught them: résumés, interviews, strategy, referrals. Due to lack of training, PhDs assume that an industry job search mirrors an academic job search. Or even more ignorantly, they believe it mirrors the peer-reviewed publication process.

• •

Let's see … so I need to write a document similar to an academic paper (résumé) and send it off to reviewers (employers) and then if the reviewers like my work they will ask me to come in and defend my position (interview) similar to the way my thesis committee would. Wrong. The academic social norms you are following now will not get you hired in industry.

• •

This is why so many PhDs spend most of their time writing and rewriting their résumés or LinkedIn® profiles. Then they spend the second most amount of time fantasizing about a phone screen or interview they have yet to schedule. Then they spend very little time, if any, creating and recording a job search strategy or building and reactivating their job referral network. If you want to get hired into the best possible job for you, you need to flip this sequence on its head.

Another reason many PhD-level job candidates perform their job searches in reverse order is because they are incorrectly aligning their efforts with what the hiring funnel looks like from an employer's perspective. When I say hiring funnel, I mean a company's increasingly stringent workflow that job candidates go through on their way to being hired. For example, the average industry company receives 250 résumés per day.[14] Employers will only invite twelve to fifteen of those job candidates to a phone screen. Of the twelve to fifteen people the company finds time to do a phone screen with, they will do a video interview with three or four candidates, and then, finally, bring in one or two people for a site visit. This is why most job candidates only focus on résumés and interviews; it is all they can see of the hiring process. They're not looking at what needs to go on behind the scenes to disrupt this funnel. They're not thinking about how they can accelerate themselves through the funnel or skip certain parts of the funnel or guarantee their progress from one stage to another. Instead, they are only seeing the start of the funnel—the résumé—and the site visit interview at the end of the funnel.

Now is a good time to start asking yourself a few new questions:

- What if I could skip the résumé stage of the funnel altogether and not be one of 250 résumés?
- Who could I talk with to schedule a phone screen today?
- Could I get hired without a site visit and get a job offer right after a video interview?
- How could I make myself such an incredible job candidate that I could skip the funnel altogether?
- How could I create my own funnel and get multiple companies to fight over me?

You can do all those things. I will teach you how.

By now, you should clearly see how your academic perspective and lack of job search training has been limiting you. Now it's time to replace your academic perspective with an industry perspective. It's time to look at what a right-side-up industry job search looks like.

How to Create a Job Search Strategy

An industry job search, executed in the correct sequence, starts with understanding your career options and creating a job search strategy, and creating a job search strategy starts with realizing that sequence matters. You cannot just haphazardly execute different job search activities at different times. Your approach must be organized in the right order. You also need to record your progress. At the very least, you should have a spreadsheet with five columns:

1. Companies of Interest
2. Job Postings or Informational Interview Notes
3. Company Contacts
4. Date You Last Followed Up
5. Next Follow-Up Date

To get hired, you must design a campaign. You must map out the steps you are going to take, and you must plan for contingencies. You cannot just fly by the seat of your pants. You can't wake up on Tuesday and submit a few résumés, do nothing to progress your transition Wednesday and Thursday, reach out to a few contacts on Friday (the *worst* day to reach out to people, by the way), coast on the weekend, and then search for more online job postings on Monday. Does this sequence sound absurd? As you read it, you might have thought: *Ridiculous! No one searches for a job like this!* Are you sure? If we catalogued your job search activities in a spreadsheet hour by hour, what would the result look like?

Thinking about your job search does not count as an activity. Wanting to transition doesn't count either, nor does playing out various scenarios in your head like *If I apply to this job, will anyone get back to me?* or *Should I reach out to this person on LinkedIn®?* Thinking about, dreaming about, and considering the possibilities of your transition are not the same as executing a job search.

Where are you documenting your progress? Where are you writing down your plans for each day of the month? Do you even have a plan? Are you following a protocol?

If not, it's time to start.

Once you have a strategy in place, you must grow and engage (or reengage) your network. The major component of your networking efforts is following up consistently with an ever-growing list of contacts at the companies you want to work for, setting up informational interviews with those people, and gently guiding them to a position where you can gently ask them for a job referral. That's where you need to live.

You hate people? Great, stay poor.

You can't stomach talking to strangers? Perfect, enjoy staying on government assistance programs for the rest of your life.

If you want a job that pays well and allows you to do your best possible work, you must get comfortable with seeking job referrals. The good news is I share a painless process for doing this in later chapters—so painless that even the most intensely introverted PhD who hates networking with a passion can follow it.

Next, you need to craft your professional profile carefully and correctly. Your professional profile includes your industry résumé and your LinkedIn® profile. You can expand your profile to include other documents and other social media profiles, and we will discuss this in later chapters, but your résumé and LinkedIn® profile are required. That being said, you should spend very little time adjusting your professional profile. You should establish your profile and then only slightly adjust it as needed based on the jobs you target. If you're applying to a new job online and uploading a résumé, the résumé you upload should be highly targeted to that position. It should not just have one or two skills from the job posting slapped into it (although most PhDs don't even do this, by the way). Instead, it should have every technical skill and transferable skill from the job posting inserted into the résumé. We will discuss exactly how to design your résumé and LinkedIn® profile in later chapters.

As a PhD working to transition into industry, you need to be prepared to present yourself as a credible and viable solution to the problem an industry employer is facing. After all, the employer has a job opening because they have a need. Do you know what that need is? Do you have any idea why the job is open in the first place? If not, you need to find out before you interview with the company. To get a job offer following any real-time interviewing interaction with an employer requires you to display a certain level of mastery—not mastery over your skills or over the job at hand but mastery over yourself. Self-mastery, more than anything else, is what you are being evaluated on during any industry interview. Most PhDs find this very hard to believe, but it is absolutely true. Few employers will require anything beyond answering a few questions during an interview, which, if you think about it, is absolutely nuts. Industry employers will pay you tens of thousands of dollars a month based on the answers you give during a few short meetings. They're going to commit not only their money but their people and numerous other resources to *you* based on what you say about yourself during a few real-time interactions. How ridiculous is this? Yet, unfortunately, this is still the most reasonable means of hiring top talent today.

Imagine applying to an industry job only to have the hiring manager bring you into the interview and say, "Okay, today you're going to manage three of our team members all day while we shadow you and evaluate your every move." Or "Today, we're going to stand over you while you run ten different lab experiments." This doesn't happen for a variety of reasons. To start, you have not been onboarded by the company or trained in the company's processes. The company's team of current employees does not know who you are or how to work with you. Then, of course, there are numerous liability issues.

Sure, some companies for certain jobs might have you complete a take-home test, submit a writing sample, or take a few technical support calls before hiring you, but that's it. They're committing to you based on very little information. So, instead, these employers will evaluate your behavior. They will see how you master yourself under stress. This is why studying common interview questions is a waste of time. It is also why waiting until you get an interview to prepare for an interview (or "cramming") is ineffective. You need to practice interacting with other professionals in a very professional way *behaviorally*, and you need to start now.

By executing your job search in the right sequence, you will save valuable time when it comes to getting hired. Unlike most job candidates, you will avoid the trap of chasing one lead at a time via the outdated process of uploading your résumé to a job site whenever you feel like it, waiting to get a reply that never comes, only to start all over again a few days, or even a few weeks, later. You will be able to rise above the grueling process of injecting yourself into the job market repeatedly to make daily progress. Most importantly, if you follow the right strategy in the right sequence, you will end up with touchpoints with multiple companies so that when you do get an industry job offer, you can quickly obtain additional offers and leverage those offers against each other to dramatically increase your salary.

It all starts with putting first things first, and when it comes to your job search, the very first thing you need to do is determine your target career path, which is where we are going next.

Chapter 2

You Can't Hit a Target You Don't Set

· · · · · · · · · · · · · · · · · · · ·

First things first, you must decide what you want your professional lifestyle to look like. Only then can you start matching job titles to that vision. Do you know which career is right for you? Most PhDs never set professional goals even though university studies show that just writing down your goals increases your odds of attaining them by 33.54 percent.[15] Instead, most PhDs work on whatever is put in front of them. They fall into whatever position academia gives them permission to hold. The few PhDs who start searching for a job outside of academia and do the research necessary to start understanding the industry landscape, sectors, and job titles often get lured into chasing a title that sounds impressive but will never lead them to the professional lifestyle they truly want. Who cares if Medical Science Liaison is trending if you don't want to travel and hate giving presentations? Sure, the title of Management Consultant demands respect and recognition, but does that matter if you hate Microsoft Excel and your personal situation would never allow you to work eighteen hours a day, five days a week, on site in a different city every week, fifty-two weeks a year? Chasing job titles is a losing strategy when it comes to getting hired in industry. If you're reading this book, you've likely come face-to-face with the pitfalls of not considering the professional lifestyle you were chasing.

Perhaps you thought becoming a PhD and being called "Doctor" was going to automatically result in a tenured, untouchable position that came with respect, rewarding work, and all the resources needed to excel. How did that work out for you? How is that working out for your advisor or for most lifetime academics? What if you could go back and shadow your advisor or any professor or principal investigator (PI)? Would you have planned your career differently? Would you have created a better target for yourself?

Job Titles Have Pitfalls

Job titles can be rat poison to your job search as they can distract you from the professional lifestyle that will actually give you the sense of achievement and fulfillment you are looking for in your career. Job titles can also be used against you, either to compensate for a lower salary offer or refusal to promote you in terms of salary or to lure you into a job that is not the right fit for you. Your performance is the most valuable asset for employers. Not titles. Not experience. Your ability to drive the right results is what matters.

Companies spend most of their budgets on hiring, onboarding, and developing performance-based talent. You are the talent in this equation. Companies will do whatever they can to find, influence, poach, and retain talent with the goal of keeping as much of the best talent as possible. They will invent job titles to get talent. They will hire recruiters to take talent from their competitors. They will spend billions of dollars to send you and everyone like you advertisements about how great it is to work at their company or, more subtly, how impressed your friends would be if you were called a Senior XYZ versus a Junior XYZ, even though they pay the same. The only way for you to keep someone—in academia or industry—from implanting their career goals into your head is to actively set your own career goals. The key, however, is to start by setting goals for your dream professional lifestyle—not your dream job title.

Ask yourself: What is important to me in life? What am I chasing? Why?

If you can't answer those questions, you're in trouble. Without those answers you have no idea what you're doing or why you're doing it. Like every human on the planet, you're likely chasing happiness of some kind, but the problem is that you've never defined what happiness means for you. Happiness is just a feeling, and that makes figuring out what will make you happy right now incredibly simple. All you must do is figure out which actions give you the feeling you're chasing most frequently.

If you put this in the context of your career, the question becomes: Which activities do you want to spend your day doing? Which will make you feel the happiest? I'm not talking about overly simplistic, hedonistic happiness like overeating pizza, drinking too much wine, or binge-watching TV shows. I'm talking about deeper, more complex fulfillment—the lasting happiness that comes with meaningful achievement. What daily professional actions will lead you to the most meaningful achievement? What characteristics of your career would lead to those actions?

Let's find out with some simple questions you've likely never asked yourself.

For example, do you want to work with a large team or a small team? Or perhaps no team? Do you want to work with numbers? If so, are you interested in large data sets or smaller data sets? Do you prefer to collect and analyze quantitative data (e.g., the user metrics that are produced when consumers use a company's software application) or qualitative data (e.g., survey responses from a company-funded focus group)? Or both? Do you want a position where you have to read and write a lot? If so, you will want to consider writing-intensive positions. Do you want to work at the company's headquarters or at one of their smaller, remote, satellite locations? Or do you want to work full-time in the field (or at a home office)? What about travel? Are you willing to travel and, if so, how frequently? Most importantly, when it comes to a company's operations, where on the spectrum of innovation and commercialization do you want to be?

Industry Job Titles on a Spectrum of Innovation and Commercialization

All industry job titles can be considered in terms of where they are on a spectrum of innovation and commercialization. This may be a new concept to you if you've been in academia your entire life where nearly two-thirds of all research is basic,[16] so let's break it down.

The world of business has innovation on one side of a spectrum and commercialization on the other. The innovation side might start with a company's intellectual property (IP), or perhaps the very beginning of an idea before it becomes a company's IP. It includes ideation (brainstorming ideas), validation (validating the best ideas based on what a company's clients want, need, and might buy), and the creation of a value proposition (an offer to solve a problem that a client has). Across the spectrum, these phases of conceptualization (or innovation) slowly transform into production, or the commercialization of products and services. There are many phases and job titles that span the middle of the spectrum, including ones in manufacturing, quality control, and quality assurance. Once the product or service is complete, it would "go to market" and be put on shelves (physical, online, or otherwise) to be sold. These products and services would then need to be supported by sales teams, marketing teams, customer services teams, and even installation and engineering teams. The question you should aim to answer is, where do you want to participate on this spectrum?

I alluded to dozens of different careers, or job titles, as I was discussing the spectrum of innovation and commercialization above. Did you catch any of them?

On the innovation side, an employer might need a Patent Examiner, Patent Scientist, Technical Advisor, and Patent Agent. They might also need a Regulatory Affairs Associate, or perhaps a team of Recordkeepers or Documentation Specialists.

As an idea is turned into a product, the company would need Project Managers, Product Managers, R&D Researchers, Scientists, Engineers, Quality Control and Quality Assurance Specialists, Data Analysts, Data Scientists, Informatics Specialists, Clerks, Technicians, Operational Support Specialists, and more.

Once production crosses from early stages of development to manufacturing and distribution, Manufacturing Agents, Product Engineers, and factory positions of all kinds are needed, such as Shippers, Truckers, Distribution Agents, and Delivery Agents. Additional marketing positions would be involved throughout this process, including Strategic Marketers, Tactical Marketers, Marketing Communication Specialists, Medical Writers, Technical Writers, Marketing Education Writers, Editors, Translators, Portfolio Managers, and more Project Managers and Product Managers.

Once the product goes to market, Technical Support Specialists, Customer Service Representatives, Sales Associates, Sales Managers, Application Specialists, Retail Associates, User Experience Researchers, IT Specialists, and Storefront Support and Online Support positions of all kinds are needed. There are distinct projects throughout this spectrum that need to be managed by more and more Operations Managers, Project Managers, Department Managers, and Team Managers of all kinds.

The questions to ask yourself again are *what activities do you want to do on a daily basis and where do you want to be on the spectrum?*

If you don't care because you're so desperate to get hired (or clueless when it comes to the landscape of industry) that you'll take any job doing anything, then stop reading this book and take a moment to remind yourself that you and your PhD are valuable. You must leverage this value discriminately because it's your moral obligation to have the biggest and best impact possible on humanity. You owe yourself, your family, and those who have supported you to do something that matters, and it's on you to decide what matters. You are the one who must care the most about the qualities of the industry career you're chasing. These characteristics will determine the impact you have and the quality of your professional lifestyle, as well as your personal life.

The Top Twelve Job Characteristics to Consider

After helping tens of thousands of PhDs get hired into thousands of different job titles at thousands of top companies all around the world, I can tell you that every PhD has a unique set of professional lifestyle characteristics they consider most important to them. Those who define those characteristics and consider them before starting their job search get hired more quickly, get paid higher salaries, and enjoy their work more. Everyone, including you, can create your own list of characteristics, and I encourage you to do so. However, to give you a starting place, I'm sharing the twelve most popular characteristics that the PhDs I've worked with privately in the Cheeky Scientist Association consider when they complete this exercise. These twelve are listed below in random order. Write the twelve characteristics down on a piece of paper or type them into a document and then rank them in order of importance to you. Note: you must rank them in terms of order of priority for *you* and *your* ideal professional lifestyle, not someone else's.

- High salary
- Remote position
- In-house position
- Innovation
- Commercialization
- Management
- Entry-level position
- Writing-intensive position
- Numbers-heavy position
- Traveling over 30 percent of the time
- Customer-facing position
- Highly technical position

Once you have your characteristics ranked, you have the beginning of a target for your job search.

Next, you will need to further define your target so you can get hired into the right position for you quickly with an incredible salary offer. However, before zeroing in on a single position or job title, you need to consider which of the six major industry career tracks are a good fit for you and your professional goals.

Chapter 3

All Industry Jobs Fit into Six Career Tracks

· ·

To transition into the business world, you must first understand how business is perceived. In this chapter, I often substitute the term "business" for "industry" because one of the frameworks I use divides the world of industry into component parts and uses the word "industry" to describe the smallest of those parts. After all, it's only us academics who routinely refer to the nonacademic landscape as "industry." Most others refer to it simply as "business."

Business Frameworks

There are many different frameworks for breaking down the world of business into discrete components. One of the simplest to understand is the S&P 500 framework, in which business is divided into distinct "sectors" and further broken down into each sector's component "industry." The S&P 500 is one of the most commonly quoted stock indexes, and if you look at the business sectors and the industries it tracks,[17] you can quickly understand the business landscape. The S&P 500 index is broken down into eleven sectors:

1. information technology
2. healthcare
3. communication services
4. consumer discretionary
5. financials
6. industrial
7. consumer staples
8. utilities
9. real estate
10. materials
11. energy

Each of these sectors is broken down into at least five different industries. For example, the consumer staples sector is broken down into household products, soft drinks, personal products, drug retail, food retail, food distributors, agricultural products, and more. Likewise, healthcare is broken down into pharmaceuticals, suppliers, technology, facilities, life science tools and services, and more.

While the S&P 500 framework is useful when it comes to understanding the breadth of the business landscape and the diversity within it, it's of little value when it comes to finding the right PhD-level career. If you're getting your MBA and want to learn how to organize business the way a taxonomist organizes different animal species on a chart, the S&P 500 framework and other more didactic frameworks are useful. But when it comes to getting hired, they are effectively useless. Remember, your goal is to get hired doing something you enjoy and be paid well for it. The key to doing this, as we discussed in the previous chapter, is focusing on the professional activities that are going to bring you the most professional satisfaction, not learning the names of business sectors and industries. By focusing on the activities you'll be doing daily in your career, you can narrow down all the possible career tracks in business into six major tracks, only two of which require segmentation into three subtracks. That's it.

This means, as a PhD, there are six major career tracks in the entire world of business for you to choose from. This is a good thing. If you're reading this book, your goal is to get hired, not just learn about getting hired. You want to enter the world of business, not reorganize it. As such, you need to execute a job search, not critique it or create a complex model for it.

The world of business is not complicated. Every business needs to make revenue, and every business will have a certain amount of profit depending on their costs. If the business cannot sustain itself on its profits, donations, or other sources of money, it ceases to exist.

Likewise, all businesses produce a widget that needs to be sold. The widget can be an advanced medical device, a Hershey bar, a smartphone application, or a chiropractor. All business is the business of exchanging value for widgets. Of course, you will want to work for a company that produces a widget that gives you a sense of meaning and ideally does some good in the world, but at the end of the day, what's driving that business to success or failure is just math and exchanging value for a widget. You need to be able to look at all careers with this kind of simplistic view. Otherwise, you will be overwhelmed by all the options and complexities available to you. Always keep in mind that at the end of your transition is only one job title and one company. You can work for other companies and in other jobs in the future, but first you must get hired into just one position, and every position can fit into one of just six career tracks.

The Six Career Tracks

It doesn't matter whether a person works for a hotel chain as a Housekeeper cleaning rooms, a Front Desk Clerk checking other people in, or a User Experience Researcher analyzing data from the customers who are using the hotel's mobile app to book their rooms, every position involved at that company, all the way up the chain of command, will fall under one of these six career tracks:

- Research and Development
- Sales and Marketing
- Healthcare, Clinical Research, and Wellness Services
- Hospitality Service, Performance, and Entertainment
- Information Aggregation, Technology, and Creative
  - Intellectual Property
  - Writing and Editing
  - Information and Data Management
- Classical Business, Finance, and Regulation
  - Financial Services
  - Business and Strategy
  - Regulation, Policy, and Government

Before getting sidetracked by diving deeper into this framework, which again would just be an exercise in semantics and organizing information, let's talk about how you can use those six career tracks combined with the twelve characteristics in the previous chapter to zero in on the job title that's perfect for you. You likely already find one or two of the major six career tracks above appealing to you based on your preconceived notions of what is involved in those tracks. Perhaps you know someone who became a Management Consultant, or you just like the sound of that job title, thus the Classical Business, Finance, and Regulation track appeals to you. Or perhaps you are a life scientist, and it seems like everyone you know who left academia got into a Research Scientist position of some kind, so the Research and Development track is both familiar and comfortable. Or maybe you have a PhD in engineering with a touch of programming experience and have been strongly considering Data Scientist positions already. Then the Information Aggregation, Technology, and Creative career path might be instantly attractive to you, specifically the Information and Data Management subtrack.

There's no point in giving you an exhaustive list of job titles or categorizing them under each of the above career tracks here. I've done this in part for you in Appendix A; however, even that list is incomplete because every list of job titles is incomplete. Job titles change and trend over time the same way baby names do. Your grandma may have been called Beverly (like mine) and she may have been a Phrenologist, Switchboard Operator, Typist, Clockwinder, Eggler, Fuller, Hobbler, Hush Shopkeeper, Lung, Haberdasher, Redsmith, or Bowling Alley Pinsette, but that's not going to help you get hired in today's job market. Instead, you should leverage today's technology—specifically today's best search engines—to find job descriptions that match your ideal professional lifestyle and then work backward to find the titles most often paired with those job descriptions and the companies that are currently offering those job titles in the marketplace.

Returning to previous examples, if you want to work in a highly paid User Experience Researcher position at Hilton Hotels (like a PhD named Erika who I helped transition into a Senior Experience Design Researcher at one of the world's largest hotel chains), do what you do best—research—by searching "user experience research," "hospitality," "job openings," and "high salary" online.

Likewise, I helped another PhD named Camillia transition into a Software Engineer role at Google by first researching industry sectors, companies, and job titles that might be right for her interests. You can watch Camillia's and others' transition stories at: https://cheekyscientist.com/transition-book.

In yet another example, if you want to work as a Principal Scientist within the Research and Development career track in-house at a large biotechnology or pharmaceutical company but prefer to focus on improving the company's current products (referred to as "r&D" in industry) versus creating new products ("R&d") then search "Research and Development" or "R&D," "Principal Scientist," "commercialization position," "in-house position," "biotechnology companies," and/or "pharmaceutical companies." Of course, your online searches can likely be much simpler than this using today's algorithms and career-specific applications like LinkedIn®.

Despite everything discussed above, you may still struggle to decide which job title is right for you. That's okay. Future chapters will explore in detail how to find the industry companies that can provide your ideal professional lifestyle and the people at those companies who can get you hired. This chapter is only meant to start shifting your academic mindset to a more business or industry mindset.

The goal thus far has been to show you what is possible for your future in industry, to produce a kind of paradigm shift in your mind, removing limiting beliefs related to your job search and the careers you can get into and replacing those limits with possible targets to explore. Most importantly, I want you to realize that it's not your niche PhD background, your citizenship status, a gap on your résumé, the length of time you've been in academia, your lack of industry experience, clinical experience, coding experience, or anything else that's holding you back from getting hired in industry. There are literally thousands of jobs you can get right now, regardless of your situation.

The only thing holding you back is deciding what you want and then making yourself visible to those who can give you what you want. As the next chapter explains, the latter will be the biggest struggle you will face in your job search once you decide on the right industry career for you.

CASE STUDY 1
Sarah Yunes, PhD

I am thrilled to finally have a transition story of my own and to be a case study in this book. I was hired as a Regulatory Medical Writer but initially planned on moving into an R&D position because it seemed like the most obvious choice given I was a bench scientist in graduate school. As time went on, however, I became more and more dissatisfied with being a researcher. I started thinking about other options. Eventually, though, I became totally lost. Worse still, I started seeing myself as a complete failure. What kind of PhD can't make up their mind about what to do with their career? How did I let myself get hired?

My academic advisor had a very clear bias against PhDs who went into industry. There was no discussion about industry careers at my university. No training or help what-soever ... nothing. Soon, I became convinced that I was completely unqualified for any position outside of academia and would be doomed to the bench at some university forever. Still, I went on. I kept trying to get hired on my own—haphazardly and intermittently. This didn't work. I knew I needed help but suffered from analysis paralysis. I played out scenarios in my head but only rarely executed anything related to getting hired in the real world. I became increasingly bitter, and my anxiety worsened.

I wanted out of academia so bad. One of my lowest points occurred after my advisor told me with confidence that she would recommend that I set a date for my defense at my next committee meeting. But when I went to the meeting and presented my data, my com-mittee decided that I still wasn't ready to graduate—after nearly seven years! I was stunned and confused. Worse still, my advisor acted completely unsurprised. She didn't fight for me. She didn't offer any solutions. She just played dumb. It was right after that committee meeting that I joined a group called the Cheeky Scientist Association. I had reservations about joining because my academic mindset kept saying "this is a scam—only university training is real." I knew I couldn't stay in academia any longer though. I had to do some-thing radically different if I wanted a different result.

In the program, I worked with Isaiah directly and my classmates to apply the princi-ples in this book. The structure and accountability ensured that I did everything I needed to get hired. I gained momentum and finally enough understanding of the job search pro-cess to see the entire framework of an industry job search clearly. I realized that I was my own biggest obstacle. I was making my job search harder on myself by experimenting with résumés and my LinkedIn® profile—as if I was going to just tweak my way to getting hired. That was my academic mindset again. I learned that hard work can't overcome a bad strat-

egy. Once I started doing things correctly, I began getting contacted by recruiters—a lot of recruiters. I credit this to getting my LinkedIn® profile done right (finally!). One recruiter invited me to a phone interview and then to a virtual panel interview. To my surprise, I was offered the job without meeting anyone in person. It was a whirlwind!

One of the reasons I was given the offer so quickly is because I demonstrated complete commitment to the job at hand, just like Isaiah taught me. I'm so grateful for all the support I received, and I hope my story and this case study give you the confidence you need to commit to the job that's right for you and to make the decision to take your career into your own hands. No one is going to make this decision for you.

***

If you're ready to transition into your dream industry position, you can apply to book a free Transition Call with me or one of my trained Transition Specialists at: https://cheekyscientist.com/transition-book.

Chapter 4

The Number One Reason Industry Employers Are Ignoring You

· · · · · · · · · · · · · · · · · · · ·

The number one reason employers are not hiring you in industry is because you are invisible to them. We live in the attention economy, and as a PhD who has spent their entire life in academia, you are attention-poor. Your résumé is being ignored due to obscurity. Despite what they admit publicly, most industry companies care very little about your technical skills. They can teach you the technical skills you need to learn on the job.

With attention to technical skills off the table, industry employers are not hiring you because you are invisible to them. Everything else you tell yourself about why you are being ignored is a waste of time and is a cover for your unorganized, inactive job search.

It is so much easier to blame lack of success in your job search on the lack of some skill, certification, or degree when the hard truth is that you can't get hired because you refuse to reach out to meet employers or employees. It is your refusal to have challenging conversations with people in industry that is keeping you from transitioning.

The Tools at PhDs' Disposal to Get an Employer's Attention

Think of all the tools you have at your disposal today for getting an employer's attention. You can find everything you need to know about an employer on their website. They might even have a careers page that gives you specific information about how to get in touch with them. You can find these employers on LinkedIn® too, including every employee who works at these companies. You can email these employers or simply pick up the phone, call their offices, and ask to speak to someone in the hiring department. So let's not pretend like you can't get an employer's attention. Instead, let's admit the truth: you are invisible by choice (you may have been invisible by ignorance before reading this book, but now you know the truth and it is your choice). As PhDs, we are trained for years and years to keep to ourselves, and, over time, we have become isolated in our ivory towers. In our isolation, we tell ourselves stories that fit our situation and shift blame off ourselves and onto imaginary forces. We imagine that we are not being contacted by industry employers because our PhD has made us overqualified. We imagine that our PhD background is too niche or that we lack some specific skill on a job posting. In reality, we just don't want to reach out to anyone because it's too uncomfortable.

Nobody in industry knows you, and nobody will know you if you keep doing what you're doing. In the chapters that follow, I'm going to tell you how to communicate your skills and show you how to write your résumé and your LinkedIn® profile in a way that will get any employer's attention. That being said, none of these strategies will fix your number one problem: your lack of network and your lack of drive to network.

You must understand that the things in this book can only be used as a tool to get you hired once you become visible to an employer who can hire you or an employee who can refer you to be hired.

Most of the strategies we are going to discuss, by themselves, will not get you hired. Having the best résumé in the world will not get you hired if you are uploading it to a Fortune 500 company's job site because 98 percent of Fortune 500 companies and 99 percent of all companies use applicant tracking system (ATS) software to instantly filter out more than half of all applications.[18] Spending three days completing every section of your LinkedIn® profile can increase your visibility on LinkedIn®, but your time will have been wasted if you fail to correctly reply to the recruiters who reach out to you.

You must also understand that there is a cost to playing the attention game incorrectly. Many hiring managers and recruiters will never come back to a job candidate's LinkedIn® profile once they have decided that you lack industry credibility. Worse, many top employers have a mandatory six- to twelve-month waiting period before they will reconsider you for a position at their company once they have reviewed your résumé and rejected your candidacy for a position. Your industry job search is not a trial-and-error affair. This is not academia. If you are performing a poor and sloppy job search, you are burning bridges, and it is time for you to stop.

Attention is a Double-Edged Sword

Attention is the cure for obscurity, but it is also a jealous friend. If you stop pursuing attention in your industry job search at any time, whatever attention you gained will quickly leave you for another job candidate. Consider the position of the hiring manager or recruiter whose attention you are trying to command. If I'm a hiring manager who's going to hire a PhD for a position at my company, I want my job to be easy, let alone if I have to hire job candidates for twelve different positions. On top of this, I need to hire someone to fill a need the company has *right now*. This is the state in which you will meet—*or not meet*—most hiring managers and recruiters.

You must also consider that the vast majority of hiring managers and recruiters are not PhDs, and they do not enjoy research. They are not highly trained researchers like you. In fact, like 27 percent of the population, they probably have not read or even started reading a book—paper or electronic—in the past year.[19] Do you really believe that the hiring managers and recruiters whose attention you are desperately seeking are joyously reading through hundreds of résumés and doing intensive research in hopes of finding wonderful you? Negative. Instead, they are skimming résumés for five to seven seconds (according to annual résumé eye-tracking studies). They are in a hurry, and they want to hire someone who is right at their fingertips. Or better yet, someone who is delivered on a silver platter by another employee at their company à la an employee referral.

If you have never viewed the *other* LinkedIn®, LinkedIn® Recruiter (or whatever it's called today), which is the LinkedIn® that large companies use to find and screen talent, I highly recommend it.[20] When you do, you will see that the LinkedIn® Recruiter interface is focused on only three major search fields: Job Title, Location, and Skills. Finding talent is an exhausting job, and most hiring managers and recruiters simply want to avoid exhaustion. They are looking for the candidate they can find easily. The problem is you have done nothing to make yourself easy to find. In fact, you have likely made yourself harder and harder to find over the years. You stuffed your résumé and LinkedIn® profile full of academic titles like "Graduate Research Assistant," "Teaching Assistant," "Postdoctoral Fellow," and "Adjunct Professor," and jammed every bullet point or sentence with commonplace technical skills and specialty methods that you were told were cutting-edge in academia, like HPLC, cell culture, flow cytometry, MATLAB, R, Python, next-generation sequencing, narrative therapy, or the ethnography method. As a result, there are no eyeballs on you or your résumé.

This might seem like bad news, but really, it's good news. It means you can instantly put yourself in a better position to get hired just by becoming more visible. The more people you get in front of, the much higher your chances of getting hired. This should be your priority from this point forward: increasing your visibility to as many people as possible. Forget your skills for now. Forget carefully choosing the right words for your résumé and forget preparing for imaginary interviews that you hope to have one day. Instead, get your name and face in front of as many people as possible.

Getting attention when it comes to getting hired in industry does not have to be hard. You can increase attention simply by putting yourself into the right LinkedIn® groups or other online meetups and forums. You can show up to in-person networking events and conferences too. Or put your résumé on your own free personal website or send personal messages to people you are already connected to on LinkedIn®. You can leverage the bevy of networking social media platforms that are being rolled out on a near daily basis to increase your visibility and keep your ear to the ground in terms of opportunities. For now, just start showing up—*everywhere*. Do not overthink who you are connecting with or which groups you are joining. There will be time to qualify your connections and job leads later. For now, just get some eyeballs on you.

Take a few minutes and do an internet search on the definition of impressions, engagement, and conversions when it comes to advertising. The impression metric, or reach, of an advertisement simply refers to how many people view that particular advertisement. When you are looking for an industry job, guess what? You are the advertisement. Alas, you currently have no impressions; no eyeballs are on you. In advertising, engagement refers to how many people interact with an advertisement. How many clicks does the ad get? How many people comment on an ad post? How many people drive by the billboard daily? When it comes to transitioning into industry, the number of people you send a message to on LinkedIn®, or have any type of conversation with, is your engagement metric and will be covered later in this book along with conversions. For now, you should just be focused on increasing your impressions. Impression gives birth to attention, and that's what your job candidacy is starved for right now. Impression is also at the top of the hiring funnel from your point of view. By getting attention through impressions, you can start conversations, set up informational interviews, generate job referrals, get interviews, and attract job offers. The rest of this book is going to outline how to increase your success at every stage of this hiring funnel, but first things first: start getting attention by increasing your impression count.

STEP #2:

Communicate Skills Employers Actually Care About

"An alleged scientific discovery has no merit unless it can be explained to a bartender."

— Lord Rutherford of Nelson

Chapter 5

Your Technical or "Specialty" Skills Won't Get You Hired in Industry

· ·

When I landed one of my first industry jobs, I was obsessed with adding value by talking about things like "statistical significance," "reproducibility," and one hundred other academically minded concepts. What I didn't realize then was that this language was awkward and irrelevant for the position I had just been hired into. So, when I brought these topics up, the people who hired me said, "What are you talking about? Are you trying to teach us a basics stats class right now? We're not an academic lab functioning on $50,000 a month; we're a $100-million-a-year company. We need you to focus on bigger, business-minded concepts like integrating your efforts within our agile project management system, increasing brand awareness, helping us develop some new conference collateral, and ensuring our R&D product pipeline stays full."

What? Come again?

This was all a new language to me. "Agile project management," "brand awareness," "conference collateral," "product pipeline" … yes, I knew the general definition of those words and could somewhat understand them in context, but I could not converse intelligently about them relative to the company's specific goals, products, processes, and larger vocabulary.

If you want to get hired into an industry job, you must start speaking the language of industry, and this starts with understanding which skills industry employers value the most.

Identifying Transferable Skills

The idea that you will be hired because of your technical or specialty skills is a lie. That is one of the last things employers truly care about. Sure, if you put buzz words on your résumé that match the words in the job posting (a strategy I recommend in later chapters), you might get a callback, but those skills are not going to get you a job offer. There is an immense amount of data showing that the number one reason employers hire PhDs is because of their transferable skills. Your transferable skills are the softer skills that transfer from sector to sector, company to company, and job to job in industry.

Unfortunately, most PhDs cannot swallow their skills being labelled as "soft." Most PhDs struggle to list even the most basic skills industry employers are hoping to see: project management, time management, writing and editing, and market knowledge. These sound too simple, and academia has taught you that simple means less intelligent and less valuable, when most often the opposite is true. Most PhDs don't even list research, analysis, work ethic, innovation, comprehension, or problem-solving on their résumés or LinkedIn® profiles. They would rather posture and list niche-specific skills that sound impressive (but are skipped rather than read) like fluorescence microscopy, real-time PCR, quantum mechanics, artificial intelligence, machine learning, and anything with the word qualitative or quantitative in it.

I know what you are thinking: … *but … but … I have a PhD! What did I do all my advanced technical training for if I can't use it to get hired?*

You have a PhD? Me too.

So what?

Guess who are some of the most overworked and underpaid people in the world right now? Guess who has more debt than anyone else?

That's right—PhDs.

Despite all the education and advanced technical training, most PhDs are unsuccessful in their careers. Perhaps you spent your time in academia developing some extraordinarily complex laboratory technique. Perhaps you became an incredible computer programmer or an expert at designing retrospective surveys. Did you learn advanced molecular biology techniques or how to rewire commercial electrical systems? Did you study for two years straight to master a field and then spend several years compiling a thesis that helped push a niche scientific or interdisciplinary field forward? While that's great, the technical skills you learned along the way will be obsolete in a few years, if not a few months. In fact, many of them are obsolete already. And the specialty methods you learned, while useful in academia, have been streamlined or completely replaced with more innovative methods in industry.

I still remember walking into my first site visit at a Global 500 industry company. As part of the visit, we were allowed to tour the facility, and we were taken to gigantic labs that were each the size of a football field and full of hundreds of millions of dollars of advanced robotics doing thousands of experiments in real time. I couldn't believe what I was seeing. I couldn't fathom the amount of data that was being generated every minute.

That's when I came face-to-face with the reality that all the technical skills I learned in academia were meaningless. The only skills of any value were my ability to understand the robotic systems, manage them, manage the technicians working alongside the robotics, and strategically map out which experiments to run next.

In short, I realized that my transferable skills were valuable—not my technical skills. The only skills that you have that will never be obsolete are your transferable skills, and these skills come in three flavors.

The Three Flavors of Transferable Skills

Transferable skills fall into one of three categories: systems-oriented, people-oriented, or self-oriented. You must communicate two to three skills from each of these categories on your résumé and LinkedIn® profile, and you must be able to discuss them during the interview process. You must also communicate how these transferable skills have helped you achieve relevant results in the past and how they will help you perform better than other candidates in the job at hand.

Your previous academic experience—and even life experience—is proof that you are an expert in at least one subject or discipline. For example, you already have many systems-oriented skills associated with your academic expertise. The key is phrasing these skills in a more universal way. For example, if you helped manage your lab's budget, you could list "financial acumen" as one of your job skills. If you had to ensure that certain antibodies or other reagents were always in stock so that everyone could continue executing their experiments, you could list "risk mitigation" or "resource management." Do not underestimate the importance of systems in business. Systems are entirely responsible for allowing a business to scale. The good news is that as a PhD, you have lived and breathed systems for most of your life. The only difference is you called these systems by different names in academia—names like protocols, procedures, methodologies, and lesson plans.

If a PhD-level job candidate does not understand systems and cannot communicate that they are systems-oriented in today's job market, they will not be hired. So take time to carefully brainstorm, understand, and communicate your process-based skills during your industry transition. Other potential options for this category of transferable skills include documentation, recordkeeping, writing SOPs, regulatory acumen, production, quality control, quality assurance, creating return on investments, or simply "systemization."

Employers report that 57 percent of their bad hires were job candidates who lacked people-oriented transferable skills, namely poor interpersonal skills and poor cultural alignment.[21] PhDs with people-oriented skills can adapt to sudden changes in circumstances and effectively communicate with team members who may or may not be in the same office (or country). Are you flexible, versatile, and well-adjusted to remote work? Can you flexibly work with other personality types in an office? Can you mentor, train, and otherwise work with people who have less technical expertise than you? Can you work with people messier, angrier, less intelligent, and more annoying than you (from your point of view)? Can you work cross-departmentally to accomplish goals that will affect the entire organization? Can you handle digital cross-functional collaboration? Do you know what "organizational behavior" is? Other examples of people-oriented transferable skills include performance management, change management, personnel development, virtual training, project management, task delegation, and chain of communication.

When employers see relevant transferable skills that are people-oriented, it indicates that you would be a good leader and collaborator. But, even more importantly, it means you can take orders from your superiors, and you can both influence others and be influenced by others for the good of a project without anyone holding an official position of authority.

As a PhD, you might think that you work hard, take initiative, and quickly grasp new concepts, but do industry employers know this about you? Do you really think a stranger who is considering hiring you or a slew of other job candidates automatically assumes you are a hard worker just because you have a PhD? No, of course not. You must show them. You must prove that you can manage yourself. The self-oriented transferable skills you take for granted are the most in-demand skills in industry. Besides hard work, initiative, and learning quickly, other self-oriented skills include completeness, stress management, innovation, research, technical literacy, and autonomy.

While industry employers need to know you can collaborate with others without constantly annoying those around you, they also need to know you are a competent person who can get things done. This is why studies done at Talent Works have found that adding the words "team player" to your résumé actually decreases your chances of getting a phone screen by 51 percent.[22]

That's right. You cut your odds of getting a callback in half if you highlight teamwork incorrectly. This flies in the face of the misconception most PhDs have about being "overqualified" for industry roles or employers seeing them as "too independent" to hire. These academic assumptions about industry simply aren't true. You might think the difference between saying you are a team player versus collaborative is small, but it's quite substantial. Collaborating means you are getting work done yourself and somebody else is getting work done themselves—together. It means there are two people working very hard interdependently to complete a shared goal and communicating as needed. Being a team player, on the other hand, implies that everyone's work is dependent on everyone else's, which of course means nothing worthy is getting done. It's a recipe for death by committee—a standard way of making decisions in academia but one avoided at all costs in industry. Your self-directed ability to bring your own ideas to the table and to think strategically and creatively to solve existing problems are the self-oriented transferable skills that will make you an asset to any organization.

Chapter 6

Could Anyone Work with You for Eight Hours without Going Insane?

· · · · · · · · · · · · · · · · · · · ·

I
f invisibility, or obscurity, is the number one reason employers aren't hiring you
right now, ignorance of likability, personality, and your professional brand is the
number two reason. When I say likability, I don't mean winning a popularity
contest. I don't mean trying to be nicer, funnier, or more agreeable. The truth is that
some people hate all those qualities while others value them. That's the problem with
likability: everybody likes something different, and what they like changes depending
on their mood, which can change by the hour.

So, when I talk about personality, I don't mean changing your personality. Rather,
I mean putting the best qualities of your personality forward through proper communication, both verbal and nonverbal.

Which qualities you put forward is for you to decide. And once you do decide,
either actively or passively, those qualities make up your professional brand.

Finding Your Professional Brand

Imagine giving everyone you know plus a handful of strangers Post-it notes and asking them to write down three things they can always count on you for, as well as three things they can never count on you for. What are the people who know you best going to write down? What are the people who barely know you going to write down? The sum pattern of their answers is a strong indication of your professional brand—or how you will come off to employers prior to being hired and certainly after being hired. You could take the above exercise a step further—and I recommend you actually do—by asking different questions to tease out exactly how people see you.

You could ask: What three traits describe me best? What did you think of me when we first met? How has this changed over time? What made it change?

The key to understanding your current professional brand is understanding how you come across to others holistically. Once you understand this, all you have to do is either find an employer who is aligned with your professional brand or adjust your professional brand to align with an employer whose brand you value. You will likely end up doing some combination of the two.

Once an employer is aware of you—you've crossed over from invisible to visible—they carefully evaluate whether you are going to disrupt their professional lifestyle, their team's current dynamic, or the company's overall culture. In short, they are looking for red flags. That's right—every employer you interact with during the hiring process is asking themselves, *Can I stand to be around this person for eight hours a day, five days a week?* You want to avoid them thinking, *My God, I can't even stand talking to this person on the phone for five minutes, let alone having to interact with them day in and day out.*

If you come across overly awkward, arrogant, defensive, boring, or negative, what does it say to your potential employer? Behold, this is my professional brand: Mr. Awkward, Ms. Arrogant, Dr. Boring, or Mrs. Negative.

What person in their right mind would recommend that their company hire such a person?

This may seem overly critical to you, but their scrutiny during the hiring process is justified. Consider it from the employer's perspective. Even if you have twenty interviews with an employer and talk to dozens of people at the organization, they still have very little information about who you actually are. Employers can't "try out" someone for a full-time, PhD-level position for two months and then decide if they want to hire you. It would be too disruptive to their current team members and the company culture, not to mention the legal and administrative complications. Instead, employers must carefully evaluate your candidacy and make certain you will not have a negative impact on them. They must also—and this is good news—go into the hiring process with positive intent. The intent must be to hire you, train you, and keep you on for years to come.

There's no way around it. You must start considering yourself from the employer's perspective because no employer will sacrifice their job for the sake of yours.

Hiring managers and internal recruiters put their own job at risk by hiring job candidates who are a horrible fit for the organization. Such a mistake can cause an external recruiter to lose their contract with a company. There's much greater risk for the gatekeepers hiring you than there is for you during the hiring process; therefore, you should develop a heightened sense of professional awareness by deepening your understanding of how you are perceived by others. This is best done by carefully considering and crafting your professional brand.

Your professional brand will follow you throughout the entire job search process. It will be communicated on your résumé, told as a story in your LinkedIn® profile's summary section, showcased by your pacing and tone on a phone screen, and indicated by your nonverbal cues during video interviews and visits.

As a PhD, though, I'm guessing you didn't spend much time thinking about how you were perceived by others behaviorally. Does your professional brand say you care more about competency than likability, or the other way around? Does it say you are technically superior in a niche field but are underdeveloped in core transferable skills like time management, project management, and chain of communication? Does it say you are management material and should be put in a senior, principal, or executive position? Or does it say you need five to eight years of entry-level training first?

If you do not have a strong sense of your professional brand yet, that's okay. You can start developing a sense of it by first considering the professional brands of the employers you are most interested in. What are the top companies you want to work for? Dig into their brands by doing research on those companies. How do they market themselves? What is their mission statement, and what are their company values? What are they broadcasting on their social media pages and their home page? Do they seem to value innovation or sustainability most? Diversity and work ethic or communication and community? It could be any quality or combination of qualities. The question is, can you recognize it?

Once you familiarize yourself with the process of quickly understanding a company's brand, you can start to align your own brand with those that appeal to you most. This doesn't mean that you start wearing Pfizer T-shirts or hats with embroidered Tesla logos; it means that you elevate the company's brand qualities in yourself and bring them to the forefront during the hiring process. If a company's brand is one of innovation and diversity, you bring those qualities to the surface by reigniting your joy of discovery and building more diverse professional relationships. Those two qualities are in you somewhere. They might be buried or ranked poorly in terms of how you've been prioritizing your life recently, but you can change that. There are very few qualities that a company would showcase as part of their brand qualities that you wouldn't be able to identify with. Plus, you'll only be focused on companies with values that appeal to you in the first place. Thus, there will be a way for you to align your professional brand with the brands of the companies you want to work with.

There's No Value in Being Mysterious

No one wants to work with, let alone hire, a mysterious person. When it comes to hiring, industry employers are risk-adverse. If they can't figure you out, they will not risk hiring you and putting you on their team. By failing to communicate a clear professional brand, you fail to sell yourself to the employer. From the employer's point of view, if you're incapable of articulating who you are and what you stand for, you are also incapable of doing the work at hand.

There are only three ways a PhD comes across to an employer when they fail to communicate a clear professional brand: annoying, awkward, or intimidating. You may not have these traits, but I assure you that as a PhD, if you do not define and communicate a clear professional brand, you will be perceived as having them, especially by people who are not PhDs. Would you want to work with someone you couldn't figure out? Would you want to sit next to a colleague you perceived as annoying, awkward, or intimidating? Absolutely not. Instead, you would want to work with someone who is approachable and who you knew how to approach, which is what professional branding provides.

Professional branding also encompasses rebranding yourself from an academic researcher to a credible industry professional. This is something you can do before getting hired in industry, regardless of how long you've been in academia. I remember when I started working with Nathalie, a PhD and good friend who is now a Director at a major pharmaceutical company. She was in academia for over seventeen years after getting her PhD, thirteen of which she spent as a professor. When Nathalie and I first talked, she was convinced she had spent too much time in academia to ever get into industry. She wondered how anyone would see her as more than an academic professor. But not only could we adjust her LinkedIn® profile to showcase her as a credible industry professional using the language of industry, but we could also reinvent her overall professional brand to showcase her as director-level material given her extensive experience.

Shortly after rebranding Nathalie, she was hired as an Associate Director and has since been promoted to Director with a Vice President position in her sights.

Once your new professional brand is in place, it's time to show that you care.

Yes, care.

You can't get hired without being engaged in the opportunity. This takes energy and positive emotion. Despite what you've learned in academia, emotion is not bad. Enthusiasm, when expressed intelligently, is magnetic to employers, which is why you can't afford to be noncommittal to those you talk to during the hiring process.

Chapter 7

No One Wants to Hire the Posturing PhD Who Can't Commit to Anything

· ·

You probably figured out somewhere along the way that life became just a bit easier if you didn't commit to everything that came your way. You figured out that committing your time and your resources to everyone and everything was unsustainable; therefore, you learned to "play it cool." You learned to "posture" or pretend that you didn't really care about an outcome, even if you deeply cared about it.

Playing it cool came with other advantages too. Perhaps as an adolescent, or maybe a bit later in life, you learned that when you didn't commit to someone, it made that person want you and your time more. After all, nobody finds desperation attractive, right? As you grew older, you likely wielded this aloof attitude successfully more and more.

Then came the world of academia, which taught you that emotion is the enemy of logic. Enthusiasm is for children or only a character trait found in certain cultures and countries, but it's not for you. You're above excitement. You've outgrown wanting something so much that you express it openly with high levels of energy. The world may have reinforced your "no emotion" stance by beating you down whenever you got your hopes up. It's better to stay level-headed than to care because rejection won't hurt as much.

Whether or not you identify with any of this, it's very likely that somewhere along the way, you decided to stop showing enthusiasm because you didn't want to seem like you wanted something too much. Maybe you were burned too many times by somebody using what you wanted against you or being rejected so hard that you vowed to never care that much again. Now you hedge in life. You play it safe. You play it cool. This is particularly true for PhDs during their job searches. Most PhDs never go all in on any particular résumé submission, phone screen, interview, or company. They never give 100 percent effort or engage with 100 percent positive energy—and this is their undoing.

Employers Don't Want to Waste Their Time

Employers don't want to hire a job candidate who's not fully committed to the position they're hiring for. One of their biggest concerns is that they're going to spend a lot of time, effort, and human resources on you throughout the job search process, only to give you a job offer that you reject because you weren't really serious about the job in the first place. Even after a site visit, employers don't know you well enough to fully trust you. All they know about you is what you say about yourself or what preselected references and referrals said about you.

> Remember, they are constantly scanning for reasons to stop investing energy in you during the job search process. They're looking for signals of mistrust, noncommitment, and lack of seriousness. Do you know that 60 percent of job candidates give up on their online applications due to tech issues alone and 5–15 percent of job candidates don't show up for their interviews at most companies even after committing to them?[23] Many of those who do show up start the conversations with statements like "Can you remind me of what the position is again?" or "Oh, I forgot that I applied here."

The average industry employer's hiring experience is three out of ten people wasting their time and behaving like unorganized buffoons. These job candidates want employers to pay them tens of thousands of dollars a year but can't even show enough respect or desire for the role to prepare for a simple phone call. Ask yourself: How much do I care? Do the employers I'm talking to know I care? Am I willing to take the risk of caring as much as possible for the industry position I want and to communicate how much I care? Or will I pull back to protect my fragile ego and pretend that I'm too smart to care?

The worst place to posture during your job search is during the interview process. Why would you work so hard to finally talk to an employer only to pretend like you don't really want the job in the first place? How could you possibly get on a phone or video interview without being 100 percent ready to articulate why you are the very best person for the job and why you really, really want the job?

As we will discuss in later chapters, the main reason employers are interviewing you is to gauge your desire for the role. Only once they know you really want to work with them will they move on to evaluating your fit for the role. When interviewing, you better have dozens of reasons written down for why you're the best person for the job and why working at that company is your number one choice. Every company you apply to can be your first choice for at least one reason because every company wins in the marketplace in at least one area or they wouldn't be in business in the first place. Even if another company is your top choice holistically, there is at least one thing about every company you're interested in that they're better at than any other company. Find that reason and lean on it. You must believe that the company across from you is highly desirable. They have to be your first choice for some reason.

You must really, really want the job in front of you, and it has to show. You have to believe it, and you have to believe that you can do the job. If you don't, hiring managers and other decision-makers who sit across from people like you ten times a day will sniff out your uncertainty.

How can you expect an employer to extend you a job offer if they aren't certain that you will likely take it (after negotiating)? Therefore, you must project certainty at all times. You must convince them that you want the job and build a case for why you want it and why you're the best person for it.

Hiring managers and recruiters will know that you're a phony and that you're not serious if you don't truly commit to the job at hand. They will know that you're unsure of yourself or unsure about whether you should work for them. And if they detect that you are unsure, they will see no reason to continue the job search process with you.

Of course, none of this means you can't get additional offers and continue interviewing elsewhere. It doesn't mean you can't leverage multiple offers against each other. It also doesn't mean you want to work at the company you're interviewing with forever and ever. But if you're there now, investing your time and taking their time, you better know why you want to work at that company, where they win in the marketplace, and how you can help them win more in the marketplace.

The hiring process is the process of making your case to an employer. Your goal is to lay out an argument for why you're the best job candidate for the position and why you want to work there more than anyone else. This argument must be made, in part, by writing a cover letter specific to the job you want, addressed directly to the person responsible for placing someone into that job.

CASE STUDY 2
Eric Johnson, PhD

I know many PhDs think they cannot get into careers outside of their niche academic discipline, so I wanted to start this case study by assuring you that this is not true. I'm an example here, as I got my PhD in Chemistry and transitioned into my first industry role as a Data Scientist. I also want to stress how important it is to determine what you want to do before starting your job search. As Isaiah says in this book, you can't hit a target you don't set. You have to have a target position, and you have to update your professional brand in order to demonstrate that you can solve the problems that this role requires. Do you know the problems you'll be asked to solve? Which problems do you want to solve in the first place, especially on a daily basis? What do you want your professional life to look like? Answer these questions, and then start your job search.

The strategy you apply to get hired must have a target but must also have a process. This process can only be successful if it's executed in the right order. When I started my job search, I thought that uploading a few applications would be enough to be successful. Upload a few applications, have an interview, get hired. I was a bit clueless as to what the actual hiring funnel looked like, including what to expect in terms of attempts, rejections, and stages. I also wasn't sure how to spend my time. In my own journey, I applied to 407 jobs. Yes, 407. (I wanted to be a Data Scientist, so of course I counted.)

There were many rejections along the way. For instance, I was offered the perfect job offer in Silicon Valley, but the day I was supposed to sign the contract, the company froze all their new hires because they were about to buy Yahoo! I interviewed at the Mayo Clinic and failed, and I interviewed with a local software company who withdrew the offer when they found out I needed a work visa. I interviewed with Uber, who didn't offer me the job because they "went with someone more experienced." I made it to the final round of interviews against one other person at Amgen and was rejected. I was able to keep going through all of this because I knew what I wanted and because I had a healthy support network of other PhDs.

The network of PhDs I was in, called the Cheeky Scientist Association, led to many informational interviews and eventually a phone screen with a top company. That first phone screen was an hour long with their Head of Analytics. We talked about my résumé and my background, and then the Head asked a few technical questions. My second phone interview was with a Senior Data Scientist who focused mainly on how I approached situational problems. I was invited for an on-site interview that lasted about five hours and included meetings with seven different people from the company's analytics team. During these interviews I was asked tough behavioral questions and more problem-solving questions. I even had a second on-site interview.

During the second site visit, I was asked technical questions, probability and statistics questions, brain teasers, and even physics questions. I was offered a verbal offer on the phone but didn't commit. Instead, I said I looked forward to seeing the offer on paper. Once I had the offer, I negotiated, but they stayed firm until I called the Head of Analytics to ask if there was any way we could bump up the salary. He agreed, and they updated their offer by adding an 8 percent "Key Contributor" annual bonus. I signed the next day. It was quite the process! I hope this helps you understand what to expect in a PhD-level job search. Remember, as a PhD reading this book, you are going for one of the top jobs in the world and must set your expectations accordingly!

***

If you're ready to transition into your dream industry position, you can apply to book a free Transition Call with me or one of my trained Transition Specialists at: https://cheekyscientist.com/transition-book.

Chapter 8

Confirming Your Career Interest
with a Cover Letter

· ·

Including a cover letter in your job application will make you stand out from other job candidates. It's also a great way to prepare your rationale for why you want the job in the first place and why you are the best candidate for the job. As I mentioned earlier, you must build a strong case for your commitment before any employer will commit to giving you a chance in that position.

The most important thing to bear in mind when sending a cover letter is that you should address it to an actual person. You want to avoid using vague, general salutations like "To Whom It May Concern" because such introductions indicate laziness (Why didn't you do your research and find out who was responsible for the position?), disinterest (Why don't you care enough to connect with the person in charge of the job?), and disrespect (You can't be bothered to address your letter to the hiring manager personally?).

If you can't even put forth the effort to find out who will be reading the cover letter, how will you ever convince them to hire you?

Today, many job postings, especially those on LinkedIn®, mention who is responsible for hiring for the position. If the responsible party is not obvious, go to the company's LinkedIn® page, click on the link for a list of the employees who work there, and perform filtered searches to find employees at the company who have job titles like "Hiring Manager," "Talent Acquisition Specialist," or "Recruiter." We will discuss how to do these filtered searches in detail in a later chapter. Here, your goal is to simply put the name of someone responsible for hiring at the company—whoever your best research efforts indicate—on your cover letter. You can also use websites like Hunter.io (a link to which can be found at: https://cheekyscientist.com/book-resources) to find employer email addresses or call the company directly and simply ask who is responsible for filling your position of interest. By identifying the best person to address your cover letter to, you present yourself as a much more serious candidate and dramatically increase your chances of getting invited to a phone screen.

How to Structure a Cover Letter

Your cover letter should only be one page. If it's longer, you must shorten it. As with your industry résumé, which we will discuss in the next chapter, you need to show respect for the hiring manager's time by only including information that is relevant to the job and using short, easy-to-read paragraphs with lots of white space around your text.

The first paragraph of the cover letter should mention three things: the person who referred you for the job, the position you are applying to, and the name of the company offering the position. If you haven't been referred for the job by anyone, mention the name of someone at the company who you've had an informational interview with. If you haven't had an informational interview with anyone at the company, start networking and set up an informational interview (we will discuss this in later chapters as well).

The second paragraph of your cover letter should detail how your experience matches the role you want, including what differentiates you from other job candidates. Here, focus on what makes you uniquely fitted for the role. Don't stuff this paragraph with cookie-cutter descriptions of your skills and experiences. Instead, discuss why you specifically are the best fit for the job and can achieve the results the position demands. Why should they hire you over someone else? Why should they not hire anyone else over you?

The third paragraph should move beyond your unique skills and experiences to a discussion of how you and your personal working style will fit into the company's current culture. This paragraph is where you should showcase your knowledge of the company's mission statement, corporate strategy, values, and, again, culture. How do your goals align with their goals? How do your values align with theirs? Why do you want to work with them over anyone else?

In terms of overall formatting, there are only two cover letter templates you should consider: the standard business format and the newer, very popular T format. The standard business format includes the three written paragraphs we just discussed, as well as formal address and signature sections. The entire letter is left justified except for your name and contact details at the very top, which are right justified. You can see an example of this cover letter formatting on the next page.

The T format, on the other hand, completely replaces the second paragraph with a two-column table. In the left-hand column, you add the most important transferable and technical skills and requirements listed in the job description. In the right-hand column, you match these requirements with your qualifications by discussing the skills and experiences you have that exactly match the requirements, as well as the relevant skills and experiences you have and the skills you have the ability to learn. The rest of the T format cover letter is the same as the standard business cover letter, and an example of the T format can be seen on the next page.

With the below two cover letter templates in your toolbox, you are ready to start exploring the five most popular résumé templates that are proven to help get PhDs hired in industry, including PhDs who have no industry experience.

Niles Crane, PhD

[Street Address] • [City], [State] [Postal Code]

Phone: [Your Phone] • E-Mail: [Your E-Mail]

LinkedIn: [LinkedIn URL]

Date: [Insert Date]

[Recipient]
[Title]
[Address 1]
[Address 2]
[Address 3]

Dear [Recipient]:

Fusce neque mi, consectetuer gravida, convallis ac, varius a, pede. Fusce pellentesque pretium quam. Ut luctus, justo id volutpat iaculis, est diam pulvinar sem, quis bibendum turpis dui eget mauris. Sed in mauris. Ut massa. Pellentesque condimentum felis nec sapien. Integer posuere elit at turpis. Nulla facilisi. Sed sapien ipsum, commodo ut, facilisis vitae, ultrices non, metus. Aenean non nulla. Curabitur mollis volutpat magna. Vestibulum tempor faucibus nisl. Pellentesque vitae enim.

Aliquam rhoncus volutpat mauris. Sed auctor. Donec tincidunt velit et tellus. Donec sed augue eget lacus placerat adipiscing. Ut convallis suscipit nulla. Morbi posuere ullamcorper ligula. Duis sit amet odio nec lorem ornare gravida. Suspendisse ante nulla, gravida quis, eleifend sit amet, placerat eget, purus. Sed egestas magna at erat. Vivamus euismod, odio id mattis porttitor, tellus nisl consectetuer turpis, ut auctor enim justo euismod nulla. Fusce eget diam vulputate massa tempor tempor.

In ante. Phasellus convallis, nisl in vestibulum facilisis, lacus pede bibendum urna, dapibus pellentesque eros magna sed nibh. Etiam tortor arcu, porta nec, laoreet quis, mollis in, libero. Aenean dapibus est a metus. In sit amet elit. Pellentesque luctus lacus scelerisque arcu. Cras mattis diam. Sed molestie, lectus id bibendum luctus, magna orci luctus quam, et auctor urna diam sit amet ligula. Sed purus dui, suscipit et, malesuada non, consectetuer in, augue. Proin et sapien. Maecenas aliquam, nibh id aliquet tincidunt, ante neque pulvinar mauris, sit amet fermentum nibh augue mollis risus. Mauris porttitor varius mauris. Vivamus in urna et sem accumsan imperdiet. Aenean fringilla, eros tincidunt gravida elementum, justo eros pharetra felis, in rhoncus arcu lectus non enim. Phasellus odio tortor, mattis ut, mattis elementum, luctus at, orci.

Sincerely,

Niles Crane, PhD.
[Your Title]

[Your Phone #]
[Your Email Address]
[Your LinkedIn]

[Date]

[Name of the Person]
[Company Name]
[Mailing Address]
[City State Postcode]

Dear _____,

I am writing to express interest in the position of X (reference #Y) in Company Z. I have included a copy of my resume for your review. You will find that I have extensive experience in X, Y and Z, which makes me a perfect fit for Position X.

Below is a comparison of your job requirements and my qualifications:

Your Job Requirements	My Qualifications
• ABC	• DEF • GHI • KLM
• OPQ	• RST • UVW • XYZ
• Abc	• Def • Ghi • Klm

I look forward to the opportunity to discuss the job requirements of Position X and my qualifications with you.

Thank you in advance for your consideration.

Sincerely
[Your Name]

STEP #3:

ATS-Proof (and Garbage-Proof) Your Résumé

"Well done is better than well said."

— Benjamin Franklin

Chapter 9

Why No One Is Reading
Your Industry Résumé

· ·

B e honest, you did the bare minimum amount of work on your current
résumé. You did just enough to feel like you made an adequate effort to
get hired. Or maybe you paid just enough to have somebody else do your
résumé, and the amount you paid them was proportional to how much effort you
thought you would've had to put in to create a good résumé.

Either way, your threshold for the quality of your résumé is much lower than
it should be. I can tell you this after looking at tens of thousands of PhDs' résumés.
Most of them are awful, plain and simple. It's almost as if most PhDs writing their
first industry résumés are trying to make them unreadable or unenjoyable to read.
And it's not only due to a lack of training on how to write industry résumés; it's also
due to laziness.

Instead of putting forth maximum effort on each and every industry résumé,
PhDs falsely believe: (1) they can get hired without investing significant effort into
their résumés and (2) they can always tweak their résumés and try again later. These
beliefs are false because every résumé should be highly targeted to an individual job

51

description, to the point that there are thirty to fifty keywords from the job posting in the targeted résumé (more on this later).

Approaching your résumé efforts as a trial-and-error affair is a dangerous experiment because many employers will not consider you for another position for six to twelve months after rejecting one résumé from you.

That's right. If you're uploading multiple résumés to employers instead of carefully curating your efforts, you're likely burning bridges in your transition.

Investing Time in a Résumé

Yes, writing a résumé is painful, but that pain indicates a point in your job search when you can set yourself apart from other job candidates. If you actually take the time to format your résumé correctly and target it specifically to the job at hand, you will put yourself ahead of all the other PhDs who are uploading the same résumé for every position. The "spray and pray" résumé strategy is a losing strategy, yet so many PhDs resort to it because they don't want to invest in the painful process of targeting a résumé to each position without a 100 percent guarantee that they're going to get a phone screen for their efforts. So, these PhDs hedge their efforts by doing the bare minimum. This way they can throw their hands up if they don't get a response and say, "See, I knew it wasn't going to be worth the effort anyway."

When I talk to PhDs about investing in their résumé writing efforts, I often compare the process to the writing they did for their thesis to reframe those efforts. Or I tell them about how long it took me to write my book. Do you know how long it took me to publish it? Two years. The first draft of this book had over 80,000 words, and I worked on it every morning before Cheeky Scientist opened for business. For those first nine months, I was writing the rough draft only, meaning I wasn't catching typos, doing developmental edits, or refining anything. I did those more time-consuming writing tasks for an additional three months. And then my editors and publisher took over, spending even more time on it.

Sure, I could've taken shortcuts. I could have crammed it all into a few weeks. But the result wouldn't have been the same.

What result do you want? Are you chasing the quick dopamine hit that uploading your résumé online and clicking "Enter" gives you? Or are you chasing a phone screen and ultimately a job offer? If your answer is the latter, do your efforts match the result you want?

How many hours total have you spent actually writing your résumé? Not thinking about writing your résumé. Not staring at a half-finished page thinking about which skills to list. Not formatting. Actually writing high-quality, highly targeted bullet points for maximum impact on the specific employer hiring for a specific position.

The average two-page résumé templates I'm going to recommend in the following chapters are between four hundred and eight hundred words on average. For the best targeted résumé possible, you should spend a solid two hours working on it. If you can't do that, then you don't deserve a PhD-level industry job. You might need to spend four or more hours writing the first version of your résumé, but after that, the process of targeting each résumé to the position at hand becomes increasingly easier.

As I previously mentioned, a quarter of the population has not picked up a book or any long-form reading material in the past year. Beyond this, people between the ages of fifteen and forty-four read for less than ten minutes a day.[24] This is your audience—the recruiters and hiring managers who are (not) reading your résumés. These people likely do not read very much for pleasure, and when it comes to the unpleasant reading of someone's résumé, they most certainly are not reading it carefully line by line. Instead, they are skimming. Even if, by some form of magic, your résumé was the only résumé submitted to a particular job posting, the gatekeeper for that job would not read it carefully line by line.

. . . .

Here's an important lesson: employers do not care about you and your work experience as much as you care about you and your work experience. You can barely find time to write your own résumé. How could you think hordes of employers are finding time to carefully read your résumé?

. . . .

Stop writing your résumé for yourself and start writing it for someone who isn't invested in you (yet) and has very little incentive to read your résumé over someone else's résumé. Studies show that even when a gatekeeper becomes invested in your résumé, they will spend, at most, five to seven seconds on it.[25] This is only the start of the obstacles between your résumé and getting hired.

There are Layers of Barriers between Your Résumé and a Hiring Manager

There are layers and layers of barriers between your résumé and a hiring manager, recruiter, or any gatekeeper. Large companies, like the Global 500 companies referred to previously, can receive up to two thousand résumés per open position, with the average sitting at 250 applications per open position.[26] Only three or four of those candidates will be interviewed face-to-face, by video or in person. That's a 98.4 percent drop-off rate. Importantly, your résumé will follow you through the entire hiring process. It will be one of the first things an employer sees about you and the very last thing they pass around the hiring committee table after your site visit when deciding whether to extend you a job offer.

A good résumé is not enough to get you hired, but a bad résumé can keep you from getting hired. In fact, a bad résumé can sabotage your job search at multiple points in the hiring funnel. Even if your résumé gets into the hands of a hiring manager and you are contacted for a phone screen, most of the questions you will be asked on that initial call will stem from your résumé.

"You mentioned XYZ on your résumé. Can you tell me a little bit more about this? Why did you spend this much time at ABC institution? You achieved # of DEF results—how?"

If you wrote your résumé correctly, you will be prepared for every question the employer asks.

That's right. You can use your résumé to play a game of inception with employers by putting content in your résumé that makes them ask for clarification on points that you can back up strongly.

The same is true of video interviews and in-person interviews; employers will go back to your résumé during these stages of the hiring funnel. Your résumé will be passed around the hiring committee table *after* every interview is over. It will be the very last touchpoint employers have with you prior to deciding whether to extend you a job offer. Think about it. Not everyone who is on the hiring committee will meet you. Instead, they will have to rely on word of mouth from those who have met you—and from what they read about you on your résumé.

One of the reasons your résumé is so important is because of how easily it can be passed on. Regardless of how powerful LinkedIn® has become in the world of talent acquisition, the résumé will never die. This is because a résumé is short and succinct. It can easily be printed and passed hand to hand between people on the hiring committee very quickly.

I saw the power (and sloppiness) of this firsthand when I was in my first industry role at a large global corporation. A typical hiring scenario would look like this: the morning a potential hire was coming in for a site visit, the head of the department would walk into my office and say, "Hey, we have Jane Doe coming to the office today, and I need you to sit down with her for forty-five minutes and talk to her about what it's like to work here and if she would be a good fit for your team. Here's her résumé. You good?"

That's it. That's all that was offered, and it's all that's offered for most employees prior to the candidate coming in. Sure, the hiring manager whose entire job revolves around hiring will be better prepared to speak with you. Others, though, will not be prepared. They will have received your résumé but very likely will not have read it. They won't know who you are. After all, hiring is not their job, and they have their own work to do. They're just meeting with you because their boss told them to meet with you. Don't imagine that there's some kind of command center at these companies digging deeply into who you are and what you can offer the company. They don't have a Polaroid of your headshot on a wall with forty other candidates and fifty large-screen TVs on the wall streaming live information about each candidate with tickers tracking your progress through the hiring funnel, calculating the likelihood that you'll be successful in the company. Unfortunately, even at large companies, most hiring happens much more on the fly with far too little information about each candidate. But this can be good for you if you step into the driver's seat and start controlling the information you put out about yourself from the start.

Recall that the first problem you must overcome in your job search is obscurity. Once you beat this problem, there is no reason you shouldn't be hired, because from that moment forward you completely control the information the employer has about you. You can put anything on your résumé that you want. You can craft your LinkedIn® profile and your interview responses as you choose. The question is whether you will do the necessary research to position yourself correctly—on your résumé or otherwise.

Ultimately, your résumé is subjective leverage that you control. It's not objective. It's not a peer-reviewed timeline of your work. No, it's a persuasive marketing document that should build the strongest case possible for why you're the best fit for that position. Far too many PhDs are really good at coming up with all kinds of reasons why they are unqualified for the position at hand, both on paper and in their own heads. This imposter syndrome, coupled with analysis paralysis, results in terribly written résumés.

Whenever a PhD starts telling me all the reasons why they can't get a job or they won't be successful at it, whether it is because they don't have previous industry experience or because they don't have a particular skill on the job posting, I always ask, "So what?" Job postings are just recycled employer wish lists. These wish lists are additive too; they grow in length every time an employer decides to add a new skill or requirement. Nothing is ever subtracted. Many employers use their job postings as a net to catch as many candidates as they can. This is especially true of employers who are experiencing a labor shortage or need to hire quickly. Start seeing everything that's written on a job posting as an indicator of what the employer wants, not a hard-and-fast requirement.

Previous experience, degrees, certifications, and skills are all just credibility indicators. Did you catch that last word? **Indicator.** They indicate credibility; they don't prove it. The only way to prove whether you can do a specific job is to do that specific job, which you can't do until you get hired. Displaying confidence in your ability to learn and competency in any question thrown at you will go further than any indicator. Indicators are not what will get you hired in today's modern job market, and they are not what will prevent you from getting hired. Employers care less about indicators than self-efficacy because indicators like experiences, skills, and training can all be gained in the future.

As a PhD, you can learn how to do a technical skill on the job. You can get another certification. You can learn a certain project management methodology once you're hired. You can gain the experience quickly and catch up to everybody else. What employers can't train you on is how to be enthusiastic about the role and committed to doing it well. They can't give you self-confidence or self-efficacy either. Your résumé is just a launching pad for them to test you and figure out whether you believe in yourself and can convince them to believe in you too; therefore, the best starting point for crafting your résumé is deciding how the information you're going to express will be formatted to invoke confidence and certainty in yourself and your skills.

Which format would most concisely showcase who you are and why you're the best candidate for the position? Which format would exhibit confidence through simplicity? How can you get the maximum number of skills and experiences from the job posting into your résumé, even if you don't have those skills and experiences yet?

It all starts with choosing the right résumé format, and that's where we are going next.

Chapter 10

The Gold Standard
Résumé Format for PhDs

· · · · · · · · · · · · · · · · · · · ·

I f you can't explain why you're the best person for the job succinctly, you aren't the best person for the job.

There is an overabundance of advice on how to format a résumé. Most of it is unproven and based on how one person in one sector of industry feels at one specific time in history. Or it's based on a blog article or book written by someone who doesn't have a PhD, has never worked in a PhD-level industry job, and has never hired PhDs at a company. Far too often—and for far too many PhDs—it's based on what a friend of a friend said worked for them. As a PhD, you know that this all adds up to advice from noncredible sources and very small sample sizes.

When it comes to résumés, and to your entire job search, ignore any advice from someone without a PhD who hasn't looked at over ten thousand résumés and who hasn't hired PhDs directly for a company they represent. Of course, if the advice is contextual, such as the hiring manager from Pfizer recommending that you use a one-page résumé instead of a two-page résumé when applying for their Medical Science Liaison role, follow that manager's advice. But advice from an external recruiting shark who is not affiliated with a company, let alone familiar with the company's long-term goals, is not contextual.

External recruiters often operate by getting a list of skills from an employer, or worse, by merely trolling LinkedIn® for new job postings the same way you find job postings on LinkedIn®. These recruiters then make their own assumptions about what that employer would want to see in terms of a résumé, and they offer unsolicited advice based on their assumptions. Even advice from experienced recruiters can be faulty. Imagine a recruiter at a large firm who has been in a particular sector of industry for more than ten years; it's very likely this person will not have a PhD and will be beholden to, or at least strongly influenced by, the bureaucratic rules, regulations, and unspoken guidelines created by that recruitment firm. Still others have been in one niche sector of industry for so long that they now have the curse of knowledge; they have become too elitist in their views and too inflexible in terms of keeping up with current trends in the hiring industry.

Of course, you can't write off everyone as wrong but you (or me). You must seek training and diverse opinions. My point is simply that specificity and context matters.

You have a PhD and want to get into a PhD-level job—that's my assumption. The résumé advice you're about to get is based on this assumption and is backed by getting tens of thousands of PhDs hired into PhD-level jobs, often working with employers as part of their hiring committee to choose the best candidates and occasionally by hiring them into my own company.

Choosing the Right Résumé Format

The key to choosing the right résumé format for getting hired into industry is understanding your positioning in the job market. There are five types of positions you will find yourself in when applying for an industry job.

The first position you will find yourself in is what I call the "Gold Standard" position. This is when you are uploading your résumé online, giving your résumé directly to a hiring manager or some other decision-maker who's not a recruiter or to an employee working at a company who's going to refer for a job. We will discuss the details of the Gold Standard résumé format in this chapter, but generally, this format is two pages or less with a lot of white space and six different sections. Use this résumé format if you're adapting your CV to an industry résumé for the first time or whenever you're not sure which résumé to use for an industry position. Don't use the Gold Standard format if you have no experience in a particular industry, are handing your résumé to a recruiter, or are trying to crack into one of the few niche fields we will discuss later.

One of the first PhDs I worked with after starting Cheeky Scientist was Arya. She had been unemployed for six months, during which she had uploaded hundreds and hundreds of résumés to different job postings and job sites. Worse, she needed a visa to work in the United States and was struggling to communicate her skills and experiences in a way that industry employers found valuable. After reviewing her résumé, I could see why she wasn't hearing back from employers. Her résumé was dense and focused on academic skills and experiences that were not relevant to the positions she was applying for. She wasn't targeting her résumé specifically to each role, and her résumé format was similar to that of an academic CV. I helped Arya change her résumé to our Gold Standard format so that her skills and experiences could be easily read (and skimmed) by employers. I also showed her how to craft the information she presented in her bullet points the way industry employers wanted to see it, not the way academics wanted to see it. As a result, she was quickly hired after using her new résumé and has since been promoted in industry four times. Another PhD who struggled with an industry résumé was Umar. Once he followed my methods, he was hired at Intel. You can watch Umar and other PhDs share their transition stories at: https://cheekyscientist.com/transition-book.

The key characteristic of the Gold Standard format is that the Work Experience section is in reverse chronological order. As I mentioned, the format is two pages or less with six sections, starting with a Contact Details section at the top followed by a Professional Summary section (for certain countries like Germany and the Netherlands, they will expect a headshot of you in this section as well). These two sections make up the top one-third of the first résumé page, which is also known as the "visual center" of your résumé because eye-tracking studies show this is where employers spend up to 80 percent of their time when they do read your résumé.[27] The majority of this "gaze time" is spent on only six data points: the applicant's professional summary, current title and company, previous title and company, previous position start and end dates, current position start and end dates, and education. Beyond those data points, recruiters merely skim for keywords that match the words in the job description. Likewise, ATS software programs weight keywords in your résumé's visual center more heavily than keywords in the lower sections.

After your Professional Summary are your Work Experience, Education, and Technical Skills & Certifications sections. The Technical Skills & Certifications section can include instruments, devices, systems, machines, certifications, second languages, programming languages, software programs, proprietary ways of doing things, trade secrets, and other technical-based skills or specialty methods you have that are highly specific to the job at hand.

The final section of this résumé format is your Honors, Awards, & Hobbies section, which should include volunteer experiences, nontechnical affiliations, and at least one hobby that humanizes you and serves as an icebreaker for the employer to bring up on a phone screen. This hobby should be one that most of the local population (local to the company) would understand, enjoy, and admire. As you can see in the image below, the Gold Standard résumé format is highly structured with lots of white space. Importantly, the text in the image below is not in a readable language. The text is simply gibberish meant to show you where the lines of text should be located and about how much text there should be in each section.

The above résumé format is exceedingly easy to skim, and the formatting is basic on purpose. There's only one font style and one font size (Arial 11 point on the example above). The title of each section is denoted simply by increasing the font size by one point (11 point to 12 point in the example above) and bolding the font style. There is only one style of bullet points, and they are all left justified, indented 0.5 inches or 1.25 centimeters, and aligned with each other. Do not use numbers or other bullet point styles. The document's margins are set to 1 inch or 2.5 centimeters on all four sides of the page, and paragraph spacing is 1.5.

All the specific formatting information is simply for your reference. Don't get caught up in the exact font size or spacing because this is not going to be your key to success. What matters the most is consistency and staying within the bounds of what is reasonable. That being said, **never decrease the margins to squeeze more information onto each page**. As PhDs, we think shrinking the margins to add more words is normal. It's time for you to realize that this is abnormal. Most of the population, perhaps even those you went to undergrad with, *increase* the margins of their pages when writing. Unlike you, they are trying to write (and read) less, not more. This is how everyone else in your undergraduate university was able to turn a three-page essay into a five-page essay. Meanwhile, you were stressing out and manipulating margins, fonts, and spacing to fit seven pages onto five.

Trying to get more information into your résumé has a massive cost. You will pay for your greedy wordiness with employer apathy.

Don't try to make your résumé fancy either. Avoid images, multiple colors, and shapes. You're applying for a serious, PhD-level position, and the last thing you need is to lose out on an opportunity because someone doesn't like your artwork or color choice. Your goal is simply to keep the employer reading, and that's best accomplished through simplicity and relevance with relevance best accomplished through function.

Chapter 11

How to Format Your Résumé if You Have No Industry Experience

· ·

M any PhDs do not have any post-PhD industry experience. Yet, most job postings ask for at least two to five years of industry experience.

Remember, this is just another line item on an employer's wish list. It's not required, even if the job posting literally says it's required. Don't use your lack of experience as a crutch in your job search. Instead, work around your lack of experience. Someone had to get hired without experience, and if they did it, so can you.

· ·

So, again, you do not need industry experience to get into an industry job. I'm going to repeat that: you do *not* need industry experience to get into *any* industry job.

· ·

Sure, you might need a formal degree or certification for number of hours worked in very, very rare circumstances, like to be a clinician or a barber, but as a PhD, you already have everything you need to get hired into a PhD-level career: competence, logic, and the ability to make a strong argument backed by your ability to learn and your past relevant results. You don't need to have experience in everything the role asks for. You simply need to show that you can learn on the job quickly and have learned similar skills successfully in the past. In this way, you can boldly show employers the abilities and skills you already have that are relevant to the job you want. There is a special résumé format for this called the "Functional" format.

The Functional résumé format is very similar to the Gold Standard format with only one key difference. Instead of drawing attention to your job titles, which are likely academic in nature and irrelevant to the hiring manager without a PhD reading your résumé, you draw attention to the transferable and technical skills you have that are *relevant* to the job at hand. The reason so many PhDs fail to get their résumé through employer ATS software programs is because their Work Experience sections all start with an academic job title, such as Postdoctoral Fellow, Academic Research Associate, or Adjunct Professor, followed by a second title such as Graduate Research Assistant, Research Technician, Teaching Assistant, Lecturer, or similar.

Why are you adapting your academic job titles to look more like industry job titles? Who are you fooling? Why are you bolding those titles to draw even more attention to them? Why are you including the name of the university in bold next to those titles? Are you actively trying to make the employer see you as a lifetime academic and totally irrelevant candidate?

You have to start seeing your résumé through the eyes of the person who will be reading it. You must start formatting it like an industry professional, not an academic. What keywords are likely in the ATS database? How can you get those words on your résumé? How can you call attention to them? What information is the hiring manager looking for? How can you help them find it faster?

The answer lies in the Functional résumé format, which you can see on the next page.

Notice the change to the Work Experience section in the above résumé versus the Gold Standard résumé format we discussed in the previous chapter. Here, your transferable skills and technical skills are at the top of each Work Experience subsection, not your academic job titles. Directly below those key experiences (which should match experiences on the job posting) is *where* (in which role) you gained each experience.

This résumé format is not new. In fact, it's been around for decades. The functional résumé format is not illegal, forbidden, or manipulative. What's manipulative is forcing an employer to read through job titles and things they don't care about just to get to the skills you might have that are relevant to the job. You won't get

Jane Smith

City, State
Your Phone
Your Email
Linkedin URL

Summary

- Etiam cursus suscipit enim. Nulla facilisi. Integer eleifend diam eu diam. Donec dapibus enim sollicitudin nulla.
- Nullam dapibus elementum metus. Aenean libero sem, commodo euismod, imperdiet et, molestie vel, neque. Aenean libero sem, commodo euismod, imperdiet et, molestie,
- Pellentesque interdum, tellus non consectetuer mattis, lectus eros volutpat nunc, auctor nonummy nulla lectus nec tellus.

Work Experience

Transferable or Technical Skill

Gained as a Job Title at Company or Institution

- Pellentesque interdum, tellus non consectetuer mattis, lectus eros volutpat nunc, auctor nonummy nulla lectus nec tellus. Pellentesque interdum, tellus non consectetuer mattis, lectus eros volutpat nunc, auctor nonummy nulla lectus nec tellus.
- Pellentesque interdum, tellus non consectetuer mattis, lectus eros volutpat nunc, auctor nonummy nulla lectus nec tellus.
- Pellentesque interdum, tellus consectetuer mattis, lectus eros volutpat nunc, auctor nonummy nulla lectus nec tellus. Pellentesque interdum, tellus non consectetuer.

Transferable or Technical Skill

Gained as a Job Title at Company or Institution

- Pellentesque interdum, tellus non consectetuer mattis, lectus eros volutpat nunc, auctor nonummy nulla lectus nec tellus. Pellentesque interdum, tellus non consectetuer mattis, lectus eros volutpat nunc, auctor nonummy nulla lectus nec tellus.
- Pellentesque interdum, tellus non consectetuer mattis, lectus eros volutpat nunc, auctor nonummy nulla lectus nec tellus.
- Pellentesque interdum, tellus consectetuer mattis, lectus eros volutpat nunc, auctor nonummy nulla lectus nec tellus. Pellentesque interdum, tellus non consectetuer.

Transferable or Technical Skill

Gained as a Job Title at Company or Institution

- Etiam cursus suscipit enim. Nulla facilisi. Integer eleifend diam eu diam. Donec dapibus enim sollicitudin nulla. Nam hendrerit. Nunc id nisi.
- Nullam dapibus elementum metus. Aenean libero sem, commodo euismod, imperdiet et, molestie vel, neque. Duis nec sapien eu pede consectetuer placerat.
- Etiam cursus suscipit enim. Nulla facilisi. Integer eleifend diam eu diam.

Education

Aliquam dapibus. Insert Dates
Nam ut est. In vehicula venenatis dui. Vestibulum ante ipsum primis in faucibus orci luctus et ultrices posuere cubilia Curae; Praesent venenatis gravida justo. In hac habitasse platea dictumst. Suspendisse dui.

Aliquam dapibus. Insert Dates
Nam ut est. In vehicula venenatis dui. Vestibulum ante ipsum primis in faucibus orci luctus et ultrices posuere cubilia Curae; Praesent venenatis gravida justo. In hac habitasse platea dictumst. Suspendisse dui.

Techniques, Software & Instrumentation

Suspendisse potenti.	ut, fermentum at, blandit vitae,	Vestibulum metus ligula,
Vestibulum rhoncus. Ut	ligula. Vestibulum	volutpat vitae, feugiat at,
rhoncus turpis a massa. Vivamus	diam. Etiam ut velit nec lacus	blandit quis, lorem.
adipiscing quam, laoreet	consectetuer libero.	

Affiliations & Hobbies

- Pellentesque interdum, tellus non consectetuer mattis, lectus eros volutpat nunc, auctor nonummy nulla lectus nec tellus. Pellentesque interdum, tellus non consectetuer mattis, lectus eros volutpat nunc, auctor nonummy nulla lectus nec tellus.
- Pellentesque interdum, tellus non consectetuer mattis, lectus eros volutpat nunc, auctor nonummy nulla lectus nec tellus.

Jane Smith

hired doing this. It's time to start bringing the skills employers are looking for to the forefront of your résumé. Use the Functional résumé format to make your relevant skills and experiences extremely noticeable so employers can find them immediately. Put them where the job titles would be, and underneath them simply put where you gained those skills, which should include the academic title or job title you held when you gained that skill and the organization at which you gained that skill. Using this method, you could turn the following start to a Work Experience section …

Graduate Research Assistant   University ABC, 20XX to Present

… into something more relevant and functional, such as:

Next-Generation Sequencing Experience
Gained as a Graduate Research Assistant at University ABC

Can you imagine the difference this change makes to employers? Instead of employers skimming your résumé, seeing irrelevant information pulled out as a bolded subheading, and immediately getting the impression that you are a student with no experience who can't do the job, they read on. With the Functional format, their attention is immediately grabbed by the skills they are looking for, and their interest quickly deepens as they read the information in your bullet points backing up these skills. The Functional résumé format should be the first choice for any PhD who does not have relevant experience or relevant job titles for the position at hand.

That is, unless the person you're handing your résumé to is a recruiter.

Chapter 12

Three Additional Résumé Formats for Unique Job Search Situations

· ·

T he only way to get noticed in the modern job market is to see your résumé from the vantage point of those who will be evaluating you for the position at hand. One of the first interviews I did with a recruiter after founding Cheeky Scientist really opened my eyes to how different their role is compared to a hiring manager. During the interview, the recruiter told me, "I hate when job candidates use the same résumé format for me as they would for a hiring manager."

Wait, I thought, *there are different résumé formats for different people?*

I knew that each résumé needed to be targeted to each individual position, but now they needed to be targeted to the role of the gatekeeper who was going to read the résumé first?

The answer was—and is—"yes."

You must target your résumé to the reader, not just the role. And this targeting extends beyond the keywords that you put on the résumé. As I mentioned previously, many recruiters do not work directly with the company they're representing. In fact, many recruiters do not even have a contract in place at the hiring company. Instead, they are headhunting to find a qualified candidate for a role that a company posted and only once they've found a potential "head" do they reach out to the company to offer the candidate to them in exchange for a finder's fee.

Did you catch that?

. . . .

Many recruiters, whether they're contacting you or not, do not officially represent any company.

. . . .

Even those who do represent the company officially or work internally and exclusively with that company are going to prioritize information differently.

Since most external recruiters and many recruiters overall have relatively little, if any, knowledge of the company or the company's needs, they rely heavily on technical skill lists gleaned from company job postings or provided directly to them by these companies; therefore, you should adjust the formatting of your Gold Standard or Functional résumé by putting the technical skills list at the top of the first page of your résumé, directly under the Professional Summary section, as seen below.

As you can see above, the only difference between the résumé formats we have previously discussed and this Recruiter résumé format is that the technical skills section is moved above the Work Experience and Education sections, rather than being below them. The impact of this simple shift is more dramatic than it might seem because by correctly prioritizing the information the reader cares about most, you have elevated your candidacy in the reader's mind.

Combining Résumé Formats When You Do Have Industry Experience

I already discussed how to fight the main killers of your PhD job search—obscurity, not communicating your transferable skills, and failure to show commitment to the position at hand. I've also talked about how overcoming those obstacles should be prioritized over any obsession with years of experience, technical and specialty skills, or degrees and certifications.

But what if you have a lot of experience in a particular industry? What if you have the exact skills that the employer is looking for? What if you are an expert in your space?

The answer is simple: exploit your expertise. Dominate your domain. Your home base during your job search should be your Unique Selling Proposition, or USP, which is discussed in detail in later chapters. For now, just understand that your USP is just a fancy way of describing where you stand out and win compared to other job candidates. Getting hired is not about blending in. It's not about listing skills that every other job candidate likely has. If you're working to get into a different industry in which you lack experience and you focus on skills that every other PhD has, you will get lost in the crowd and lose out on the best roles in industry. But if you focus on presenting your unique combination of technical and transferable skills, you will win. Likewise, if you have extensive experience in a specific area of industry and are applying to a job within that area, the surest way to win is to leverage your expertise. This is what the Combination résumé format allows you to do.

A Combination résumé, you guessed it, *combines* the Gold Standard and Functional résumé formats from previous chapters. The unique feature of the Combination format is the addition of a Key Industry Skills section between the Professional Summary section and the Work Experience section (which is still in reverse chronological order). If you have already gained the skills you need to perform at a very high level in a role, you'll want to highlight them at the very beginning of this résumé format in the Key Industry Skills section. The Key Industry Skills section should be approached as an extension of your Professional Summary section (which has three bullet points and showcases your three biggest and most relevant career highlights).

Since you have experience in the field already, you will want to further highlight your experience with an additional five bullet points in your Key Industry Skills section, for a total of eight bullet points and eight career highlights (three in your Professional Summary and five in your Key Industry Skills section). Then you will further exploit your experience and associated job titles in the Work Experience section that follows. You can see an example of this Combination format below.

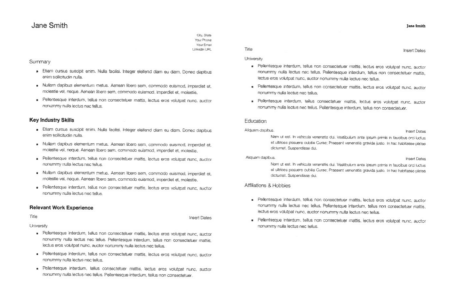

The Ideal One-Page Résumé for Competitive and Client-Facing Industry Roles

The more competitive or client-facing the industry role, the shorter your résumé should be. Recall the eye-tracking studies I referred to earlier that found employers only spend five to seven seconds on a résumé.[28] Think more carefully about what that means for you. Your résumé had to be filtered with hundreds, if not thousands, of other résumés successfully through an employer's ATS software and a real person had to select your résumé from dozens of résumés that survived the filter, if not more. Then that person cared just enough to skim it for a maximum of seven seconds before looking you up on LinkedIn® and deciding whether to invite you to a phone screen. Now the brevity of this process should excite you, not depress you, because if you can be brief but impactful, you will stand out. This is especially true when competing with other PhDs who haven't read this book and will be trying to add as much information to their résumés as possible.

How can you make your résumé pop? How can you make it stand out over every other PhD-level job candidate? How can you help your audience consume as much relevant information about you as possible in the shortest amount of time?

An easy answer is to draw a line down the middle of the first page of any of the above two-page résumé formats and put everything on the original first page on the left side and everything on the second page on the right side, then cull as much text as necessary to reach a clean, one-page "Sidebar" résumé. The Sidebar résumé format is the preferred format for employers hiring PhDs into top competitive positions in industry like Data Scientist, User Experience Researcher, and Medical Science Liaison, as well as those hiring for more client-facing roles like Technical Sales Specialist and Marketing Communications Specialist. As shown below, for this Sidebar résumé format, your Contact Details, Technical or Specialty Skills, and Education sections should be on the left, and your Professional Summary, Work Experience, and Honors, Awards & Hobbies should be on the right.

Jane Smith

Contact

Phone
(123)456-7890
Email
Yourname@email.com
Website
Janesmith.com
Address
1234 Parkway Dr.
New York New York

Skills

Business Development

Associate Manager

Graphic Design

Photoshop

Website Design

Education

DOCTOR OF PHILOSOPHY
New York University

2006-2009
BACHELORS OF ARTS
New York University
2002-2006

Professional Summary

Lorem ipsum dolor sit amet, consectetur adipiscing elit. In eu felis at augue hendrerit | mollis. Integer in tristique eros, vitae varius lacus. Ut et mauris eleifend, hendrerit mauris a, hendrerit diam.

Work Experience

Drug Discovery & Development
Company | 2015- Present
- Lorem ipsum dolor sit amet, consectetur adipiscing elit. In eu felis at augue hendrerit mollis. Integer in tristique eros, vitae varius lacus..
- Lorem ipsum dolor sit amet, consectetur adipiscing elit. In eu felis at augue hendrerit mollis.
- Lorem ipsum dolor sit amet, consectetur adipiscing elit. In eu felis at augue hendrerit mollis.

Drug Discovery & Development
Company | 2015- Present
- Lorem ipsum dolor sit amet, consectetur adipiscing elit. In eu felis at augue hendrerit mollis. Integer in tristique eros, vitae varius lacus..
- Lorem ipsum dolor sit amet, consectetur adipiscing elit. In eu felis at augue hendrerit mollis.
- Lorem ipsum dolor sit amet, consectetur adipiscing elit. In eu felis at augue hendrerit mollis.

As a PhD, you can't go wrong using a one-page résumé format, and a Sidebar résumé format is the best one-page résumé format available. As a PhD, industry employers know you can be complex. They expect it. Their concern is that you can only be complex. Using the Sidebar résumé format will show them that you can communicate clearly and concisely, alleviating any concerns they have about whether you can work with their nontechnical team members or with their nontechnical clients.

Now that you see the value of having less on your résumé, let's address what you can—and should—leave off your résumé.

What to Leave Off Your Résumé

The most notable thing—maybe the only notable thing—to leave off your initial résumé is your publications. There is no place for your publications on any initial résumé you submit to an employer. If you're adding something akin to a Works Cited section to your résumé, you've completely misjudged your audience and will be seen as completely ignorant when it comes to industry and the role that hiring managers and other initial gatekeepers play in the hiring process. Realize that most of these gatekeepers do not have a PhD. They do not understand your technical skills and likely know nothing about the technical skills they're hiring for. They're certainly not asking themselves, *Hmm ... I wonder what the volume and issue numbers are for every article this job candidate has published?*

• •

Seriously, they're not looking for publications on your résumé.

• •

It doesn't mean your publications are meaningless. It means that if they can help you get hired, they will come up later in the hiring process. For now, save space on your résumé and showcase yourself as industry-minded by adding a link to your publications on Google Scholar or similar, or by putting "Publications Available Upon Request" at the bottom of your résumé. You can and should still highlight the number of publications you have and even name one or two of your top publications succinctly in one or two bullet points (more on this in the next chapter), but that is as far as you should go.

Likewise, you should not waste precious résumé space on the contact information for your professional references. In today's world, you do not even need to waste space on "References Upon Request." Employers know that you have references and will ask for them if and when the time is right. Focus instead on communicating your skills, experiences, and abilities in carefully crafted bullet points, which is where we are headed next.

Chapter 13

The Perfect Three-Part Résumé Bullet Point

· · · · · · · · · · · · · · · · · · · ·

A re you excited about the résumé formats you just read about? If you are like most PhDs, you think discovering a proven résumé format for industry is the be-all and end-all of getting hired. Now you have that résumé problem solved, right?

No.

Your résumé problem has just started.

I routinely talk to PhDs who have spent two hundred dollars on a downloadable résumé template from Monster.com, Career Builder, or a similar company, only to continue being ignored by employers after uploading it to job sites, and it's because they haven't learned to craft solid bullet points.

The Typical Bullet Points

The most challenging part of putting your résumé together is carefully crafting the bullet points that will go on your résumé, especially in the Professional Summary and

Work Experience sections. Think about the last résumé or academic CV you created. What did you write for the bullet points? Was any research involved?

Here's what I'm guessing you did: you either found a job posting you liked or merely thought about a job title you liked and started crafting bullet points you assumed would sound impressive for that job based on your experience. You focused on the complex technical skills you learned in academia and emphasized the number of years in your PhD field or other academic field. You didn't talk to a company who was actually hiring for the role. In fact, you probably didn't even look at the job posting carefully. Instead, you skimmed the posting to get a "feel" for the role. There was no keyword research involved—no data, no inquiry—just you writing whatever you could pull from your memory at the time. This unstructured and sloppy résumé strategy is a losing strategy, and it's why your résumé is not getting any responses from industry employers.

If you want to use your PhD to transition into industry, you need to get serious about the information you are writing on your résumé. You need to look at every bullet point from the viewpoint of the employer. What is the number one thing they care about over everything else? (I've already discussed it, by the way.) It's your ability to get hired, learn the role quickly, get along with everybody else on the team, and fit in with the overall culture of the company. This is what industry employers care about first and foremost. They want to know that if they hire you, you will not disrupt their current team or their current processes. They care more about what is working already and who is working for them already than anything you can bring to their organization.

Also consider that the hiring manager's own job is on the line if they hire a PhD who torpedoes the company's already highly functioning team. Your résumé will be carefully evaluated to ensure that you are not an awkward, arrogant, or defensive PhD coming out of academia.

Crafting New-and-Improved Bullet Points

The only way to ensure that you understand what is important to industry employers is to start every bullet point with what those employers prize most: transferable skills. As I mentioned previously, you want to include two or three transferable skills from each of the main transferable skill categories: systems-oriented, people-oriented, and self-oriented.

While employers care about transferable skills first, quantified results are a close second. I've worked with many recruiters and hiring managers over the years, and I've seen more than one snicker when they get a résumé that starts with "Ten years of experience in …" and then fails to mention any achievements during that time.

Do you know how bad it looks to say you have a lot of experience and then not mention anything you achieved during the time you spent gaining that so-called experience?

After the laughter subsides, these industry employers ask, "So what?"

You have a PhD. So what?

You have the exact skills the position calls for. So what?

You worked with a Nobel laureate. So what?

Ask yourself "So what?" over and over again as you write your résumé bullet points until you get to a result that matters, and then quantify that result. What good are your skills if you haven't used your skills to achieve anything? Who cares if you have ten years of microbiology experience? What have you achieved during those ten years? Anything at all? Or were you hoping to get hired based merely on your tenure in a field? Academia rewards tenure (or at least it used to), but industry does not.

The good news is that you have achieved meaningful results in your academic career whether you know it or not.

The better news is that the exact results you achieved matter less than your understanding of the importance of results and your ability to communicate your results.

Every single bullet point on your résumé needs to end in a quantified result. You can easily transition to this part of your bullet point using language like "resulting in," "as demonstrated by," or "as evidenced by." It is challenging to sit down and figure out your results and then quantify them. It is certainly more challenging than just listing skills, duties, and experiences in your résumé, but is the only way to move past the résumé stage to the phone screen stage. Remember the résumé eye-tracking studies I referred to earlier? Those same studies showed that employers' eyes pause at length on numbers. But there's a catch. The numbers must be written numerically, as in the number "10" rather than "ten" spelled out.[29]

Examples of quantified results include:

- "resulting in 5 reports on ABC research area"
- "resulting in 3 poster presentations on ABC topic"
- "resulting in 2 publications including a publication in ABC journal"
- "as evidenced by 8 collaborations, including a collaboration with ABC research group"

The main reason this process is so hard for PhDs is because many PhDs experience a sense of imposter syndrome when formulating the results section of their bullet points. In short, they don't think they have achieved any worthwhile results.

PhDs often feel like they can't claim a result as an achievement if anyone else was involved. If somebody else touched the figure, paper, or presentation, PhDs see it as a joint effort and feel guilty writing "resulting in XYZ." They feel like they are writing "resulting in XYZ that I achieved all by myself without anyone's help." This is ridiculous. You need to claim the results that you were a part of because no one is going to claim your results for you. If you do not have the courage to claim ownership in part or in whole for your achievements, why would any employer ever hire you? Because you want others to have the credit? Because you are a passive team player? These are not the values industry employers are looking for; they are seeking those who have the courage to stand up and say "I did this" and "here's why it matters." If you are stuck determining which results to claim on your résumé, consider the following list of examples (additional examples can be found in Appendix D).

- Number of publications
- Number of presentations
- Number of reports
- Number of discoveries or innovations
- Number of volunteer experiences
- Number of optimized or innovated systems
- Number of collaborations
- Number of completed projects
- Number of teams led or mentored
- Number of team outcomes
- Number of students taught
- Number of certifications
- Number of grants or patents
- Amount of grant funding

To finalize the perfect three-part bullet point for your industry résumé, you need to sandwich the transferable skills at the beginning of your bullet points with the quantified results at the end of the bullet points. You make that sandwich with your technical or specialty skills, but only those that are relevant to the job at hand.

Examples of how to structure these technically stacked connecting phrases, along with their content, include:

- "with in-depth knowledge of XYZ research technique"
- "and experience in XYZ instrument including XYZ instrument"
- "with an ability to develop and test questionnaires related to XYZ field"
- "with an ability to interpret study results related to XYX field"

Complete examples of these three-part bullet points include:

- Cross-functional collaborator with expertise in automated technologies including XYZ technology as demonstrated by # of SOPs on ABC topic.
- Project management expertise with expertise in XYZ technical processes resulting in # experiments that led to # discoveries in ABC field.
- Ability to delegate tasks and expertise in designing novel processes such as XYZ process resulting in discoveries, including ABC discovery.
- Documentation and reporting skills as well as expertise in XYZ related data analysis skills as evidenced by teaching # professionals on ABC topic.

By correctly connecting the three parts of your résumé bullet points, you will launch the reader of your points into the future. You want any employer who reads your résumé to see you in the position at hand *as they read* your résumé.

This is called *future pacing*, and it's what this three-part bullet point process is designed to do. Future pacing is made possible by a strong understanding of the key-words related to the job you want, which is where we are going next.

Chapter 14

Keyword-Hacking
ATS Software Programs

· · · · · · · · · · · · · · · · · · · ·

Y ou can't get hired in industry by using academic language. If you're like me when I started my first industry job search, the extent of your online research for companies that would hire you was typing "top jobs" into a search window and pressing enter.

Maybe you went one step further and typed "top jobs UK" or "top companies UK." Or maybe you just typed in "job openings." Whatever the specific case, this is a very poor job search strategy and a very, very poor research strategy in general. You can't find unique opportunities specific to your situation by relying on short-tail keywords. Short-tail keywords are not specific; therefore, they are likely to pull up many results but few that fit you, your goals, and your overall circumstances.

Long-tail keywords, on the other hand, provide very specific information as an input to the search browser and yield very specific information to you that fits your very specific situation.

So, instead of searching "top jobs" or "top companies UK," try searching things like "midsize engineering companies, greater London area" or "fast growing R&D

companies, Manchester" or "small biotech companies, project manager, Sydney." These long-tail keywords will inevitably turn up aggregated lists of companies you've never heard of.

Did you get that? These lists have already been aggregated for you.

Companies make revenue. Where there's money, there's documentation. We will explore how to use this strategy to further your networking efforts in great detail later. For now, understand how critical word choice is in your job search.

By using long-tail keywords in your research efforts, you'll go beyond just identifying the same handful of companies that everyone already knows—Pfizer, Intel, Apple, Google, Amazon, etc. When you start searching for small to midsize companies as well, you reveal millions of other companies in your space ready to hire you right now. Small to midsize companies are often in the fastest part of the industry growth phase, which means they are hiring aggressively.

You might want to work for a large company, and that's certainly an option. But does the company size alone matter? Small companies can have anywhere from ten to one thousand employees and midsize companies go from one thousand to several thousand employees. Even if you get hired at a very large Global 500 company, you're only going to be working with a few hundred to a few thousand people in one office building. They may have many other locations, but those additional locations are not going to change your day-to-day, on-site environment much.

The overarching point here is that if you want to master your job search, you need to master keywords, and you need to start opening your mind to new definitions, labels, and frameworks.

Mastering Keywords

The reason you need to master keywords as part of opening your mind is because keywords and their rankings are what employers use to find job candidates. You don't need to be some technical wizard to understand how keywords and the ATS algorithms work. You only need to understand three things: crawling, indexing, and ranking.

Crawling is when a company's server or a software application, such as LinkedIn® or another ATS software program, sends out search robots (often referred to as "spiders") to scour their directory profiles or résumés. These spiders review all the text in your profile or résumé, as well as the metadata of the pictures and URLs you added.

Indexing is when the information that is found during a crawl is organized and stored in the company's or software program's data centers.

Once your LinkedIn® profile and résumé are in such an index, they can be displayed as a result to relevant search queries from employers. In other words, your profile or résumé receives a search ranking. This ranking provides the keywords on your LinkedIn® profile or résumé that will best answer each query or search result, and each search result is ordered by relevancy so the employer can find the job candidate they are looking for, or at least the job candidate that best fits the initial query.

All this searching and finding is made possible by keywords. If your LinkedIn® profile or résumé lacks the keywords that an employer is searching for, and if those keywords are not connected to other relevant keywords that the employer is searching for (referred to as "keyword connectedness"), you will not be found. Instead, you'll be invisible.

The good news is that keywords are easy to master. Once you understand that long-tail keywords are more effective than short-tail keyword and that doing research on keywords matters, the rest is easy. The rest starts with simply copying and pasting as many keywords as possible from the job description into your résumé and LinkedIn® profile. It boggles my mind how few PhDs do this. Understand that you can't plagiarize a job posting. There are no copyrights or special protections on keywords for skills in a job posting, and even if the job posting mentions a proprietary or trademarked methodology, skill, product, or department, the employer still wants you to put their words on your résumé and LinkedIn® profile—their *exact* words. You don't need to break out a thesaurus to find different words than what's on the job posting to impress the employer.

Now, if you're like most of the PhDs I work with, at this point you're thinking, *Well, this doesn't work if I don't have the skills in the job description.* Really? Why can't you use words like "relevant" or "similar to" to link the skills and experiences in the job description to your related skills and experiences? Why can't you write that you have "the ability to learn" or "the ability to do" a certain skill?

If a job posting asks for "personnel management skills" but you've never been a manager, you can still write "volunteer and youth mentorship skills relevant to personnel management skills" or simply "the ability to develop personnel management skills."

Likewise, if the job description asks for "Python programming expertise" but you've never programmed in Python, you can still find a way to get the keywords "Python" and "programming" on your LinkedIn® profile and résumé. You could say "Experience in R and MATLAB relevant to learning Python and other programming languages."

Do you see how this works?

The goal is to get the words that are used in the job description onto your résumé and LinkedIn® profile because that's the only way to ensure you show up in the employer's LinkedIn® or ATS search results.

Now the only challenge is going through each job description and highlighting the keywords throughout the description—namely the transferable and technical skills—ranking them in terms of which are used the most, and adding those at the top of the list to your résumé and LinkedIn® profile. Good news! I have a hack for this that will save you a lot of time. Instead of doing this by hand, you can simply copy and paste all the text form the job description, or from multiple job descriptions, into a free online word cloud.[30] (A link to a free online word cloud can be found at: https://cheekyscientist.com/book-resources.) Using a word cloud shows you which skills and keywords are used most in the job description(s). The skills and words that show up in the largest font in the word cloud are the ones that are used the most. Now you just have to select the largest words—literally the largest—and put them on your résumé and LinkedIn® profile.

While hacking keywords is valuable and will save you time, you don't want to ignore the qualitative component of a job description; you want to actually read the description. Only by reading a job posting carefully will you really be able to understand what the employer is looking for. More importantly, this is the only way to understand where you can stand out as a job candidate. By reading a job posting carefully, you can see if the employer is more concerned about people-oriented, systems-oriented, or self-oriented transferable skills. As you read, do you see words like "process," "development," "procedure," "SOP," and "design" repeatedly? If so, they are looking for someone who is systems-oriented, and you better put a lot of systems-oriented transferable skills on your résumé and LinkedIn® profile. Does the description use words like "self-motivated" and "initiative" a lot? If so, make sure you add a lot of self-oriented skills to you résumé and profile. When you read the job posting a second time, do you see any unique combinations of skill sets you happen to have? If so, make sure you exploit those when crafting your résumé and profile.

Making Strong Keyword Connections

Once you have identified a strong set of keywords to put in your résumé and on your LinkedIn® profile, you need to start thinking about keyword connectedness. Just sprinkling in a few keywords from the job description is not enough. You must ensure the keywords you use fit into the context of the associated bullet point, sentence, or paragraph. This is why creating a longer keyword list of twenty, thirty, forty, or even fifty different keywords can be valuable because it gives you a vocabulary sheet to use as you're creating your résumé and LinkedIn® profile. We will discuss exactly how to do this in a later chapter. While it might sound like a lot of work, it's worth it. Every single job posting easily has at least thirty to fifty different keywords. By extracting as many keywords as possible, you put your résumé and LinkedIn® profile at the top of employer searches.

Now all that's left to do is learn how to dominate the most popular and successful ATS software program in the history of the job search universe so far, LinkedIn®, which is what we are discussing next.

CASE STUDY 3
Ravikiran Ravulapalli, PhD

I spent over a year trying to transition into an industry R&D role. Updating my résumé according to the standards in this book is what helped me finally get hired into an R&D position at one of the largest pharmaceutical and biotechnology companies in the world, despite not having industry experience. Looking back at my initial résumés, I'm shocked at how poorly they were written. I wouldn't even have hired myself after seeing my own résumé! That's one of the biggest problems PhDs face—learning how to change an academic CV into an industry résumé. You can't ignore this transformation and be heard. You must change.

I started by updating my résumé to the Functional format prescribed by Isaiah and then diligently crafted each bullet point in my résumé so that it was relevant to the employer's job description and always ended in a quantified result. The latter took much effort and was made possible by the bullet point scripts and other tools Isaiah provided me with in the Cheeky Scientist Association. My first résumés did not lead to a single phone screen. Not one. Once I made these changes, however, I got invited to a phone screen two out of every five jobs that applied to. Yes, I went from a 0 percent success rate to a greater than 85 percent success rate.

Looking back, I wish I would've dedicated more time to my résumé sooner. In particular, I wish I would have taken Isaiah's advice on keywords to heart sooner. ATS software is just a word-matching machine. Yet, as PhDs, we try to be too clever by using all of our own words for the work that we have done and can do instead of using the employers' words. I hope you do not make this mistake like I did. I lost many job opportunities due to uploading low-quality résumés.

One final thing I wanted to mention in this case study is that if you're reading this, you do not have time to test things out in your job search. I see so many PhDs wait to take their job search seriously and then suddenly get exposed to the industry job market after ten to twenty years in academia—or more!—and fail quickly and repeatedly. These PhDs remain clueless for months, if not years, refusing to get training from other PhDs who have transitioned into industry before them. I hope this won't be you. I want to sign off by saying thank you to Isaiah and the Association and to encourage you to start changing your résumé and taking your job search very seriously right now, not later.

***

If you're ready to transition into your dream industry position, you can apply to book a free Transition Call with me or one of my trained Transition Specialists at: https://cheekyscientist.com/transition-book.

STEP #4:

Dominate LinkedIn®
(or Whatever Social Media Platform Comes Next)

"Don't compete. Dominate."

— Grant Cardone

Chapter 15

Why Employers Can't
Find You on LinkedIn®

· · · · · · · · · · · · · · · · · · · ·

U ntil now, your job search was a one-sided affair. It was all about you. You,
you, you. *I want a job! I want to be recognized for my skills!*
But ... I don't really want to do any work to get noticed.

If you've read this far, you know that needs to change. What I highlight in this
chapter is that your job search is a two-part equation: you and the employer. And
we're going to focus on the part that's not you (the employer).

Who are these people trying to hire you? How do they find you?

LinkedIn® is the Most Extensive ATS Software

I talked about ATS software that employers use as part of their internal systems for
filtering through résumés. But I have yet to talk extensively about the most successful
ATS software of all time: LinkedIn®. Understanding LinkedIn® and understanding what
employers want to see from you as a job candidate go hand in hand because, in today's
world, employers *live* on LinkedIn®. Today, 95 percent of recruiters use LinkedIn® as
their main sourcing tool to find job candidates—95 percent![31] How much time are you

investing on LinkedIn®? How much time have you spent updating your profile or reaching out to new contacts? Not thinking about doing those things but actually executing those things?

If you're like most PhDs, the answer is very, very little.

The rest of this chapter is dedicated to opening the world of LinkedIn® to you—and not just the LinkedIn® you know but the LinkedIn® employers know. Did you know there are multiple versions of LinkedIn®, including LinkedIn® Recruiter and LinkedIn® Talent Insights? Did you know that you have to tell LinkedIn® to show you on LinkedIn® Recruiter before you can even be found there by employers? Did you know that your visibility on LinkedIn® is related to your Social Selling Index, or SSI?

If not, now is the time to learn.

First, though, we need to set the table in terms of LinkedIn®'s current role and future role in the job market.

Initially, I was hesitant to write about LinkedIn® specifically because twenty years from now, LinkedIn® might be called something else. Perhaps another company will buy LinkedIn® and change the name, or maybe a new hotshot software platform will come out of nowhere and overtake the world. It's happened before. Remember Myspace? What about Friendster? They existed before Facebook, and both barely exist or don't exist now. Facebook doesn't even exist anymore (the company is now called Meta).

But I decided that LinkedIn® is too important not to discuss when it comes to a PhD-level job search today.

• •

Importantly, LinkedIn® is now owned by Microsoft, thanks to the largest acquisition in Microsoft's history.[32] For decades, Microsoft has dominated industry companies as the most popular operating system. Considering that, LinkedIn® likely isn't going anywhere anytime soon.

• •

That being said, my goal is to only focus on the evergreen aspects of LinkedIn®. The advice I'm going to give you about LinkedIn® will always be in style. The upcoming strategies will always be relevant, and they will always work to get you hired, regardless of the software platform you apply them to. On the other side of algorithms are people making a decision based on what you show them and how you show it to them. For example, making your LinkedIn® profile "future facing," as in writing about your experience in a way that shows employers you're the perfect fit for the future position, is an evergreen strategy. Using the language of industry on your profile and, even more specifically, the language of the company and position you're applying to is an evergreen strategy.

How to be Seen on LinkedIn®

If you want to be found on LinkedIn®, you have to ask yourself what would motivate LinkedIn® to make it easier for employers to find you. Why would LinkedIn® want to help you? They're not doing it out of the kindness of their heart. **They need to make money.** They are a business that is trying to grow. Yes, they want to make your *experience* on LinkedIn® as enjoyable and productive as possible, and they do so in part by giving you many, many features for free—but why? How can they afford to do that?

They can afford to provide those things to you because companies pay them an immense amount of money to find you and other qualified job candidates.

Now, here's the important part: if LinkedIn® fails to help employers find job candidates who are a good fit for their jobs, those employers will stop paying LinkedIn®, and LinkedIn® will go out of business. Above all else, it's in LinkedIn®'s best interests to make sure employers find the right job candidates. Period. And by the *right* job candidate, I mean job candidates who are not only a good fit for the position and company but also those who are serious about getting hired and are very likely to accept a job offer. In other words, LinkedIn® prioritizes job candidates who are actively looking for a job right now.

This is why it doesn't matter whether I'm talking about LinkedIn® or another platform that helps employers find job candidates in the future. Someone can read this book one hundred years from now and the goal of that platform is going to be to keep employers happy by finding them the right job candidates. The question is, how does LinkedIn® know which job candidates are actively (and seriously) looking for a job right now versus those who are just dabbling, "kind of" looking, or looking for opportunities for the future?

The number one way LinkedIn® identifies who is actively and seriously looking for a job is their profile activity. Someone's activity refers to how much a job candidate is updating and republishing their profile page. Job candidates who are updating their LinkedIn® profiles daily or even multiple times per day are skyrocketed to the top of LinkedIn®'s search results because LinkedIn® knows that you are serious about getting hired now.

You're no longer just scrolling through your newsfeed, skimming job postings, or stalking connections.

No, now you're digging in. Now you're doing the hard work of writing and rewriting your profile. Now you're serious.

This means you can boost your visibility on LinkedIn® Recruiter and the rest of LinkedIn®'s platforms by updating and completing your LinkedIn® profile and then consistently and constantly keeping it up to date.

When it comes to keeping your visibility elevated on LinkedIn®, you must turn on your visibility by choosing which jobs you want to be found for and in which locations. The location and operation of this feature has already changed numerous times on LinkedIn®, but it will always exist because LinkedIn® will always need your permission to show that you're open to work. The good news is that this feature currently allows you to limit your visibility only to paying employers (those paying to use LinkedIn® Recruiter), which will ensure that your advisor, PI, or current employer cannot see that you are open to work. While updating your profile and turning on your visibility will ensure you can be found on LinkedIn® Recruiter, there are many other aspects of your activity on LinkedIn® that can and should be leveraged to further increase your visibility.

Increasing Your LinkedIn® SSI

As I mentioned earlier, LinkedIn® has a metric for how visible you are in their search results: your SSI. A direct link to see your current SSI can be found in the endnotes as well as at: https://cheekyscientist.com/book-resources.[33] As a PhD who has spent their life in academia, your current score may only be in the twenties or thirties out of one hundred. It may even be only two or three. Ideally, you want to raise this score to somewhere between the sixties to eighties. For now, aim to just get it above fifty. Your SSI is determined by four factors:

- **How established your professional brand is**. To increase this score, fill out as many LinkedIn® profile sections as possible as robustly as possible using keywords specific for the sector(s) of industry you're trying to get into.
- **How many connections you have to people in the sector(s) of industry you want to get hired into**. The more focused the sector and the more contacts within this sector, the higher your score will be.
- **Engagement with insights by posting on LinkedIn® and by liking and commenting on other people's posts**. This is called "splashing around" in the "LinkedIn® pool" and is very important to LinkedIn®'s algorithm. You can further increase your activity here by writing and publishing LinkedIn® articles.

- **Building relationships by sending connection requests with personal notes and reaching out to new connections after they accept your request.** The deeper you go with each connection by sending more and more messages back and forth (to build a professional relationship), the more this score increases.

Chapter 16

Why You Should Delete Your LinkedIn® Profile and Start Over

· ·

I t's better for you to delete your LinkedIn® profile than to keep your incomplete LinkedIn® profile posted. A study by Statista showed that this was true regardless of whether the job at hand was entry-level, mid-level, or executive level.[34]

How could this be? Wouldn't it be better to at least have some information available about you rather than no information at all?

Not if that information is the wrong information. Not if that information portrays you as a lifetime academic who is clueless about working in industry and would be a liability to hire.

Seeing the Employer's Point of View

During the early stages of a job search, employers are looking for reasons not to hire you. They are on high alert for red flags, and your LinkedIn® profile being bare bones or academic in nature is a giant red flag. Until you are invited to a site visit with an employer, your number one priority is avoiding red flags that could trigger them to dismiss your candidacy. In other words, you're playing defense more than you're playing offense.

The comprehensiveness and specificity of your LinkedIn® profile are indicators of your competence for a particular role. If an employer reads your résumé and then goes to the LinkedIn® URL listed in the Contact Details section of your résumé—and, by the way, you should always include your LinkedIn® URL in this section of your résumé—they will immediately be turned off by an incomplete profile, a profile that doesn't match your résumé, or a profile that doesn't display any industry credibility.

Think about it from the employer's point of view. When an employer sees an incomplete LinkedIn® profile, they think, *What? This person isn't even dedicated enough to complete their profile, let alone hold the reins of a serious, PhD-level position here. Goodbye.* They are also going to click a little box on LinkedIn® recruiter that effectively says, "Don't show this profile to me again—ever." Now, you've burned a bridge. That's one less employer who will be able to find you when you finally get things right.

As I've said throughout this book, your industry job search is not a trial-and-error affair. You don't get rewarded for experimentation the way you do in academia. There are consequences, and burning bridges with incomplete profiles is one of them.

Creating Robust Content

LinkedIn® rewards "dwell time," which is how much time a reader (the employer) spends on your profile page. Google started doing this years ago with one of its updates to reward web pages where readers tended to *dwell*—reading more content for a longer period of time than they would on other similar pages. LinkedIn® now leverages this same strategy with their algorithm and will for the foreseeable future. This is why your LinkedIn® profile must be filled out completely, meaning you should add robust content to every section available to you. But don't just fill in the section with just any text. Instead, leverage the text you add to each section by carefully choosing your keywords and making sure your keywords are connected to each other (as discussed in the chapter about keywords and ATS software).

Also consider that your LinkedIn® profile needs to appeal to every employer at every company for every type of role you're targeting, not just one employer from one company for one role like each targeted résumé you create. This means that you need to narrow down your job search to the two or three related job titles you want most and then collect and review five to ten job postings from different companies of interest for each of those job titles. As I already mentioned, you can copy and paste the text from those job postings into a word cloud to see which words are the most relevant for your job titles of interest. Then all that's left to do is to sprinkle those keywords throughout your profile.

By starting your LinkedIn® profile fresh, or drastically renovating your current incomplete profile, you can ensure that you appear at the top of employers' LinkedIn® Recruiter search results.

If you're wondering where to start, start at the top. Just like ATS software weights the keywords in the top one-third of the first page of your résumé more strongly than the rest of your résumé combined, LinkedIn® weights the keywords at the top of your LinkedIn® profile (namely your Headline and Summary sections) more heavily than the rest of your profile combined. But this visual center of your LinkedIn® profile is different from the visual center of your résumé in that it includes pictures: a Profile Picture (or headshot) and a Banner Photo.

Unless you are applying for a job in Germany or a handful of other countries where a headshot in the top corner of your résumé is mandatory, your résumé should not include pictures. On LinkedIn®, however, pictures along with well-placed text are a must, which is what we will be discussing next.

Chapter 17

How to Make Your LinkedIn® Profile a Magnet for Industry Employers

····················

The visual center of your LinkedIn® profile is the top section of your LinkedIn® profile: your Profile Picture, Banner Photo, Headline, and Summary. The visual center is the most important part of your profile because it's the first thing that employers see. They use your visual center to decide whether they want to explore your profile further or move on to another profile; therefore, all components of your visual center should be personalized and targeted to your dream position or positions.

Choosing a Profile Picture

Your Profile Picture should portray you as a reputable industry professional. If you have a bad or nonexistent profile picture, your visibility on LinkedIn® Recruiter will nose-dive, your connection requests will be denied, and your messages will be ignored. When adding a headshot to your profile, do not add one that depicts you as a student, such as a photo of you presenting at a conference, holding a pipette, sitting at a desk or lab bench, standing in front of a tree or bookcase, or wearing your lab coat.

Instead, use a picture of you wearing the same clothes you would wear to a job interview. Put effort into this photo the same way you put effort into the other parts of your job search. Don't just take a selfie. You want to look confident and approachable, like someone who would be great to work with. A nice smile, good lighting, and high-quality photography provide a great first impression for anyone you invite to your LinkedIn® profile.

The reality of how important a Profile Picture is can be lost on a lot of PhDs, so let's explore this a bit deeper.

If you want to get hired into a PhD-level industry career, you must have a high-quality, nongrainy, non-selfie, non-self-cropped, non-leisurewear photo as your headshot. Period.

You can't opt out of having a headshot either. The days of hiding what you look like online are over. If you want to get hired, someone needs to know what you look like—before they invite you to a face-to-face interview. You can't get away with having a blank space for a headshot anymore on LinkedIn® or any other social media platform without being seen as both high-risk and awkward. You need a picture, and this picture is more valuable than everything else on your profile. Employers want to get a look at you before hiring you; therefore, you should let them see you as early as possible.

That being said, it is your responsibility to look professional in your profile picture. Most employers will decide not to hire somebody based on a picture—not because they don't like how you look as a person but because they don't like the lack of professionalism and dedication your sloppy profile picture reveals.

Whether you get your Profile Picture professionally done, which I highly recommend (very inexpensive at local department stores or easily attainable with an online search for local photographers), or you do them yourself at home, make sure your background is white or another light color and blank (no family photos or decorations behind you). Make sure the lighting is good and that your eyes can be seen even if you're wearing glasses. You should have a full smile or at least a competent and authentic half smile. Practice as many times as you need because you'll be able to use this picture for the next three to five years. Ideally, when you're looking for a job, your headshot is the same on every online platform or website. This displays consistency, which builds trust. Employers want to know you're the same person everywhere. Remember, employers hate surprises when it comes to hiring. They value security and trust, which is best displayed, especially early in the job search process, with consistent images and text.

Adding a Banner Photo

Many social media platforms, LinkedIn® included, allow you to choose a Banner Photo, which is just a long, horizontal photo at the top of your profile that's most often used to catch someone's attention. LinkedIn® provides you with a default blue or gray background Banner Photo, depending on the season. However, you can—and should—customize your Banner Photo.

Add a high-quality Banner Photo that relates to your dream job or reflects your personality. You can be creative here. For example, you can add an image from your research discipline (this works really well if you work in an imaging discipline), an image of the cityscape where you live or want to live, an image of a hobby you are passionate about, or an image with an interesting pattern.

Unfortunately, most job candidates never customize their Banner Photo, or they post a Banner Photo that says nothing about who they are, the career track they're interested in, or the overall industry sector they're seeking a job in. This photo matters to both employers and LinkedIn®'s algorithm. It's literally at the very top of your LinkedIn® Profile. Employers really will skip over your profile or quickly bounce away from it based on the Profile Picture and Banner Photo you have. Take both very seriously. When choosing your Banner Photo, make sure it's high-definition and, as mentioned, symbolic of you and your professional brand in some way. If you want to work for a biotechnology company, showcase a high-quality biotechnology image. If you're an engineer and want to work for an optical company, use a high-definition image of a series of lasers. If you want to work as a User Experience Researcher in the hospitality sector, download a high-quality image of the inside of a superior hotel chain, the inside of a resort, or the outside view of an all-inclusive ranch. Make sure these images are general enough to imply that you're willing to work for any company (i.e., don't use images with a Hilton or Marriott logo in the last example) but specific enough to indicate your career interests. There are many royalty-free websites online like Pixabay and Pexels from which you can download images for free very quickly.[35] Links to some of those websites can be found at: https://cheekyscientist.com/book-resources.

Most importantly—and this is so easy to do but so few people do it—put that image into PowerPoint or design software and add three of your key transferable skills as text in the middle of the image. Yes, you can turn the banner photo into a mini professional summary so employers can quickly identify the relevant skills you have for the jobs you want. Make sure when you upload the final photo that you test it on both the desktop and mobile versions of LinkedIn® to ensure the words are not cut off and the picture looks centered.

Crafting a Headline and Summary

After you establish credibility with your Profile Picture and Banner Photo, you must craft your Headline and Summary sections. As I mentioned, LinkedIn® weights the keywords that are in these topmost sections far more than any other sections on your profile. In particular, the keywords in your Headline can dramatically influence LinkedIn®'s algorithm in your favor. The problem is that while your LinkedIn® Headline contributes the most value in terms of LinkedIn®'s algorithm, it's often the most ignored or underutilized by PhDs. Most PhDs simply list "postdoc" or "PhD student" in their Headline along with the university or institution they are currently attending.

Don't make this mistake. Don't waste this valuable real estate on academic words that will never appear in an employer's search.

Your headline needs to include the information that employers are actually searching for. As I mentioned in previous chapters, employers do not enjoy doing research. They're trying to find candidates quickly, and the search terms they use are the simplest versions of the skills you think are so important. In most cases, they are searching for the basic transferable skills required for the job, not your highly specific technical skills. Or they are searching for the simpler, transferable versions of your technical skills. You may know how to do an advanced research technique like HPLC, but they're likely searching for "research experience" or "data analysis." You might be an expert at understanding net promoter scores and other product management metrics, but they're searching for "branding," "marketing," or just "product management."

In fact, it's highly possible that the hiring manager or recruiter looking for you doesn't even know what your technical skill means. You have to learn the language that employers for the jobs you want are using because that's the language they are typing into LinkedIn® Recruiter and other recruitment search engines. The good news is that you can find this language simply by familiarizing yourself with the job descriptions. After reading twenty or more postings for a Research Scientist, Process Engineer, Medical Science Liaison, User Experience Researcher, Clinical Coordinator, Technical Writer, Postsecondary Educator, Administrative Assistant, or any other position, you have a superior understanding of the search terms employers are using for those roles. As mentioned, you can then hack these job postings quantitatively by using word cloud software, choosing the largest words in the word cloud (those used repeatedly in your chosen job postings) to include in your Headline. Put the most important and most frequently used words in your Headline—front and center.

Consider the employer's perspective. If they want to hire a Project Manager in London, what are they going to search? Project Manager. London. Enter. That's it. That's where they will start their search. Make sure your Headline reflects this by putting the name of the job title or job titles (two at the most) at the start of your Headline. If particular transferable or technical skills are used often in your selected job postings, put them in your Headline next. Notice that you are answering key questions for the employer when you do this: What do you want professionally? Who are you professionally?

Overall, your Headline should answer the following four questions for an employer:

1. What do you want professionally? Answer this question by adding your desired job title(s) to your headline.

2. Who are you professionally? Answer this question by sharing the technical and transferable skills you have that are relevant for the job. Aim to include three to four skills here. You can also include key accomplishments related to these skills.

3. Where do you want to work? Answer this question by adding your preferred location. LinkedIn® gives you the option to add a location to your profile, but you can also add one or more locations directly in your Headline. If you want to relocate, add the location where you want to work, not your current location. You can also indicate your willingness to relocate by adding "Willing to Relocate" to your Headline.

4. Who are you personally? Answer this question by adding at least one hobby to your Headline. Most hiring managers don't come from a technical background, so hobbies serve as conversation starters that humanize you. Hobbies also strongly differentiate you from other candidates who only mention their technical skills.

Overall, your Headline should be structured like the following:

Desired Job Title | Transferable Skill | Technical Skill | Transferable Skill | Location | Accomplishment | Hobby

Appendix E is an extensive list of Headlines from PhDs who have been hired in industry after updating their LinkedIn® profile Headline using the above methods.

Once you update your LinkedIn® Headline, you want to reinvent your LinkedIn® Summary section. Your Summary is not a place to copy and paste your résumé. This section is crucial to getting a phone screen because it's the first place employers will click to learn more about you and find your contact information. It's the major hook of your profile. Here, unlike your résumé, you should write in the first person and let your personality shine instead of sounding robotic and boring. That said, you should still use keywords and maintain a professional voice throughout your summary.

Start by introducing yourself and your professional brand in narrative form. Make your narrative "future facing" and focus on what you can contribute to an organization. Doing so will help the employer picture you in the position they are trying to fill. Then add three bullet points explaining your major achievements. The layout of your Summary should be clean and include lots of white space. Write in short paragraphs and leave space between your paragraphs and bullets. This makes your summary much more readable and encourages the viewer to continue scrolling to the rest of your profile. Below is an example of a properly formatted Summary section. As with the previous résumé images, the text in the image below is not in a readable language. The text is merely gibberish meant to show you where the lines of text should be located and approximately how much text there should be in each section.

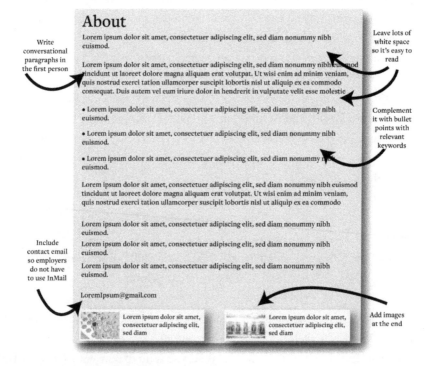

Finishing Your Profile

After you complete your visual center and Summary on LinkedIn®, turn your attention to your Experience and Volunteer Experience sections.

In the past, LinkedIn®'s Experience section was more specifically termed Work Experience. The change to Experience is significant because it encourages job candidates to include all relevant experiences in their profiles, not just past job titles. Add all relevant experiences to your LinkedIn® Experience section, including work, non-work, and volunteer experiences. Like your résumé, you will want to include at least three bullet points for every entry in your Experience section.

· ·

Remember, your bullet points must start with a transferable skill and end with a quantified result, with a technical skill sandwiching the two together. Focusing on your results and positioning them as evidence that you can achieve similar results in the future for your companies of interest helps employers envision what you can achieve for their company. Though you may feel like you have not achieved any results relevant to industry, you have. These can include number of publications, number of presentations, number of reports, number of discoveries or innovations, number of volunteer experiences, number of optimized or innovated systems, number of collaborations, number of completed projects, number of teams led or mentored, number of team outcomes, number of students taught, number of certifications, number of grants and patents, and funding amounts.

· ·

The above process should be duplicated for your Volunteer Experience section because employers place high value on this particular section. Don't make the mistake of just listing the name of the institution you volunteered with. Instead, take this section as seriously as your Experience section and add bullet points with key skills and results to showcase what you accomplished as a volunteer. Show that you take your volunteer work seriously.

Whenever you can, add images to your profile, whether that means uploading images directly or adding relevant URLs that pull in featured images from the associated web pages. You can do this in most sections of your LinkedIn® profile, including the end of each of your Experience sections. The human eye rests on images, just as it does on numbers. Some examples of appropriate images for your Experience section include an article you wrote, a picture of you conducting a work activity, or a URL to a web page that features your past work or working environment (the URL will pull the featured image from the web page into your profile as a thumbnail).

One final piece of advice for creating an Experience section that attracts employers is to format your Experience section functionally instead of chronologically. Similar to swapping out your reverse chronological résumé for a résumé that features your most relevant skills by function, you can adjust your LinkedIn® Experience section to highlight your relevant skills rather than your job titles. This is particularly useful if you spent your career in academia and have yet to work in industry. To do this, simply click "edit experience" in your Experience section and enter a technical skill or transferable skill in the Title space for each Experience. Then select your employer type and enter the company or institution name under company name just as you would otherwise.

There are many other sections of your LinkedIn® profile that you can—and should—complete using the methods above, including your Education, Honors & Awards, Publications, Organizations, Courses, Languages, and more. As you fill out each of these sections, make sure you are asking yourself the following questions:

- Is this section "future facing?"
- Does this section include keywords for the industry position(s) I want?
- Is this section personalized and "on brand" professionally?
- Does this section include keywords and a pitch that distinguishes me from other candidates?
- Have I taken this section seriously?
- Did I add bullet points, and is each bullet point results-oriented?
- Have I included images and other media in this section to make it even more eye-catching?

Once you have completed the key sections of your LinkedIn® profile, it's time to start adding some relevant, social proof to your profile through Endorsements and Recommendations. Then you can finally leverage your profile and social proof to gain exposure to industry decision-makers.

First, however, you need to be fully prepared for the process of networking—both online and offline. Connecting and networking to get hired is an art and a science; it moves fast and changes quickly. If you're not aware of the right order of things, you will burn bridges with top employers. The good news is that I have a strategy for ensuring your success in networking, even if you're a PhD who doesn't particularly enjoy reaching out to people you haven't met yet (like me).

STEP #5:

Crack into Any Career Network (and Stand Out)

·····················

"Be so good they can't ignore you."

— Steve Martin

Chapter 18

The Crucial Difference between Connecting and Networking

······················

I wasted the first three years of my graduate school career networking the old-fashioned way. I would go to internal seminars with the same people over and over again, arriving just in time and leaving right after it was over. Once or twice a year I would go to a conference and stand in front of some poster I made last-minute, like a used car salesman begging people to care. I would collect business cards and university cards at my poster and think, *I'm networking! I'm networking! It's happening! I've been discovered!* only to never have anyone who took my card or gave me a card reach out to me. Then, like all PhDs, by the time I reached my last year of graduate school, I complained about not having any industry connections or career options outside of doing a postdoc. What I didn't realize at the time was that I had never done any networking in graduate school. Sure, I connected with people. But I never networked.

Connecting is Different than Networking

Connecting is what happens when you meet someone. Networking is what is happens when you follow up with them to build a professional relationship. Most PhDs never network. They meet someone at a conference, seminar, or poster section in person, or they press the blue connect button on LinkedIn®, and that's it. When you're a job candidate searching for a job, it's *your* responsibility to turn connecting into networking. There is no substitute for networking, and your career will never reach its full potential if you don't network. It's been proven time and time again, even in academia, that networking is the key to funding and success. *Nature, Science, Cell,* and the like have reported over and over again that it's not the best research that gets the most funding; it's the most well-connected researcher who gets the most funding. Period. We live in a relationship-driven world, and love it or hate it, your relationships and access to decision-makers will dictate your industry success.

You Have to Spend Time Networking

If you want a PhD-level job in industry, you must build a bigger network. A key part of building a bigger network is improving your interpersonal skills. These skills are important not only for networking but also for getting and passing an industry interview. Numerous studies, including some reported by the National Academies, show that interpersonal skills are measurable and important.[36] Several surveys, reported by the Workforce Solutions Group, Adecco, and the ManpowerGroup in *Upstart Business Journal*, show that interpersonal skills, matter more than technical skills, no matter the profession.[37]

Improving your interpersonal skills is important, but it's only the first step. The next step is leveraging your interpersonal skills to grow your network and get an industry job. Studies in the *Academy of Management Journal* show that successful industry professionals spend nearly 70 percent more time networking than their less successful counterparts.[38] The *New York Times*, among other sources, reported that over half of all job hires at top-tier companies are from networking referrals.[39] On top of this, a study by Achievers found that the two-year retention rate of a job candidate increases from 20 percent to 45 percent if the candidate is hired from a referral over an online application.[40]

Along those lines, the fastest and most effective way to get an industry job is by getting referred for one. A referral is the result of building a strong professional relationship and can be achieved consistently by following a proven networking process.

In terms of sequence, you will connect with an industry professional, network to build a professional relationship, and then ask for and receive a job referral for an upcoming or open position at a company.

• •
Connect. Network. Get referred.
• •

A referral most commonly comes in the form of an industry employee who works at a company of interest to you passing your résumé on to the hiring manager for an open position or giving you permission to use their name or referral code when applying online. It could also come in the form of receiving an email introduction to a hiring manager or another decision-maker at the company, being introduced to another employee at the company who can tell you more about upcoming positions and the company as a whole, getting permission to mention the employee's name on a cover letter, or simply being told insider information about jobs that are about to open but are not posted yet. It is easier than you might imagine to be referred for a position if you have networked confidently and appropriately because industry employees are often incentivized to refer you, with the average employee referral bonus at $2,500.[41]

Still, referrals don't just happen, and neither does networking. You will have to get organized, create a strategy, and work for it.

Networking is kind of a second job (without pay) that will take up at least half of your time during your job search. Too many PhDs think that getting published and having an almighty PhD is going to lead to industry exposure and thus job opportunities. That is not the case. If you want to get hired, you must start building your network.

The new rules of networking as a PhD involve both online and offline techniques targeted at three types of professionals: gatekeepers (e.g., hiring managers, recruiters, talent acquisition specialists), decision-makers (e.g., directors, executives, operations managers, those who you may directly report to once hired), and proximally positioned peers (i.e., those with the job title you are seeking or other PhDs at the company in similar positions). While your networking activities must be robust and consistent to get hired, there is no need to be overwhelmed. Networking, like any transferable skill, can be learned, improved, and mastered. It's a matter of simply following the right steps in the right order.

As you move through the next few chapters, focus your initial efforts on gradually branching out and slowly increasing your risk tolerance until you're comfortable contacting anyone—online, in person, or otherwise.

While that might sound easy, I know networking—or even just the thought of networking—is extremely painful for many PhDs, and that's what we will discuss next.

CASE STUDY 4
Emma Lirette, PhD

I'm a humanities PhD, and worse, my PhD is from an interdisciplinary program. When people ask what my PhD is in, I usually say American studies, but it's closer to cultural anthropology, archival history, and comparative literature. Or something. I taught as a Visiting Assistant Professor for a year, and while I loved teaching and the respect regular faculty give visiting folk, the lack of permanence, the puny paycheck, and the insularity got to me. So I decided to transition into industry and, like too many PhDs, tried to do it on my own at first. Most of my time was spent honing my résumé and cover letters, so I never really got anywhere. Family obligations made sustaining in-person networking efforts difficult, and what little networking I was doing wasn't yielding any significant results. That's when I joined the Cheeky Scientist Association and shifted my focus to my LinkedIn® profile and networking on LinkedIn®.

After I joined the Association, I started spending most of my time reaching out to people on LinkedIn®. I would follow up with people I met at in-person networking events on LinkedIn® too. While I did go to some PhD-specific and tech-specific networking events, I followed Isaiah's recommendation and also went to random ones with different professional organizations unrelated to PhDs or anything technical. Isaiah calls these types of events "Blue Ocean Connecting" events because they are events where you will be highly differentiated as a PhD. There likely won't be any other PhDs "in the water," so to speak. One of the events I went to was run by a real estate agent and a shoe store owner. I was one of the few people trying to break into a PhD-level role and the ONLY person there with a PhD. Talk about standing out! At the event, I was introduced to someone who was working with a Global 500 retailer as a consultant. This consultant offered to pass my résumé along to the Head of User Experience there.

After the event, I fired up my LinkedIn® networking game and began deepening the relationship with my contact from the event. He had forgotten to pass along my résumé, which made me realize Isaiah was right about something else: the ball was always in my court when it came to my job search. It was on me to drive each networking relationship forward, and LinkedIn® was the best way to do this. I got a call from the hiring manager at the company the next week, had a phone screen two days later, followed by a case interview and a marathon site visit. I received an offer and signed it shortly thereafter.

Transitioning into industry, especially with my interdisciplinary background, would not have been possible without elevating my activity on LinkedIn®. Most importantly, I followed the strategies in this book for updating my LinkedIn® profile. Every time I met someone at an online or in-person event and followed up with them after, the first thing they saw was my LinkedIn® profile. Once I started demonstrating industry credibility on this profile, opportunities really started opening up. The same will happen for you.

***

If you're ready to transition into your dream industry position, you can apply to book a free Transition Call with me or one of my trained Transition Specialists at: https://cheekyscientist.com/transition-book.

Chapter 19

How to Participate in In-Person Networking without Feeling Awkward or Exhausted

. . . .

Most of the remaining chapters about networking focus on building professional relationships by following up online with contacts and setting up informational interviews to get job referrals. But first, this chapter focuses on what most PhDs truly dread the most: in-person networking.

On a long enough timeline in your job search, you will have to meet someone in person. And you will have to get that person to like you. Even if you secure a remote position, there will be a team event at least once a year you will be expected to attend. If you want to elevate your career beyond technical support, freelance technical writer, or the like, you will need to get in front of other professionals.

I definitely avoided doing this in graduate school. During the last year of my PhD program, I made every excuse imaginable to avoid networking in person. I knew it was important for my job search and would be a deciding factor in my career options, so I would sign up for networking events that usually happened at the end of the day or over the weekend.

Of course, the end of the day and the weekends were the times when I least felt like traveling to a networking event to stand around awkwardly for three hours. And why were these events always so long—three hours!? What was I going to do for three hours? It wasn't until years later when I was setting up my own networking events that I realized organizers make the events three hours long because people get off work at different times and they want to accommodate as many people as possible over the course of that time, not keep everyone there from start to finish. Understanding this changed everything for me. I realized that the networking event's timetable was there for me to use as I liked. I could walk in, have professional conversations over the course of fifteen to twenty minutes, get three business cards, and leave. This was much more manageable—and much less painful.

Networking Doesn't Have to be Painful

Networking can be leveraged for maximum impact with very little input. The key is to plan your networking activities in advance. Networking should be a strategic venture, not a random one. Start by mapping out a list of events to attend in the next three months. Next, call the organizers and hosts of those events, tell them why you're coming, and ask for help preparing for the event. Ask how you can get the most out of the event. They will be eager to help you.

Think about it. If you're hosting a networking event—putting extensive time and energy into the event to make it successful—what are you most hoping to get out of the event? What would make it, in fact, successful? People networking.

If someone shows up, feels uncomfortable, and has a bad experience, that is death to a host. By reaching out beforehand, you are helping them make the event successful. When you talk to the host, ask if it would be okay for you to find them when you show up and introduce yourself in person and if they would be okay introducing you to one or two other attendees once you get there. They will usually agree do this and, in doing so, will do most of the networking for you.

When you arrive at the event, don't be surprised if you see people congregating into groups of two to eight people. On the outside of these groups, it may seem like joining is an impossible feat, but it's not. Still, many of us PhDs can recount multiple times when we have stood alone, awkwardly near a wall, clutching a drink in our hand, watching these circular conversations from what felt like miles away. In those situations, it's important to know with 100 percent confidence that you are the only one who can make yourself engage with others. No one is going to come save you from your solitude. No one is going to relieve you of the mild discomfort of meeting new people. It's all on you.

That being said, you can follow proven processes for entering these groups that will make you feel much better and will successfully integrate you into informative and entertaining group conversations. The strategy you can use to join one of these groups is actually simple and easy to execute—you just have to do it.

How to Join a Networking Group

First, find a group you want to join. Aim for a group of four or fewer people. Approach the group, look the person who is currently talking in the eyes, smile, and say, "Excuse me, I'd like to join in and introduce myself." Be kind, but don't apologize, and don't ask permission. Most importantly, remember that this is expected and acceptable behavior at networking events. You are not interrupting. Then, introduce yourself, shake hands with everyone in the circle, turn back to the person who was speaking, and say, "Thank you so much, please continue." Done. You have successfully entered a networking circle.

• •

To successfully join a networking circle, you are going to have to interrupt someone who is talking. There is no way around this. There will never be a pause. Again, this is not only perfectly okay but is also expected and encouraged.

• •

Remind yourself as many times as you need to that people expect you to come up and talk to them randomly at a networking event. You are not bothering them. It's called a "networking event" for a reason—so people can network. Everyone is eager to have a conversation, and everyone is worried about standing awkwardly alone. Others will be excited to have a conversation with you. Yes, networking is hard. For many it is an uncomfortable experience, but you have to do it. It is an essential part of your job search, a lifelong transferable skill, and will play a larger and larger role in your career success once you get into industry.

During your networking conversations, always make sure to get the contact details for people you are interested in making a more in-depth connection with. This is the only way to move from connecting with people at an event to networking with them, which occurs after the event. True networking can only be done by following up with the people you meet later—but not too late. Most importantly, it is your responsibility—and your responsibility alone—to follow up. You cannot rely on other people to reconnect with you after the event. You must get their information so that you can follow up within twenty-four hours. Consider how many people you have met at conferences, poster sessions, or other networking events. These may be people you had great conversations with and collected business or university cards from, only to never hear from them again. How many? Each of these is a lost opportunity because you did not follow up. As a PhD, you know how to set up a system, you know how to follow through, and you know how to be determined. To network successfully, you need to call upon those strengths. After each networking event, you can send a quick email or LinkedIn® message to the people you met as early as right after the event and no later than twenty-four hours after the event. Your note should remind the other party about the conversation you had and express your gratitude for your time together. Then you should set up a plan to follow up every one to four weeks with your new connections, depending on how soon you need a job referral to get hired.

Having the Actual Conversations

As far as the individual conversations you have with people during networking events, your overall goal should be simple, small, and measurable. As I mentioned earlier in the chapter, a good starting goal is to connect with three people (yes, just three) by getting their contact information and following up with them within twenty-four hours of the event. Each interaction should only take five minutes, and four and a half minutes of that time should be spent listening to the other person. Your goal is to get them to talk about their interests. Studies in neuroscience and behavioral psychology continue to show that the more the person you're talking to talks about themselves and their interests, the more they end up liking you.[42]

Did you catch that?

You do not need to posture. You do not need to talk much at all.

Instead, say something like, "Nice to meet you. So what's something you're working on right now that you're excited about?" Or, even more generally, "What's something going on in your life that you're enjoying right now?"

Notice this question is framed to get them to easily respond with something that is positive, about them, and at the top of their mind. If you do this well, the other person will talk at length about themselves and something positive going on in their life. After they share, you can ask a few follow-up questions about their initial response, such as, "Wow, thanks for sharing. It sounds like you have your hands full. What are some challenges that have come up in that project/venture/goal?" or "Very interesting. Thanks for sharing. How did you get involved with that project/role/goal in the first place?"

I discuss how to extend those conversations in future chapters, but remember, you are just connecting here. The actual networking—following up to build a professional relationship—occurs after you first meet someone.

After a few minutes of talking about themselves, the other party will usually realize it's been a one-sided conversation and pause to say something along the lines of, "Well ... enough about me. What about you?" Silence. Drumroll. This is it. This is the rare moment in life when you have a few minutes of someone's undivided attention. Will you leverage it and leave them wowed and impressed with your candor, clarity, confidence, and professional awareness—or will you make their eyes glaze over? The only way to avoid the latter is to develop an elevator pitch that goes beyond who you are (which I share how to do in the next chapter). Once you've delivered your elevator pitch, all that's left to do is ask the other person for their business card or contact information, thank them for their time, and excuse yourself without making a scene.

You don't need to explain why you are leaving, apologize, or hang around the other person awkwardly. You can simply say, "Thank you again. Enjoy the event. Excuse me," and walk away. There is no need for a goodbye production. Instead, just leave. Do the same thing when you want to leave any networking circle and the overall event. But before you leave the overall event, thank the host, and thank both the host and anyone else you met after the event.

Chapter 20

Turning Your Unique Selling Proposition into a Rationale-Based Elevator Pitch

. . . .

T he more you know who you are, what you want, and why, the more influence you carry in your job search and in life. If you follow the methods in the previous chapter for getting the most out of in-person networking events, you will gain moments of focused attention from those you're connecting with, whether those are after they talk about their interests and pause to ask about you or when you start an in-person interview by answering the classic "Tell me a little about yourself."

These moments are very fleeting, so you need to be prepared. You will literally only have seconds to impress the other person. You won't impress them with your accomplishments but with the concise delivery and impact of your elevator pitch.

This is your chance to break free of the academic stereotype (nonsocial nerds who can only hold conversations with other nonsocial nerds about their latest experimental findings). A recent report in *Nature* showed that many postdocs struggle to communicate their knowledge to nonscientific audiences. As the article notes, "[PhDs deliver an elevator pitch] the same way as they would do it to a lab colleague—resulting in a lot of glazed eyes and wrinkled brows."[43]

But you can be different.

You can craft an intelligent, succinct, and rationale-based elevator pitch.

The key is to practice and revise your pitch until you have developed a winning introduction that can be expressed in a conversational tone. An elevator pitch is a personalized, top-of-mind script you can deliver in a connected way that shows confidence during impromptu encounters with decision-makers (whether at formal events or in elevators). It's a powerful tool that you can use when a professional at a networking event says, "Enough about me, what about you?" or when hiring managers ask, "Can you tell me a little about yourself?"

The Parts of an Effective Pitch

To create an effective pitch, you must answer three questions about yourself:

1. Who are you (both professionally and personally)?
2. What do you want?
3. Why should someone else care?

For example, you could say, "I'm an immunology specialist but I enjoy going to craft fairs on the weekends, and I'm here to grow my industry network because I'm interested in developing new skills that will help me translate my knowledge of the immune field to a product that will help people."

With your pitch in place, all you have to do is present it to your target with confidence and good body language.

Of course, truly pinning down who you are professionally in addition to what you want and why is not an easy task. It takes careful thought and execution to arrive at a simple sentence that communicates your professional who, what, and why. And before you can pitch yourself to someone else, you first must understand what makes you unique in the first place. Then, you must position your unique qualities as a proposition that will benefit someone else. In other words, you have to craft a Unique Selling Proposition (USP).

USP as a Venn Diagram

The term Unique Selling Proposition or USP (sometimes referred to as a Value Proposition) comes from the world of advertising, marketing, and branding. A USP is a description of the factor or factors that differentiate a company's product from its competitors. It's the main reason the company communicates to consumers to convince them to choose their product over others. As a job candidate, *you* are the product that you are trying to sell to employers. When employers are reviewing your application, they are asking:

- How will this unique candidate solve my problem and help my organization succeed?
- What is different and better about this candidate that warrants my time and attention?
- Why should I choose to work with this candidate and not the other job applicants?

Your USP should address these questions. In doing so, it will help convince employers that you are uniquely qualified and that they should hire you over other candidates. To arrive at your USP, you need to consider three factors from an employer's perspective:

1. What the company needs
2. What you do well
3. What other job candidates do well

Imagine each of these factors as a circle in a Venn diagram (as a reminder, a Venn diagram typically has three overlapping circles with an overlap between every combination of two circles and an overlap of all three circles in the center). The purpose of visualizing a USP in this way is to show you what you want to avoid and what you want to focus on when crafting your USP.

Consider the three areas of overlap in such a Venn diagram. First, imagine the overlap of the "What the company needs" circle and the "What other job candidates do well" circle but not the "What you do well" circle. Clearly, you want to avoid this area altogether in terms of your résumé, LinkedIn® profile, or any networking conversations or interviews you have with employers.

Second, consider the overlap of all three circles: "What the company needs," "What you do well," and "What other job candidates do well." You might think this is a safe place to be, but it's not. This is a very risky zone. At best, you're calling attention to the skills and experience you have that many other candidates have, and at worst, you're putting another job candidate with the same skills and experience back into the employer's awareness. Unfortunately, this is the zone that most PhDs play in when trying to transition into industry. These PhDs list their technical skills and niche-specific specialty skills on their résumés and profiles and talk incessantly about their PhD training and education. Of course, every other PhD-level job candidate they are competing with is communicating in the exact same way.

The only way to differentiate yourself from other job candidates and arrive at your true USP is to focus exclusively on the area of overlap between the "What the company needs" and "What you do well" circles but not the "What other job candidates do well" circle. This is where you win intelligently in the job market. This is your area of differentiated strength. This is your USP. The only question that remains is which skills can be found in this particular overlap for you. The answer lies in your transferable skills and the unique combinations of your technical skills and transferable skills. You can see the above areas of overlap, including the areas to avoid and the area of overlap to focus on when creating your USP, in the image below.

The simplest way to arrive at your USP for any individual position, as well as any company or sector of industry, is to fill in the three circles with the technical skills and transferable skills found in the individual job posting or collection of job postings. You can easily visualize the most popular skills across multiple job postings with the word cloud strategies discussed in previous chapters. Start by creating a spreadsheet with three columns, titling the columns: "What the company needs," "What I do well," and "What others do well." Review a job posting for a position you are interested in. Carefully read through each word of the job description, realizing that every word is in the description on purpose. Pull out as many descriptive words as you can, including words like "self-motivated," "global sites," "scientific knowledge," "communication with team members," and "fast-paced." There are no right or wrong words to use here, and there is no limit on how many words can create one "keyword." For example, one keyword might be "downstream development purification and optimization activities" while another might be "data analysis." Use these keywords to fill in the "What the company needs" column in your spreadsheet. Pay particular attention to the words that describe the technical skills and transferable skills needed for the job. Next, let's turn our attention to the "What I do well" column.

Despite what your academic advisor, imposter syndrome, or overly critical academic mindset might tell you, you do *a lot* well. You would not have earned or be in the process of earning a PhD if you did not have valuable skills and qualifications. It takes a certain level of research, communication, strategic thinking, and other skills to create new knowledge. Few people possess skills at that level. Even fewer have demonstrated that they have those skills by earning a PhD. Many PhDs focus on what they don't have for their target industry role. If that describes you, *stop*. Instead, focus on what you *do* have as well as what you have the *ability* to do, not just what you already have experience doing. Be sure to focus on relevant skills you already have that are related to those on the job posting. Additional questions that can help you realize just how many skills you've gained include:

- What did you excel at during your PhD training?
- What skills and methods did you find yourself training others on?
- Did you give seminars that those outside your niche subject area could understand?
- Did you compare different products to find out which would be best for your research group or project?
- Did you keep organized records of safety protocols or the research group budget?

Academia, with its hyperfocus on publications and grants, may not honor these accomplishments, yet they are extremely valuable in industry because they are transferable and give rise to many other niche skills.

Now carefully consider all the keywords you listed in the "What the company needs" column. Copy and paste any of the skills you already have *and* any of the skills you have the ability to learn, including skills that are related to skills you already have, into the "What I do well" column. Be bold here. You want to claim as many of the keywords as possible. Remember, you don't have to be an expert in a particular skill to leverage it in your final USP; you only have to be able to do it or have expertise in something relevant to it. Once you've claimed the skills that you do well, you need to recognize and move away from the skills that your competitors will likely claim.

As a PhD, you've probably noticed that you have certain traits in common with those already working in your target industry. Hopefully this realization encourages you to further realize that you are already a good fit for the roles you are pursuing. However, you should also realize that others looking to enter the industry—your competitors—also possess those traits. What are the traits that seem to be shared amongst those interested in your target industry role? (Hint: You are a PhD and will likely be going up against other PhDs for the roles you are targeting.) Prior to reading this book, what was your sole focus when it came to your so-called qualifications and skills? The answer, of course, is your technical or specialty skills.

When it comes to filling out the final "What others do well" column, you want to imagine what the average PhD without career training—one who is obsessed with only their technical skills—would include on their industry résumé or in a conversation with an employer. Or just look back at your very first industry résumé. What were you focused on? Did you start a bullet point on your résumé with "10 years of experience in XYZ scientific field"? Did you list technical skill after technical skill and complex duty after complex duty? Did you start your first résumé with your education? Did you tell people about your research background initially? This is what your competitors are still doing, and you need to differentiate yourself from them.

So copy and paste all the keywords associated with technical skills from the "What the company needs" column into the "What others do well column." Don't copy keywords that you don't have experience with because other PhDs applying may not have that experience either. Also don't copy keywords that you're concerned others who are more experienced than you *might* be able to claim on their résumés. That is a biased assumption that most often turns out to be false. Now see what's in the "What I do well" column that's not in the "What others do well" column. This is the beginning of your USP.

Honing the USP

Your USP needs to be honed into a USP statement before it can be further refined into an elevator pitch. The keywords in your "What I do well" column but not your "What others do well" column can be used to write your USP statement.

Please note that the key to an effective USP statement is often combining the technical skills you have that the company needs with the transferable skills you have that the company needs because the latter will almost always be ignored by other PhDs applying for any industry role. So your USP statement may sound like the following: "I'm a cross-functional collaborator who can work with global teams to achieve goals related to protein purification and column chromatography, as well as other lab-based techniques." In this example, the USP is that you are trained in lab techniques **and** are skilled in communication and managing team relationships.

Another USP example is, "I'm a bottom-line-focused project-management professional with PhD-level experience in research, data analysis, documentation, and budgeting." Here, the USP is that you are a PhD skilled in research and analysis **and** have strong project management skills and understand their importance.

A last USP example could be something like this: "I'm a published scientist and humanitarian with expertise in molecular biology and a passion for sustainable systems and improving human health." The USP is that you are published in a highly technical field and excel in the quantitative aspects of industry **and** have a heart for working with people to improve their lives and the world as a whole qualitatively.

Once your USP statement is written, you can quickly and easily trim it down into an impactful elevator pitch. Recall that your elevator pitch is a personalized, top-of-mind script you can deliver in an encounter with decision-makers. Like your USP, your pitch should sell you to a prospective employer. It should highlight what you can uniquely offer the company to advance its mission and goals. Your elevator pitch should answer who you are (both professionally and personally), what you want, and why someone other than you should care.

. . . .

Notice that the first question asks you to explain who you are both professionally and personally. For the personal component, consider one of your hobbies that is not related to your PhD work and is qualitative in nature. This personal addition to your pitch humanizes you and helps hiring managers and recruiters who may rarely encounter PhDs, much less have one themselves, identify with you. Playing an instrument, playing a sport, gardening, arts and crafts, traveling, and cooking are all good examples.

. . . .

An example of an effective elevator pitch is, "I'm an immunology expert who loves to bake—German chocolate cake is my favorite recipe—and I'm seeking a project management role because I want to help coordinate research into treatments that will help cure XYZ disease and improve patient lives."

Armed with your USP and knowledge of how to engage with professionals in person, it's time to turn our attention to your online networking efforts. If this seems intimidating to you at first, fear not. As a PhD, you have a secret weapon that will allow you to succeed in networking where many others have failed.

Chapter 21

Networking Online Starts with Discovering Your Target Companies and Contacts

. . . .

A large part of networking is identifying the companies you want to work for and building a network of employees who work at those companies.

To successfully network your way to a job referral, you must build a bridge between connecting with people in person or online and following up to build a professional relationship. But who are you connecting with in the first place? Who are you targeting? What are you targeting?

Why PhDs Fail in Their Networking Efforts

The number one reason PhDs fail in their networking efforts is that they fail to follow up repeatedly with those they've connected with. You cannot build a professional relationship, let alone get a referral, without following up online to establish rapport and trust.

The second reason that PhDs fail in their networking efforts is that they fail to establish clear goals. They have no target. They have no system. Their documentation efforts are nonexistent. Their reach-out is haphazard. Most PhDs don't even know who they should be reaching out to.

Who are you reaching out to? Who would you start reaching out to right now if you woke up tomorrow with the goal of sending a connection request and message to three industry professionals? Have you even considered it? If you're like most PhDs, you have not.

Let's turn this around and start at the end of your networking efforts.

What's your goal? Your goal is to get hired into an industry position at an industry company. Earlier chapters focused on helping you narrow down which positions might be right for you. Still, you may feel overwhelmed (or underwhelmed) by your options. So what's left to define? What have you yet to consider?

I have done thousands of Transition Calls with PhDs in over one hundred countries. The majority of PhDs I talk to cannot give me the name of a single industry company they would prefer to work with. The rest can name one or two companies but know nothing—I repeat, nothing—about those companies beyond what the average person on the street knows, e.g., Apple makes computers, SpaceX and Tesla hire for AI, or BASF deals in chemicals.

How can you get hired at a company if you don't have any target companies? And how can you connect and network with gatekeepers and other employees at those companies if you haven't targeted those companies?

Finding Your Targets

Networking starts with creating a list of target companies. Essentially, it starts with research, which, as I've mentioned, is something you excel at. Research, or discovery, is the first step for you, even if you're not sure which industry sector you want to enter yet. You can always qualify and refine your research results later.

As a PhD, you have spent countless hours searching for and finding information that very few people in the world would have the perseverance to discover. You've likely spent hours just in this past week researching something completely unrelated to your work, just because you wanted to know more about the topic. Not only do you have an intense thirst for knowledge but you are also very, very good at researching. Have you ever had the displeasure of watching someone who is not a PhD do a web search? If so, what did that person do differently than you—or any other PhD for that matter?

First, they likely searched for one search term. After searching for that one keyword, they likely skimmed the first two or three hits in the search results, didn't find what they were looking for, and gave up. Or they spent what felt like a day and a half reading a result you instantly knew was not going to help them get the answer they were looking for and was not a credible source in the first place.

In the same span of time, you and any other PhD would have done three to four different searches using different sets of keywords that quickly honed better and better search results from more and more credible sources. Then you would have dug into not only the first page of search hits but also the second, third, and even forth. At that point, you would have flown through web page after web page inhaling information and navigating deeper and deeper into the material to find the primary references. Once you found the primary sources, you would have read to the bottom, looked at the references for those sources, read those sources, and so on until you had consumed the references of the sources' sources' sources' sources. If necessary, you would also have looked at book excerpts online or made plans to go to the library to finish your research.

You must realize that this is abnormal—in a good way. It's superhuman. There's nothing wrong with people who cannot research at this level. That's not the point. The point is that training matters. You are highly trained in research, and this skill can be your secret weapon in your networking efforts.

The Strategy for Networking

Networking is not hard for you because you're a poor networker; networking is hard for you because you're executing a poor strategy. The beginning of your networking strategy is creating a document to record your efforts.

How many spreadsheets, read-outs, protocols, lessons plans, or other documents related to your research work do you currently have stored on your computer or in the cloud? Dozens? Hundreds? Thousands?

Now, how many documents do you have stored related to your job search? One? Your résumé? Two? Two versions of your résumé?

And your goal is to get hired into a top industry career that less than 2 percent of the population will ever get hired into?

Perhaps it's time to rethink your efforts.

The good news is that you can organize and document your efforts very simply. All you have to do is create a spreadsheet that I refer to as your "Job Search Sheet." This sheet will act as your home base for all your job search activities, especially the activities related to your networking and job referral efforts. Fill out nine column headers in your spreadsheet with the following:

- Company Name
- Company LinkedIn® URL
- Company Size
- Gatekeeper or Decision-Maker Contact (Embed LinkedIn® URL)
  - Date Last Contacted
  - Date to Contact Next
- Proximal Position Contact (Embed LinkedIn® URL)
  - Date Last Contacted
  - Date To Contact Next

Now, simply fill in one hundred rows in the sheet.

Yes, one hundred rows.

Oh, and it should only take you sixty minutes or less.

Can you spare sixty minutes to finally organize your job search? If you do, in my experience, you will be hired into your dream position less than sixty days after completing your sheet—sixty minutes to get hired in under sixty days. Imagine being completely organized in your efforts and knowing exactly who you are going to reach out to each day and exactly when to follow up. Imagine your networking efforts essentially being on autopilot. How much easier would your job search be?

The key to building this sheet to one hundred rows quickly and effectively is to leverage your abilities as an expert researcher by standing on the shoulders of those who have done most of the work for you already. You will also need to draw a clear line between your research and aggregation efforts and your qualification and critiquing efforts.

The value of separating discovery from analysis is something many PhDs learned to do the hard way while writing their theses, myself included. When I first started writing my thesis at the end of my graduate school career, I would write a few sentences, stop, go back, edit those sentences, write a few more sentences, stop, go back, edit those sentences, reedit the first few sentences, write again, edit again, and on and on. This was extremely unproductive, and I came to realize after only a few days that it was far easier and much more efficient and effective to just let myself write for a couple of hours before going back to edit what I wrote. Eventually, I was writing until I had all the sections of my thesis completed, and only then did I go back and start editing my thesis.

This is how you must approach your Job Search Sheet. There will be a time to qualify, critique, and edit your list later. Besides, you're likely unsure what you really want in terms of working at an industry company. Why limit yourself based on the company's location, size, or anything else related to the company until you know the full story?

A few years ago, I worked with a PhD named Erin in the Cheeky Scientist Association, and they were adamant that they would never leave Toronto, Canada, for an industry job. Their family was in Toronto, their partner had a job in Toronto, and they loved Toronto. Then Erin got a job offer from Allergan in Ireland making double the salary she anticipated and managing her own team of seven people.

Don't set limits on what's possible on your career. You might get an offer to work for a company of forty people in Singapore heading up an entire department for a very high salary. You are valuable, and you should keep your options open—for now.

What Would This Look like If It Was Easy?

I have this quote on a bookshelf in my office because, as a PhD, I tend to make things overly complex. When aggregating your list of one hundred companies, don't build your list from scratch. Countless others have already done this work for you. Simple online searches for "XYZ companies in ABC location," or even more simply, for "XYZ companies," will start to give you an understanding of all the companies in your desired field. You can take those company names and add them to the first column of your sheet.

Next, search for those companies on LinkedIn® and add the URL of their company page to the second column. Be sure to also include the number of employees in the third column. This number can be found at the top of the company's LinkedIn® page as a clickable link. Click this link to see all the employees who are working at the company and are also on LinkedIn®.

At the top of the page that follows—the page showing you all the employees at the company—you can used LinkedIn®'s advanced search filters to find employees who have "Hiring," "Recruiter," "HR," "Human," or "Talent" in their job titles. These searches will identify the gatekeepers at the company—the Hiring Managers, internal Recruiters, HR and Human Resource professionals, and Talent Acquisition Specialists. For small and midsize companies that have yet to hire dedicated hiring managers and other gatekeepers, you can seek out more general decision-makers instead, including those in operational roles like Chief Operations Officer (COO) or Operations Manager or those with "Executive," "Senior," "Lead," or "Head" in their job titles. Then type the name(s) of these professionals into the fourth column of your sheet and link their names to their LinkedIn® profile URLs so that you can see their names when scanning your spreadsheet and quickly navigate to their LinkedIn® profiles when it's time to send them a message.

Similar to your efforts above, you will want to seek out professionals at the company who are in proximal positions, or positions that are the same or similar to the position that you would like to get hired into at the company. You are specifically looking for employees who are either in the exact same role you want or in lateral roles (those you would be working with in a cross-functional capacity). For example, if you want to be hired as a Research Scientist, a proximal position could be Research Scientist, Scientist I, II, or III, Senior Scientist, R&D Project Manager, Product Manager, Data Manager, Application Scientist, or even Marketing Communication Specialist, Technical Sales Specialist, Scientific Writer, Medical Affairs Associate, or Evidence Evaluation Specialist. The key is that these proximal professionals are not in upper management, nor are they hiring gatekeepers. Fill in the names of these professionals in the seventh column of your sheet and then link their names to their LinkedIn® profile URLs.

Columns five, six, eight, and nine simply record the last time you interacted with each contact and the next time you plan to interact with them. I discuss these columns and the online networking efforts associated with them in later chapters. You can see an example of one PhD's Job Search Sheet below.

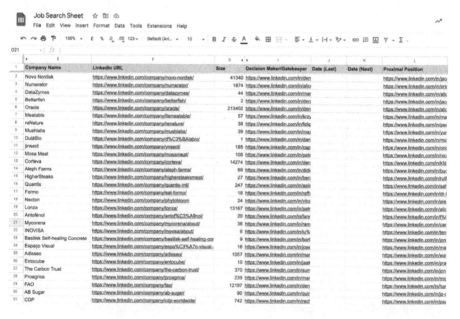

Company websites can also help you target your LinkedIn® searches. Many company websites, especially websites for small and midsized companies, have an

"About Us" section that includes biographical information for the people who work there. Very often those bios include personal information you could leverage in your first interaction with them. Knowing the name of the person you want to reach out to before heading to LinkedIn® is especially helpful when searching for prospective strategic connections at large companies because large companies have thousands to hundreds of thousands of employees, which can make it difficult to sort through the search results LinkedIn® gives you.

Likewise, company blogs can help you find specific employees at larger companies. Larger organizations often highlight specific employees or teams on their blogs. These articles can give you a reason to contact the person you are interested in. As you'll see in the next chapter, starting a conversation with someone is very easy when you can mention that you saw an article about them and found their work interesting. You can also set up Google alerts for the companies you are most interested in. This will alert you of any stories published about your target companies. You can use the information in those stories to identify and reach out to potential connections.

As a reminder, during the above aggregation exercise, it's important to resist the urge to qualify the information you record in your sheet. Do not prioritize the companies or the contacts on your list. Turn off your internal editor—the critical part of your mind that likely overdeveloped during your tenure in academia. Instead, enter a discovery mindset. This is an exploratory exercise, and the result should resemble a brainstorming list more than a carefully curated list. Only once you have 100 rows completed on your sheet (or 101, counting the header row) is it time to start qualifying the companies and contacts on your spreadsheet.

STEP #6:

Follow the Straight-Line Referral Method

"I've learned that people will forget what you said, people will forget what you did, but people will never forget how you made them feel."

— Maya Angelou

Chapter 22

Using Company Culture to Qualify Your Job Leads and Networking Efforts

· · · · · · · · · · · · · · · · · · · ·

A t an in-person event, you never want to qualify who you have a conversation with. This leads to looking over the person's shoulder for someone better to talk to or having someone else look over your shoulder for an upgrade. You must be present with whoever is in front of you at the event because you never know how connected that person might be. They could have someone in their network who is looking to hire someone like you right now, they could be hiring, or they could be about to get hired themselves at a company you'd love to work for. At the very least, it's possible they will get hired before you at an industry company and have great insights into which other people you could talk to about getting hired.

· ·

Never qualify at an in-person event. It puts you in the wrong mindset, prevents building rapport, and is ultimately fruitless.

· ·

Your online networking efforts, however, should be qualified—to a point. You want to spend most of your time and attention engaging with employees, gatekeepers, and decision-makers at your companies of interest. In particular, you want to spend the most time engaging with those who can make decisions about hiring you and those who are responsive.

Considering a Company's Culture

The best first step for qualifying your job leads is determining company fit, and the best first step for determining company fit is considering whether a company's culture is a good fit for you. It's more important for you to determine whether a company is a good match for you than whether you are a good fit for the company.

Company culture can be defined as a set of shared values, goals, attitudes, and practices that characterize an organization. In other words, culture is the way people feel about the work they do, the values they believe in, where they see the company going, and what they're doing to get it there. Collectively, these traits represent the personality—or culture—of an organization. Establishing the culture you'd like to be associated with professionally is important to help establish patterns in your job search.

There are a variety of elements that make up company culture. Some of those elements include company mission, working environment, leadership style, values, ethics, expectations, and goals. To name a few alternate terms, company culture is also known as "organizational culture," "corporate culture," and "workplace culture." The best place to start in terms of understanding what companies and cultures would be good fits for you is to consider the following questions:

- What type of working environment motivates you?
- What type of working environment makes you happy?
- What professional lifestyle are you looking for?
- What are your professional values?

To determine what type of working environment motivates you, consider things like whether you like big offices with lots of open space. Or perhaps how an office looks does not matter to you as long as there are intelligent, motivated, and equally driven colleagues to work with? To figure out what type of environment really motivates you, think about a time when you were extremely productive. What was special about that situation? Were you working alone or with others? Did you have a looming deadline or generous time freedom? Were you dealing with people or with the product? Then do the same exercise but think about a situation in which you were horribly unproductive. In short, try to pinpoint what helps you do your best work (and your worst).

Likewise, consider what type of working environment makes you happy—productive but happy, not lying-on-a-beach-doing-nothing happy. Does working under pressure motivate you and keep you challenged yet happy? Do you thrive and really enjoy yourself when left to work independently? Or would you be more productive and happier working on a team and being held accountable? Sometimes it might help to work backward and think about what makes you unhappy. Are you cranky in the morning? Maybe you would appreciate a later start or a more flexible schedule? Is your day incomplete without witty banter about the current state of world, trends in a particular industry, or shared hobbies and experiences? For example, it's easy to be dazzled by perks like catered lunches and beer on tap, but if you prefer shorter workdays, you should be aware that this catering might mean long and inconsistent work hours.

When it comes to discovering which professional lifestyle you're looking for and what your professional values are, you will have to dig even deeper. Remember, you can't hit a target you don't set. You must do the work of figuring out which companies are the right fit for you. If you don't care which company you get hired at, what's the point of transitioning into industry in the first place? If you don't know what you want, you won't be able to convince a quality employer to hire you during an interview, nor will you have the motivation to sustain the ups and downs of a PhD-level job search.

While a job offer might be fantastic, especially after working hard to write a résumé for a specific industry position, interview for it, and negotiate a salary, none of this will matter if you end up stressed, overwhelmed, and even further from the life you've always wanted. Do you know what kind of life you want? Do you know what professional lifestyle will bring you closer to your ideal life? You better figure it out—and quickly. Consider these more practical questions: Does it matter if you leave your office before the CEO does? Or does everyone in the building get kicked out by 6 p.m.? Do you care if everyone orders lunch from the same place and you're expected to chip in? Is working late and having dinner catered in okay, or will you miss having family dinners at home? Are you okay with flying to a different location on forty-eight hours' notice or less and being there for days if needed? Do you want to spend half your time filling out regulatory documents and doing administrative work?

These are the kinds of questions you need to start asking and answering. If you find answering those questions difficult, try determining your professional values first.

How to Determine Professional Values

There are three useful ways to discover your professional values. First, try considering your "peak experiences." Reflect on meaningful moments that stand out to you professionally. What was happening to you? What was going on around you? What values were you honoring?

Now go in the opposite direction by considering your "suppressed values." Consider a time when you got angry, frustrated, or upset. What was going on around you? What were you feeling? What values were being suppressed?

Finally, consider the "code of conduct" by which you already live your life. Many people don't realize until far too late in life that they have their own life rules and that these rules collectively are different than everyone else's rules. What are your rules? What's most important in your life? Beyond your basic human needs, what must you have in your life to experience fulfillment? Creative self-expression? A strong level of health and vitality? A sense of adventure? Constant growth?

By understanding your values, you understand your priorities, which in turn helps you identify the lifestyle you are chasing and the company culture most capable of giving you that lifestyle. The good news is that industry employers spend billions creating and maintaining a culture that provides their employees with the professional lifestyles they crave.

Company culture is important to employers because employees who fit in with the company culture are not only happier but also more productive. When an employee fits in with the culture, they are also much more likely to want to stay with that company longer, which reduces employee turnover and the associated costs of training new hires. Company culture is important to employees too, of course, because the company's employees are more likely to enjoy work when their needs and values are consistent with those of their employer. If you work somewhere where the culture is a good fit, you tend to develop better relationships with coworkers and be more productive. On the other hand, if you work for a company where you don't fit in with the company culture, you are likely to take far less pleasure in your work. For example, if you prefer to work independently but are employed by a company that emphasizes teamwork, you are likely to be less happy, not to mention be less efficient.

So how do you determine what a company's culture is? How do you define it in a simple way that makes it easy to identify which companies fit your cultural ideal and which likely do not?

Defining Company Culture

The job search platform, Indeed, has a simple system for identifying which company culture you would like to target. While this platform isn't known for PhD-level jobs, its framework has been very useful when I personally work with PhDs in the Cheeky Scientist Association who are not sure which companies are the right fit for them.

As PhDs, we tend to overthink decisions like which company culture we should commit to, and our overthinking tends to inhibit us from choosing the best option. The list below is simple for a reason. You can make choices based on your first impressions or instincts. These instincts are supported by a framework of knowledge about yourself, which is called up instantly and can dim under more intensive analysis. Your goal here is simple: decide which of the below culture descriptions resonates with you the most positively and which is instantly repugnant to you.

- Detail-oriented – quality and precision-focused
- Innovative – creative and risk-taking
- Aggressive – competitive and growth-oriented
- Outcome-oriented – results-focused with a strong performance culture
- Stable – traditional, systems-oriented processes
- People-oriented – supportive and focused on fairness
- Team-oriented – cooperative and collaborative

Which of the above options best describes your ideal company culture? Prior to deciding, please review your answers to the exercise earlier in the chapter so that your choice below is framed within the context of what motivates you and makes you happy, as well as your ideal professional lifestyle and your professional values. Once again, it is important that you do not overthink this. The option that initially jumps out at you as the most ideal is often the best option for you. If you find yourself stuck, start by eliminating the options that repulse you the most. Everyone is different, and there are no right or wrong answers. If you really want to choose two options and can't decide, flip a coin. You can always change your answer later.

Now turn your attention back to the Job Search Sheet from the previous chapter, which is your home base for all job search activities. It's time to start qualifying the job leads (the rows) on your sheet by determining which of those companies are the best fit for you. Start by adding an additional column titled "Culture Fit" to the left of the current far left "Company Name" column. In this new column, you are going to rank each job lead, or row, on a scale of 1–3 with 1 being the worst fit and 3 being the best fit. Your goal is to rank each job lead according to how well your initial impression of the company's culture fits with the ideal culture you chose for yourself.

There are several things you can do to find out more about a company's culture. For example, you can check out the company website, specifically the "About Us" page if they have one. It often includes a description of the company's mission and values. Some company websites also have testimonials from employees, which can be a great way to hear about the culture firsthand. You can do additional research online too. You may also want to consider reviews of the company online but take them with a grain of salt. Glassdoor, for example, provides reviews and ratings of companies that are written by current or former employees.

· ·

Please note that most company reviews are written by a few disgruntled former employees, not current employees working at a company. Make sure you are actively seeking positive information about the company to counterbalance this negativity bias.

· ·

Additionally, you can ask past and current employees, as well as current company affiliates, questions about the company's culture. If you know someone who works for a company you're interested in, ask to set up an informational interview to learn more about the company. Check LinkedIn® or the alumni office at your college to see if you have connections at the company. The employer will likely ask you questions to assess whether you'd fit into the company culture, and you can ask them questions in return. You might ask about considerations that are important to you, such as the amount of independent work versus teamwork or what your day-to-day schedule would be. You can even shadow an employee. If you are offered the job and are still unsure of the company's culture, ask if you can shadow someone in the department for a day or a few hours. This is a useful way to see the office dynamics in play and ask any remaining questions. When having conversations with those familiar with the company, be sure to ask the following questions to get a strong understanding of the company's culture:

- How would you characterize the company's overall management style?
- What is the company's approach to teambuilding and career development?
- How does the company respond to and overcome failures?
- How are employees recognized for their efforts?
- What is the work–life balance like?

- Does the company host social outings or events for employees?
- What personality traits do you look for in your ideal team members?
- Is the company's strategic approach driven by processes or results?
- Do the company's different departments ever collaborate with one another?
- What kinds of people seem to succeed in this company/department?

After you've done your research and ranked companies for culture fit, you can get a sense of which companies are the best fit for you by sorting your sheet by the Culture Fit column so that the companies with the highest ranking are grouped at the top of your sheet. With that additional research complete, you're ready to start reaching out to the contacts you curated, starting at the top of your sheet where the most qualified job leads are now listed.

Chapter 23

Reactivating Your Current Network and Expanding It

·····················

Reactivating your current network can instantly decrease the degrees of separation between you and professionals in your target companies. Your connection efforts on LinkedIn® or elsewhere should start by pursuing your own contacts because the people you already know, even if they aren't in fields of interest to you, can lead you to people who are working at your companies of interest. This includes family, friends, past classmates, teaching assistants, postdocs, professors, and former employers. In particular, as a PhD, you should work to identify alumni from your current and previous universities to contact as they often take a special interest in "giving back" to fellow alumni (i.e., you).

There are Only Six Degrees of Separation between You and Anyone Else

It's been said that there are only six degrees of separation, at most, between you and anyone else in the world. In other words, you are only six introductions away from connecting to any decision-maker in industry.

Of course, you are likely only two or three degrees of separation away from numerous industry gatekeepers and decision-makers. You might only be one degree away. This is because, whether you know it or not, you are already in the industry you want to get into—at least in part—because you already have or are about to have a PhD. You are already trained at a very high level in your field, which gives you credibility in related fields, so by networking correctly on LinkedIn® with other PhDs in industry roles, you can cross off many of the aforementioned six degrees of separation and quickly gain exposure to decision-makers.

Imagine you have a friend from undergrad who is connected to someone who works as a Senior Scientist at your company of interest, and this Senior Scientist is connected to several Product Managers at the same company. As a result, when you reconnect with your friend from undergrad, you're reconnecting secondarily to those Product Managers because they are already your second-degree connections. Perhaps one of those Product Managers is connected to a Medical Director at your dream company and your ideal industry position is to become a Medical Science Liaison. Now by reconnecting with your friend from undergrad, you have activated your third-degree network (which this Medical Director is part of) and are only two introductions away from a referral for your dream position. You can see how that one reconnection can dramatically increase your chances of successfully establishing a professional relationship with a key decision-maker.

· ·

By refusing to reactivate your current network and obsessing over those you have yet to connect with, you fail to leverage your current shared connections, both those in your secondary and tertiary networks, who can get you a job referral in very short order.

· ·

After spending years working long hours either alone or in a small research group during your PhD journey, you might feel like you have lost contact with everyone you used to know and have no way of reactivating your network. This is simply not true. You have "relationship equity" with everyone you have ever met or spent time with, especially in person. While the level of equity will vary based on how much rapport you had with someone, how much time you spent with them, and how long it's been since you've interacted, it is never zero. You can easily build on the remaining equity by reaching out with the right networking script once you open yourself to the connections you already have. Consider connections you've already made through the following sources:

- Current jobs
- Previous jobs
- Undergrad university alumni
- Graduate university alumni
- Postdoc university alumni
- Other institutional alumni
- Family
- Volunteer organizations
- Sports teams
- Band, orchestra, or choir
- Clubs
- Places of worship
- Interest groups

Before building your list of new gatekeepers, decision-makers, and proximal contacts on your Job Search Sheet, create a list of everyone in your current network. You can do this in a separate tab on your Job Search Sheet if you want your networking lists all in one place. Think about the sources listed above to build this list. There might already be a gatekeeper, decision-maker, or contact in your current network who is working at one of your companies of interest.

Avoiding Desperation Mode

When it comes to reconnecting with your current network or reaching out to expand your network, the networking script you use in your email, LinkedIn® message, or elsewhere is critical for the kind of response you get—or whether you get a response at all.

Unfortunately, most PhDs avoid reactivating or expanding their networks until they are completely desperate to get hired. They wait until they've defended their theses and are working for free with no career options other than a postdoc or teaching assistant positions. Or they wait until there is yet another spending freeze at their institutions, one that put their postdocs, teaching positions, adjunct positions, or other positions in jeopardy.

Now it's too late to add value to their network and build a professional relationship; it's time for drastic measures.

PhDs in these situations enter "desperation mode" and start spamming would-be connections with long scripts that start by talking about themselves and end by asking the other person to read their résumés and hire them, help them get a job directly, or consider their candidacy for a position. This is like going up to a stranger on the street with a bag over your head and begging them for a job. What's their reaction going to be?

Here's an actual message (with the name changed for privacy) I received from a PhD in desperation mode. I've received hundreds and hundreds of these over the years, as have many of the Global 500 business partners and affiliates we work with at Cheeky Scientist. Messages like this will never get you hired. And those you send them to—especially those who do not understand the PhD condition—will avoid you at all costs.

· ·

Hello Sir,

I am a PhD and postdoc in Molecular Biology working at Harvard University Medical Center, and I have designed and synthesized molecular imaging peptide probes, peptidomimetics, fluorophore labeling, chelating peptides for radiolabeling, biotin-conjugated peptides, multiple antigen peptides (MAPs), peptide heterodimers, bioconjugation with proteins, phage and antibody, worked with various fluorophores to evaluate their imaging capability in pre-clinical mouse model and clinical specimens.

I saw you have an open position for a Senior Scientist at your company and I think I am a good fit for this role. Can you refer me for this position? Please review my résumé that is attached here.

—John Smith, PhD

· ·

You might think that the above message is absurd and you would never send a message like it, but your behavior might change after six months of unemployment when you start to worry about paying for rent, healthcare, or groceries for your family. The only way to avoid desperation mode permanently is to get out in front of your job search—in particular, your networking—and start reactivating and expanding your network now. This requires forethought, patience, and an abundance mentality. There are hundreds of thousands of people who can help you get hired in industry—if you approach them correctly.

Approaching Professionals Correctly

The key to connecting with any professional correctly is putting yourself in their shoes. What do they want to hear from a stranger or someone they haven't heard from in a while? What will capture their attention? What are their interests? What value could you add for them in your connection request?

In the Cheeky Scientist Association, we have a mantra when it comes to networking. The mantra is: "Add Value First," or AVF.

. . . .
"Add Value First" or AVF
. . . .

If you want someone to accept your connection request, let alone like you and trust you enough to refer you for a job in industry, you must think about them first and yourself second. This must be done authentically. Many PhDs over the years have asked, "But won't they know that I'm just being nice to get something?"

Yes, if you're just being nice to get something.

You can't just add value to capture a referral with no intention of developing a professional relationship. Likewise, you can't just directly tell an employee at a company who is not responsible for hiring that you want a job referral from them. In both cases, you are being manipulative.

Read someone's LinkedIn® profile. Learn about who they are, what they want, what they've achieved, and what their interests are. Message them in a way that serves them best. This is the opposite of manipulation. This is authenticity. You must reach out to contacts with an authentic desire to grow your industry network in the long term. You must see each connection as an end in itself. There are several ways you can add value for the other person, including:

- Show appreciation as a colleague – You can do this by writing about how you appreciate anything on their LinkedIn® profile, from their interests to experiences to posting activity.
- Compliment their work – Whether it's a peer-reviewed paper or a large project they completed, you can write about how impressive it is.
- Congratulate their career progress – It's never too late to do this for their most recent transition or promotion; you can give them a compliment on the promotion they received two years ago or their successful transition from academia to industry five years ago.
- Ask them for their opinion or advice – Other people love sharing their opinions and giving advice so much that they often do so in an unsolicited fashion; give them a chance to tell you what to do, and they will open up.

- Make a recommendation – You can easily find out what their interests are by looking at their volunteer work, their previous LinkedIn® activity, the influencers they follow on LinkedIn®, or their interests on LinkedIn®; recommend a book by one of the influencers, a restaurant in one of the travel locations under their interests, or further reading on a topic they shared in their feed.
- Make an introduction – A great way to get to know someone better or to connect with them in the first place is to ask them if you can introduce them to someone in your network you already know well; just find something they have in common and be sure you can articulate how the connection can be fruitful for both; everyone, even senior executives, know networking is important, and everyone also struggles to find time to do it; help solve this problem for them, and you will build instant rapport.

Beyond adding value, it's also important to indicate why you are connecting or reconnecting with each person. What's your rationale for sending this message?

As a PhD, you understand the importance of rationale. You also know from experience that when someone you don't know sends you an email or online message, you immediately wonder, *Why is this person messaging me?*

Don't hide from this. Give them a reason.

I recommend going to the person's activity section at the top of their LinkedIn® profile and viewing their most recent post activity. Open their posts and find one that you can comment on. Understand that the reason does not have to be impressive; it just needs to exist.

The next question people wonder is, *Who is this?* Again, make sure you answer this question simply by mentioning that you're a PhD. I also recommend mentioning a shared interest you have with the person. This lends credibility to who you are and supplies additional rationale for why you're reaching out.

Over the last ten years, I have crafted tens of thousands of networking scripts for PhDs in the Cheeky Scientist Association. The one that continues to get the most replies from industry employees time and time again is the following script.

· ·

Hi [Name], I saw your post on [post topic] in my LinkedIn® feed and thought to reach out. Congrats on your success in [job title] at [company name]. I'm a PhD in [relevant field] and saw we are both interested in [shared interest]. Would you be interested in connecting?

· ·

This script can be adapted slightly depending on your audience. If you're reaching out to a decision-maker at an executive level, you will want to adapt the message to reflect what's most valuable to them. An employee at an entry-, mid-, or even senior-level position in industry, such as those I describe as being in proximal positions, value appreciation given where they are in their careers. Many are starved for it. So show them appreciation for their success in industry. Those at the director, executive, or principal level, however, are so starved for time that they often value direct, succinct messages over appreciative messages. These professionals also have plenty of people kissing up to them in industry at this point in their careers, making it very hard to get their attention with personal flattery. They are much more focused on their careers from a company perspective, meaning their success and self-worth is tied to their team's success and the company's success as a whole. As such, aim to compliment their teams' and companies' accomplishments. For decision-makers, I recommend the following networking script.

. . . .

Hi [Name], I saw your post on [post topic related to company name] in my LinkedIn® feed and thought to reach out. Congrats on the success of your team and [company name]. I'm a PhD in [relevant field] and would love to be on a team like yours one day. Would you be interested in connecting?

. . . .

You will want to tweak this script again for industry gatekeepers, such as hiring managers, recruiters, and talent acquisitions specialists. These people are looking for talent and want to fill their open positions; therefore, you can be much more direct in your messaging. In this case, your rationale must be much more relevant to their goals. Aim to find a specific job opening they are responsible for and ask whether it's still available. If they respond with the affirmative, proceed to ask for the next best steps in applying if it's not mentioned on the job posting. If they respond in the negative, ask if there are any other positions in XYZ space they are currently trying to fill. The initial script should look like the one that follows.

. . . .

Hi [Name], I saw your post for a [job title] at [company name], and I was wondering if the position was still available? I'm a PhD in [relevant field] with experience and [relevant training]. Would you be interested in connecting?

. . . .

In any of the scenarios above, if you do not establish a connection the first time, you can send a second email or a follow-up message on LinkedIn® (if you have LinkedIn®

Premium) that is even shorter and does not refer to your first message. Understand that it will take you three or four messages on average to get a response from a new contact. Industry professionals can get over one hundred emails per day, and many of these emails, especially those coming from outside of their organizations, end up in their spam or social folders. Your messages should be sent only once per week or, if you're on a time crunch, once every three days at the most. As you send these messages, keep adding value in new ways. Eventually, they will see one of your messages, open it, and read it. Then they will review your other messages and when they see that each one adds value and was kind and professional, the law of reciprocation will kick in and they will reply. The key is to never send anything passive aggressive like "Just wondering if you saw my last message." You should also vary your efforts by using at least two different channels for reaching out, such as email and LinkedIn®. Of course, this can take immense time and effort, which is the main reason I founded the Cheeky Scientist and the Cheeky Scientist Association.

During my own transition, I realized that most PhDs enter their first job search with no industry network. A rare few have weak relationships with a few people working in industry, but such weak relationships never yield strong referrals. The data continue to show that over 70 percent of industry jobs are filled through referrals. The Cheeky Scientist Association helps PhDs sidestep this problem by giving members direct access to tens of thousands of PhDs who are already working in top industry careers. These established Associates provide referrals and personal recommendations to other, newer Associates because they can trust that these new Associates have been trained on the job search process and know the social norms of industry. In other words, established Associates can trust that newer Associates won't embarrass them after being introduced to a Hiring Manager or Talent Acquisition Specialist at their company.

Still, many PhDs opt to try connecting and networking on their own. Regardless of which route you choose, your efforts must be robust. By staying persistent and consistent in your connection efforts, you will start getting replies. Getting a reply, however, is not the end goal. The end goal is a referral, and you can only achieve this goal by guiding your connections to deeper levels of professional intimacy, which is what I'm going to show you how to do next.

Chapter 24

Guiding Networking Contacts to Deeper Levels of Professional Intimacy

· ·

T he goal of your online networking efforts is to build a professional relationship where the other party feels comfortable enough to refer you for a job at
their company or otherwise help you further your efforts to get hired. It is
a multiple-step process during which every problem is followed by another problem.

I have worked with many PhDs who thought they would get hired if only they
could finally get a reply after sending a connection request to someone on LinkedIn®.
But when those same PhDs finally started getting replies from industry employees and
employers, they freaked out, hid, and waited to reply. Some of them never replied!
Others went as far as changing their visibility settings on LinkedIn® so others wouldn't
know they were online.

They didn't know how to keep the conversation going.

They got stuck again.

Having a networking process and understanding each step of that process
ahead of time will help you anticipate future problems and avoid roadblocks in
your online conversations.

How to Gradually Build Professional Intimacy

PhDs make two main mistakes when it comes to generating referrals. They either go too deep too soon in terms of professional intimacy by asking questions like "Why did you do XYZ?" or "What specific techniques do you use for XYZ?" and other complex, intense questions, or they never go deep enough to build long-lasting relationships.

To avoid these mistakes and transform your connections into job referrals, you must understand the process of building professional intimacy and how to go from one level to the next. I created a three-step job search referral strategy for just that—a proprietary methodology that helps PhDs navigate the networking process. It takes you from initially connecting with and getting a reply from an industry professional to getting a referral. The three steps of the strategy are:

1. Getting a reply
2. Adding value
3. Informational interviewing

Of course, before you get a reply, you have to connect with someone properly. How to connect and reconnect with industry professionals is discussed in the previous chapter, and I review more strategies for growing your network in the next chapter. Here we are going to focus exclusively on how to carry a conversation with a contact forward to a job referral.

In the previous chapter, I also talk about the importance of following up with contacts to get a response. Most often, you will have to send three or four messages before getting a response. Each of those messages should add value in new and different ways; however, once you get a response, your goal shifts. Not only do you want to add value after you get a response but you also want to carry the conversation to a deeper level of professional intimacy. If you fail to do this, things will get awkward, and the other person will go silent very quickly. We have all either initiated or been part of networking conversations that went something like this:

How are you?
I'm great, how are you?
I'm great too ... you?
(awkward silence)

Circular conversations that get stuck at the same level of professional intimacy are exactly what you want to avoid. The key is realizing that *you* are responsible for carrying the conversation forward because *you* are the one who reached out to connect. If you fail to carry the conversation forward by asking questions that prompt slightly-more-intimate-yet-professional responses in a graduated way, your online rapport will break, and you will ruin your chances of getting a referral.

The other party wants to talk about deeper issues—but slowly. They want to dive deeper into more interesting and meaningful topics—but in a natural way that doesn't make them feel uncomfortable.

If you carry the conversation forward correctly, you can move the other person into an informational interview so naturally that they won't even realize—or care—that it's happening.

A networking conversation can only be carried forward to a referral successfully if it is started successfully; therefore, when connecting initially, remember to never start the conversation by talking about yourself or asking the other person to help you get hired. Asking for a referral without first investing in a contact burns bridges and can even get you blocked by other professionals or blacklisted from entire companies. You should also never mention that you're looking to do an "informational interview" with them. The phrase "informational interview" is commonly used in the job search industry when you're a job candidate, but it is uncommon with industry professionals already in their careers. The phrase typically comes across as too formal and intense, and when connecting, the last thing you want to be is formal and intense. Carrying a conversation from the other party's initial reply to adding value to an informational interview should be seamless.

• •

The key, again, is to ask quality questions that graduate slightly each time to deeper and deeper levels of professional intimacy. When done correctly, the other party will feel comfortable and even rewarded.

• •

After all, the purpose of an informational interview is to elevate the other person's credibility. You are showing appreciation for their success in industry. They have gone before you and transitioned successfully. They are where you want to be. Act like it. Serve them in the conversation. By doing so, you'll leave the other person wanting to help you and even work with you in the future. And this all starts by learning to navigate the four levels of professional intimacy correctly.

The Four Levels of Professional Intimacy

The first level of professional intimacy when talking about networking and informational interviews is termed "Topical Intimacy." The best question to ask a networking contact to get them to this level of intimacy after they reply to your initial connection or reconnection request is "What are you currently working on that you're excited about?"

Everyone is currently doing something in their work that is on the top of their mind. It might be challenging, but it's likely also rewarding. It's a healthy challenge. It's too early in your professional relationship to bring up the challenge, but it's the perfect time to ask them what they're working on and encourage a positive response by framing the question in a way that only allows a positive reply.

People enjoy talking about positive, topical experiences, especially when they're related to their favorite thing in the world: them and their life. No matter who you are talking to, they will enjoy talking about what excites them. By asking the above question, you can be confident that your connection will take this cue and give you information that will help you move to the next level of professional intimacy. While you're at this first level of professional intimacy, you can also ask questions like "What are you doing on a day-to-day basis? What parts of the job do you find most enjoyable? What surprised you when you started working in this field?" Just remember to ask positively framed questions that prompt positive answers.

The second level of professional intimacy is termed "Challenge Intimacy." The perfect question to ask a networking contact to get them to this level of intimacy is "What are some of the challenges associated with your role?" While this question is an extension of the first question, it will allow you to go a bit deeper into the other person's professional life and get to know both their personality and mindset better.

In the first level, you asked your connection to talk about what excites them about their job; most people will focus on only the enjoyable aspects of their lives and work at this stage. Once you ask about the challenges, you subtly ratchet up the rapport by offering them a new person (you) to share their struggles with while keeping the conversation focused on their job. Here is an example of how to transition from first- to second-level professional intimacy:

"Well, right now I'm working on a new project that has some amazing potential. We're all pretty excited about it at work."

"That's great to hear. Congratulations. I love when I can get my hands on an engaging project, even if it's challenging. What are some of the general challenges you're facing with the project right now?"

Notice that you're keeping the conversation light and general (avoiding intensity) by asking about "general challenges" instead of getting too specific. Here, you are identifying with the other person by showing you understand what it's like to work on an engaging project and expressing that you also enjoy it. You are also elevating their credibility and giving them a chance to shine by showing appreciation for the challenges they've overcome. Here are some additional questions you can ask in the second level of professional intimacy:

- How were you able to spearhead that project?
- Can you tell me a little about the project team that you're working with?
- What parts of the job do you find the most challenging?
- What skills do you need to leverage to be able to do that work?
- What qualifications do you need for that particular role?

The third level of professional intimacy is termed "How-To Intimacy." Here the ideal question to ask is "How did you get hired into your role in the first place?" After you've learned about the fulfilling and challenging aspects of your connection's role, it's time to go deeper in the third level of professional intimacy and ask about their professional story and how they transitioned.

Pivoting to this third level of intimacy is crucial as it will change the context of the conversation from general life and career questions and answers to job search questions and answers. You can make this pivot extremely subtle, keeping the conversation entirely focused on the other person and your interest in and admiration for what they've accomplished. For example, you might say, "I can appreciate those challenges; it sounds like you're in a complex role. I hope it's rewarding for you though. I'm curious, how did you get hired into that role in the first place?"

Always use the word "you" when asking this question. Your connection will answer more freely because they can focus on their subjective experience. They won't have to think through their answers. At the third level of professional intimacy, you can also ask:

- What did the hiring process look like for you?
- In your opinion, how has the company changed since you were hired?
- What are your plans for career progression?

At this level, aim to only ask experiential, opinion-based questions that focus on the other party's personal experience.

The fourth and final level of professional intimacy is termed "Advice Intimacy." The best question to ask here is "Which roles are about to open up in your company's pipeline?" In this final level of professional intimacy, you very subtly shift the conversation to you. You can do this by linking their transition story (how they got hired) to your transition plans. For example, you could say, "Wow. You had three rounds of video interviews. That's quite the process. Congratulations again on the role. I recently started my own job search, and it sounds like I would be a good fit for a company like yours. What positions are open or opening up where you're at?"

This is the simplest, subtlest way to set you up for a referral because they might tell you about positions that are not even open yet. If they're enjoying talking to you, they might even say, "Well, give me your résumé, and I'll keep you in mind." The steps of this informational interview process set you up for this final moment: asking for a referral.

But really, you're asking for advice—advice that will ideally lead to a referral by prompting the other person to ask how they can help you.

Since you showed interest in them at the beginning of your connection, they are much more likely to show interest in you, and since you behaved professionally and appropriately, they will know you are a serious candidate who is deserving of a referral. Here are some other questions you can ask at this final stage that will prompt the other party to give you advice or directly help you get hired:

- Who else could tell me more about the company? Could you introduce me to them?
- Could you pass my résumé on to the hiring manager in case a position opens up that I'm a good fit for?
- Do you know who the hiring manager is for this open position at your company?
- What advice would you give to someone in my position?

There may be times when you don't have a chance to ask those final questions because, as I discuss in previous chapters, the other party may stop talking about themselves and ask you about your interests and plans for the future. You should always have your elevator pitch on deck, ready to say who you are, what you want, and why they should care. In this situation, you likely have introduced who you are already and can jump right to saying something like, "I'm looking to transition into a company just like yours so that I can be a part of similar projects that are challenging, rewarding, and help other people."

By successfully guiding your networking conversations to deeper levels of professional intimacy, you master the informational interview process. Still, it's important to understand informational interviewing at an even deeper level because every individual will respond differently to your questions, and conversations with different personality types can be very unpredictable. The next chapter will help you master informational interviewing so that you are ready to respond positively no matter what turn your interviews take.

Chapter 25

Executing Informational Interviews Like a Friendly Student Journalist

· · · · · · · · · · · · · · · · · · · ·

The previous chapter covers how to follow the Straight-Line Referral method most likely to result in successful informational interviews and job referrals. It includes specific questions to ensure you take your conversations with industry employees to deeper and deeper levels of professional intimacy, simultaneously keeping them comfortable and opening them up to give you a referral.

In this chapter, I dive into why informational interviews exist, how to properly set them up in person, by video, or by phone (not just through online messaging), and how to master the interview process so that you can wrangle any conversation into a productive meeting that takes you at least one step—and likely many steps—closer to being hired.

The Purpose of an Informational Interview

The purpose of an informational interview is twofold. First, you want to gather intelligence that will help you determine whether a particular company or role is the right fit for you. Second, you want to leverage the informational interview to build rapport with the person you're talking to and get inside information about jobs that are open at the company, especially jobs that are not yet posted online or never will be posted online.

Industry experts agree that over 80 percent of today's available jobs are not advertised.[44] Those jobs are not hidden deliberately; they're not advertised because the ideal internal or external candidate has already been introduced to the hiring manager through a referral. According to a recent survey commissioned by iCIMS, a provider of talent acquisition solutions, when an employee refers someone, that candidate is hired approximately 67 percent of the time.[45]

Advertising jobs online is a painful process for hiring managers. Employers must wade through thousands of job applications from people they do not know. A company only resorts to advertising a job when they cannot find the right candidate through other channels, such as word of mouth or referrals. This is why you need to master the art of informational interviewing. Specifically, you need to master keeping the person you're interviewing on a straight line to getting a referral, or at least to getting inside information about job openings at the company.

By setting up an informational interview, you gain an opportunity to learn about a company's culture and how well you would fit into it, as well as strategically place yourself within the hidden job market of the company. Informational interviews allow you to develop contacts in your field. They also allow you to become well-informed about the industry or company you're interested in joining.

How to Request an Informational Interview

The foolproof way of securing an informational interview is to start with people you are already connected with in your network. These can be friends of family, alumni, professors, or colleagues from internships. Ask everyone you know for potential contacts in a field, at a company, or in a job that interests you. In the early stages, keep your options open. Don't limit yourself to informational interviews with only high-profile contacts. Instead, get comfortable with the process by interviewing people you already know well.

Also don't limit yourself to setting up informational interviews for only the one or two positions you want most. Even if someone's position seems outside your area of immediate interest, it can prove helpful in the future. You might learn firsthand information that makes a position more attractive to you.

The goal is to slowly build up your experience interviewing other people. Make sure you nurture these professional relationships both before and after you interview them. Build or rebuild rapport prior to the interview and follow up after the interview.

Once you've exhausted your current network, it is time to do some research. As I mentioned earlier, LinkedIn® is the best platform to use to search for employees at companies that interest you; however, before you reach out to anyone through LinkedIn®, ensure your LinkedIn® profile is complete, up-to-date, and professional. Your potential contact will absolutely look at your profile before deciding whether to reply. Lacking a professional LinkedIn® photo or having an incomplete profile will immediately end your chances for making a connection. Professionals want to connect with other professionals. They do not want to connect with people who appear unprofessional. I cover how to update your LinkedIn® profile extensively in previous sections of this book.

The most important part of an informational interview is how you request one. If your requests are open-ended or intense, the other party will pass or ignore you completely. When requesting an interview in person or by phone or video, always be very clear about how much of the other person's time you're going to take. Clarity and politeness are crucial here. Never ask someone for a moment of their time or open-ended questions like, "Do you have time later this week for a short conversation?" And, of course, as I already emphasized, never mention an "informational interview." Instead, ask for a very small and specific amount of time on a specific day during a specific block of time with only one alternate day and time. For example, ask, "Are you free tomorrow any time between 12 and 3 p.m. or Wednesday between 9 and 11 a.m. for a quick, three-minute call?"

. . . .

I recommend suggesting three or seven minutes instead of five, ten, or fifteen because it's specific and not rounded to the nearest five or ten. Rounding to the nearest five or ten is usually code for "I'm estimating and this could take much longer."

. . . .

Be exact. Show them right away that you've thought this through and are not going to waste their time. You should also specify the topic in your requests. Don't make them guess your intentions. Don't even make them guess how you're going to phrase your questions. Instead, say, "Are you free tomorrow anytime between 12 and 3 p.m. or Wednesday between 9 and 11 a.m. for a quick, three-minute call? I'd love to ask you two quick questions about how you got hired at company XYZ and what you enjoy about it."

Most importantly, keep the intensity of your request low. Don't make your conversation a big deal. Don't make it hard for them to commit by acting like they are the only reason you're getting out of bed in the morning. Never say, "I've set aside time tomorrow and would love to call you and talk with you about your career." That's too intense. Instead, say, "I'll be making some work calls tomorrow around noon and would love to give you a quick call too."

Altogether, you might say, "I'll be making some work calls tomorrow around noon and would love to ask you two quick questions about how you got hired at company XYZ and what you enjoy about it. This would only take three minutes. Are you free any time between 12 and 3 p.m., or I could do Wednesday between 9 and 11 a.m. too. No worries if not."

Once you leverage this or a similar script to secure an informational interview, it's time to prepare for it.

Preparing For and Executing an Informational Interview

Prepare for an informational interview like you would prepare for a job interview. Do background research on the company and position you are targeting and on your interviewee. Come prepared with at least ten additional questions. Desperately trying to keep the conversation afloat with no agenda in mind will make you look bad and will frustrate your interviewee. If the interview is in person or by video, you must dress and act professionally. Remember, making a good first impression is imperative. Bring your résumé as well, but only hand it over or share it online during the interview if you are asked to by your interviewee. Keep in mind that the person you're interviewing could provide additional leads or referrals that could lead to a job. If you are shy by nature and the thought of interviewing a complete stranger feels uncomfortable, remember that you are flattering this person by asking for their expert advice. You're not there to sell yourself. You're simply there to ask questions and create a dialogue.

To that end, you must practice your questions. The best way to do this is by asking the questions you've prepared to a friend, family member, classmate, labmate, or anyone else you can practice with until you feel confident and your voice sounds conversational.

During informational interviews, you are the interviewer, not the interviewee; therefore, you always want the focus to be on the interviewee. Your goal is to make the other person feel important. You want the other person to leave feeling valued, so make sure you compliment them on their accomplishments and stay authentically curious about their career and industry experiences. The more you talk about yourself, the less the other party will feel inclined to help you, and the less likely you are to get a referral. Instead of appearing professional, you will appear self-centered and arrogant by focusing on yourself.

During the interview, aim to gather as much information as possible about the company the other person represents. This is your chance to deeply understand what it's like to work at their company and determine whether the company is a good fit for you. That being said, don't interrogate the other person. Don't press them to answer certain questions, and don't be a stickler for time or topics.

Firing off a list of questions that only matter to you without engaging your interviewee will create a cold and unfriendly atmosphere. Instead, you want to approach the interview like a friendly journalist writing a "puff piece" about the interviewee and their company. Your goal is to keep the tone casual and conversational by actively listening and responding to the other person's stories. Don't be afraid to go with the flow of the conversation. If the other person veers off on a tangent, that's good! Let them veer. It means you've hit a topic of particular interest to your interviewee. If the other person becomes disengaged with structured questions like, "What is a typical day at work like?" try asking less conventional questions like "How have your work passions changed over the years?"

You should constantly be gauging their interest level and moving the conversation to what they are most excited to talk about. Finally, keep the entire interview time to a minimum. Respect the timeframe you set, but—and this is important—be ready with more questions in case they say, "I have another fifteen minutes if you'd like to keep talking."

How to Behave Like a Journalist

Behaving like a friendly, yet curious, journalist means keeping the focus on your interviewee, adapting positively to their personality, and actively listening by smiling, nodding, and taking notes. When it comes to keeping the conversation going, your aim is to be engaging but relaxing by asking questions that are career-focused and in the realm of the other person's expectations. When holding an informational interview with someone by phone, video, or in person, it's best to focus on the seven types of questions you should be asking rather than memorizing exact questions. The seven types of informational interview questions are:

1. Preparation – How did they learn about the position they are currently in, and what was the application process like?
2. Present job – What are their current responsibilities?
3. Career future alternatives – What is the career trajectory for people in this role? Can they move up the "corporate ladder"? What lateral moves are possible?

4. Lifestyle – What are the pros and cons of their position? Do they have a lot of free time outside of work, and was this an important reason for them taking the position?

5. Job hunting strategies – What advice can they give PhDs wanting to secure this type of position? Is additional training required? What qualities should you focus on?

6. Nature of organization – What is company culture like? Is there a constant turnover of employees? Is job satisfaction high?

7. Expertise and qualification matching – What suggestions can they offer to a PhD looking to be successful in their field?

Pay close attention to what's being said, and ask questions when something isn't clear. At the end of the interview, try to gather names of other individuals you can interview next. Then, depending on how the interview progressed, ask for a referral to a position that is open or will be opening at the company.

Always send a thank you note after the interview. Remember, following up is an effective way to keep in touch, be remembered, and show you are grateful for someone's time. Neglecting to follow up, on the other hand, will unravel any meaningful conversations you had. If you communicated solely by email prior to meeting, an email thank-you note can suffice. However, a physical thank-you note sent through the post is preferred as it leaves a lasting impact on the receiver.

Importantly, be specific in your message by quoting something from your interview or including a link related to a topic you discussed. Let the other person know they made a significant impression on you. This will keep the door open to develop the relationship further, and they will be more inclined to return the favor in the future with a referral.

Here is a short follow-up message you can send after an informational interview:

• •

Hi [Professional Name],

Thank you for meeting with me today.
It was great to discuss [topic] with you. I really appreciate the insight you provided and will be [action to take] just as you suggested. I'll be sure to let you know what happens, and please let me know when I can repay the favor.

Thanks again for your time.

Sincerely,
[Your name]

P.S. I've attached [link to article on discussed topic or similar]. If you find time, I would love to know what you think about [specific point]. No worries if not.

. . . .

After sending your thank-you note, continue to foster the relationship with your new connection well after your interview is over. If you have not done so already, connect with them through LinkedIn®, endorse their skills, and follow their achievements online. Act as a peer sponsoring them, not a fan kissing up to them. Find as many ways as possible to add value professionally. Congratulate them for a promotion, pass along an article or conference of interest, or simply discuss current events in the field. By continuing to foster the relationship and add value, you are in a good position to ask them for a referral when a position opens up at their company if you haven't done so already. This can be asking for the name of the hiring manager or simply asking permission to mention their name as a reference in a cover letter.

When it comes to hosting an informational interview, it's important to have this kind of long-term strategy in place. Your goal is to build a lasting professional relationship that you can add value to and turn to for help over and over again. Your goal is not to ask for a quick favor and drop the other person forever.

By staying focused on building long-term relationships, your informational interviews will lead to more referrals and give you the information you need to make a decision about which industry position is right for you. Informational interviews will also lead to actual job interviews that put you just one "yes" away from your dream industry position and compensation package.

CASE STUDY 5
Elizabeth Thatcher, PhD

My goal was to be a Medical Science Liaison (MSL), but I didn't have clinical experience or industry experience. I was an engineer. During my postdoc, for a period of about two and a half months, I applied to many MSL jobs but only received two phone screens. Nothing ever progressed. After joining a group called the Cheeky Scientist Association, which helped me implement the strategies in this book, I began reworking my résumé. I applied to five places in one week and received four phone screens this time. I was so excited, but still, nothing progressed. The problem was I was a slow learner (or hardheaded) and still refused to network. I was sort of networking, but not really ... I wasn't building deep professional relationships, and I wasn't doing any informational interviews.

Once I started taking networking and doing informational interviews seriously, everything changed. The most valuable advice I received from one of these informational interviews was that I could easily gain more clinical experience by attending Grand Rounds at hospitals in my area. I started going to Grand Rounds once or twice a week, and suddenly I was getting past the phone screen stage and being invited to site visits. At one point, I was having at least one in-person interview every one to two weeks. I was being told consistently by employers and employees at the companies I interviewed at that offers were being prepared. It was very stressful with lots of ups and downs.

Then, one day, Deepak (another Associate) posted that his company was looking for a new MSL in my location. I really can't say enough about how incredibly nice and helpful Deepak was. He referred me to the recruiter and helped me prepare for my final MSL interview presentation. Within days, I had seven interviews for the position and was offered the job! I did a little negotiating and then happily accepted the job. I became an MSL! I can't thank the Association enough. It showed me how to network and helped save my sanity by cheering me on!

***

If you're ready to transition into your dream industry position, you can apply to book a free Transition Call with me or one of my trained Transition Specialists at: https://cheekyscientist.com/transition-book.

STEP #7:

Prepare for the Three-Stage Interview Funnel

"You never get a second chance to make a good first impression."

— Will Rogers

Chapter 26

The Industry Interview Funnel Starts before You Interview

· · · · · · · · · · · · · · · · · · · ·

The interview process includes all the steps of the hiring process between the résumé screening and job offer and has three main components: the phone screen, the video interview, and the on-site visit. The number of rounds for each of these components will vary depending on the company size and the position. The number of candidates a company considers for an open position drops off dramatically after the résumé screen and dwindles with each successive interview round. The only way to make the most of the increased odds an interview provides is to be prepared and responsive.

The Speed of Industry Time Is Greater than the Speed of Academic Time

Industry time is not like academic time. Things move much faster. For instance, new job postings receive their first application within two hundred seconds of being posted.[46]

Things move even faster later in the hiring funnel. You must be ready to say "yes" to a phone screen request at a moment's notice if your dream employer asks if you're free to talk about your experiences. You must be prepared to reply right away to their LinkedIn® message requesting more information about your candidacy. You must be highly responsive, with your phone, email, and LinkedIn® notifications turned on, so you can seize the moment before the employer moves on to the next candidate who is ready and willing to meet with them right away—that candidate who started preparing for industry interviews months in advance, practicing behaviorally for dozens, if not hundreds, of hours to avoid coming across ill-prepared, awkward, or book smart without being people smart.

Employers Want to See That You've Done Your Research

The goal of every step of the interview process is to convince whoever is interviewing you that you are the best candidate for the position and a good fit for the company. You will find selling yourself during an interview easier if you lay a strong foundational mindset for approaching your interviews. You should research every company to which you apply; that allows you to demonstrate interest and commitment during interviews. Hiring managers notice when a candidate has done this homework, and it always leaves a good impression. Here are a few questions your research should answer:

- What are the company's values? What is their mission statement?
- Has the company gone through any recent mergers and/or acquisitions?
- Why do they need to fill your target position?

You should also prepare questions to ask your interviewers, which I cover more in the following chapters. Most importantly, show up to every interview prepared to convince the employer that you are the best person for the job and that their company is at the top of your list. If you fail to project certainty in either of those areas, you will fail to get a job offer. After all, why would anyone extend an offer to someone who couldn't even convince them that they were the right fit for the role or that they wanted to work for the company in the first place?

As a PhD, whether you know it or not, you've picked up some bad habits in academia that hinder your performance in industry interviews. The worst of these habits is avoiding confirmation bias at all costs. Of course, when it comes to work, especially data and information that can directly or indirectly affect patient lives, scientific funding, etc., you should avoid confirmation bias. But in your job search, you should be as biased as possible toward yourself. You must do everything you can (short of outright lying) to convince employers you are the best possible candidate for the job. You must find every angle and leverage every turn of phrase that can make you seem, even momentarily, to be the better candidate. Once you are hired, you can prove yourself and reassure them you were always the best choice—but you must get hired first. While all PhDs regularly express uncertainty in their work in sharing things like error values and the limitations of the research approaches, there's no place for this when it comes to pitching yourself as the ideal candidate for an industry role.

Sure, you will get "gotcha" questions like "What's your biggest weakness?" and "Tell me about a time when you had to violate your own ethics." just to keep you on your toes. But at no time should you build a case against your being the best fit for the role.

Answering questions about your skills and experiences with "I've never done that," "I don't have that experience," or simply "No" is a giant red flag. Instead, you must answer those types of questions with "I have many similar experience in this area including …," "I have yet to work with that specific device but I'm a very fast learner and will come in early every day until I can operate it at an expert level," or "I have the ability to do it, and here's how I will learn the skills required …." A lack of commitment in terms of your skills, experiences, or general enthusiasm for the role is one of the biggest reasons PhDs fail to convert an interview into a job offer.

• •

Companies may even try to test your commitment by asking if you are open to other roles. Don't fall into this trap by slipping back into pontificating about all the possibilities you're open to. Instead, be firm that you are open to doing whatever it takes to serve the company best, but you do believe you're the best fit for the position at hand.

• •

In addition to showing commitment to your target role, you must also show commitment to the company that is interviewing you. You need to provide rationale for why a particular company is your number one choice. Understand that every company you are targeting can be your top choice for one reason or another. Ideally, that reason relates to the company's mission, vision, or values.

The First Ninety Seconds of an Interview Are the Most Important

When it comes to executing an industry interview, a typical interview round can last anywhere from fifteen minutes for a phone screen to forty-five minutes for an individual meeting during a site visit.

However, no matter the overall length of the interview round, studies show that the interviewer decides whether or not they will recommend hiring you within the first ninety seconds.[47]

The same studies found that 55 percent of your impact comes from the way you dress, act, and walk through the door; therefore, you should prepare to make a good first impression. Much of this impression comes from nonverbal cues. Did you dress professionally? Did you smile during the interview? Does your body language portray confidence? It's a lot easier to manage your nonverbal cues and portray confidence when you have established a plan for some of the standard interview logistics ahead of time. Start planning for these by addressing the below questions in a few notes well in advance of your next interview:

- Where will you keep a copy of your résumé so that you can easily get to it for a phone screen?
- Where will you take calls for your phone screens so that you are not distracted?
- What will you wear to your video or in-person interview? Does the professional attire you selected require any care to look its best (e.g., dry cleaning)?
- Where do you plan to take your video interview? (PhD Pro Tip: Make sure it is a place that gives you good lighting and has reliable internet access.)

In general, there are only two questions that are asked within the first ninety seconds. These questions are the same for every interview type and interview round.

The first of these questions is "How are you today?" Don't start the interview by giving a lukewarm response like "Good, thank you" or similar, and certainly don't taint the interview from the outset by talking about how bad the weather is, how nervous you are, or any other random or negative observation. Instead, simply say "Perfect."[48] Replying with "Perfect" keeps your answer clean and to the point, which will keep the conversation moving forward and eliminate the urge to ramble about whatever you did that morning on your way to the interview. It also has the advantage of being a unique answer without being too unique (and thus, odd). It is the most concise and professional answer you can give, which is exactly the first impression you want to make.

The second question you will be asked is, "Can you tell me a little bit about yourself?" This is a simple Credibility Question, which is one of the four types of interview questions I discuss in a later chapter. The best way to answer this question is by delivering your elevator pitch, which I cover extensively in an earlier chapter. You want your response to explain who you are, what you want, and why they should care in one minute or less.

Now that you understand the basics of interviewing, it's time to learn the specific ways in which interviews are structured and how they progress, as well as the most common ways industry interview questions are framed.

Chapter 27

Phone Calls, Video Interviews, and Other Early Screening Methods

························

The first round of the interview process is most often done over the phone or another audio channel, so this type of interview is commonly referred to as the phone screen. During a phone screen, an employer (typically someone from human resources) has seen your résumé or received a referral from your networking contact and wants to talk to you on the phone to determine whether you should progress to the next step in the interview process.

Do Not Underestimate the Importance of Early Screening Methods

Many PhDs tend to underestimate the importance of the phone screen because it's the first round of the interview process and is not technically focused, but remember, if you got to the phone screen, you are amongst the top twelve to fifteen applicants out of hundreds, if not thousands. This is your first opportunity to talk to a company employee who is involved in the hiring decision, so you have to take it seriously. You must be prepared at all times for a phone screen because employers set aside discrete units of time to go through résumés and people who have been referred to them and make those calls. They might be calling twenty different candidates over the course of a few hours. So, you might get very short notice before a phone screen; they may email you only a couple of hours before, maybe a day tops. You can't wait to have a phone screen confirmation to prepare for this interview. The moment you apply to a company, you need to start preparing for the phone screen.

How to Prepare for a Phone Screen

When preparing for a phone screen, start by creating a checklist with all the relevant information you have gathered about the company and the position. One of the advantages that you're going to have on a phone screen versus a video interview or a site visit is that it's only audio. So, you can have papers with data in front of you and refer to that information throughout the call. Find as much information as you can online and print it out or create a list. Here are some points you will need to cover during your research:

- What are the things this company is likely going to bring up?
- What is this company like?
- What are their values?

You should also have a list of questions ready to ask at the end of the interview. Phone screens are usually not very technical. The person interviewing you will mostly focus on whether you are a good fit for the company, if you have the general qualifications for the position, and if you are capable of having the kind of friendly conversation that will happen all day long at the company if you get hired.

Continue your phone screen preparations by setting aside a silent room and clear workspace where you can take your call without interruptions. Make sure nobody will interrupt you during the screen and portray with your body language that you are interested in the position and the employer has your full attention. You might think this doesn't make a big difference during a phone screen since the interviewers can't see you, but if you are distracted or stressed out, this will show through the tone of your voice. A great way to see how you come across over audio is to record yourself answering basic interview questions. Use a smartphone or other device to do this and listen to the recording. Do you sound engaged? Is your tone uplifting? Does the pace and pitch of your voice vary, indicating enthusiasm for the role and conversation? Or do you sound like you're barely awake? Do you sound bored or boring? Do you sound monotone? Are you Ben Stein taking attendance in *Ferris Bueller's Day Off*—"Bueller ... Bueller ... Bueller"? It's worth knowing.

What to Do During the Phone Screen

As you have the phone screen, take notes. These might be useful for future interview rounds and will help you determine if the job is a good fit for you. Take notes by hand; don't type. Otherwise, the other person will hear you typing, which can be distracting. If possible, use a hardline connection instead of a cell phone. Make sure you turn off call waiting and notifications from other apps on your phone. This is something a lot of people don't think about, but just like you don't want any distractions in your environment, you don't want any distractions coming from your phone during a phone screen.

Keep your résumé in clear view. Very likely the person on the other end of the phone has your résumé in front of them and will ask a few questions based on your résumé. These are called Credibility Questions, and they test whether your answers match the information you put on your résumé. So have your résumé on hand, and make sure your answers match.

Listen carefully and speak clearly. Keep your responses concise, and don't ramble. Avoid repeating yourself. Don't interrupt the interviewer or feel like you need to fill all gaps in the conversation. Many interviewers will purposely stay quiet after you give your initial answer just to see how you handle the silence.

Will you fill it with awkward commentary about yourself? Will you offer information that doesn't reflect well on your candidacy? Will you reveal that you're not a serious candidate?

They will wait to see. You can cut this tactic short by prompting them to acknowledge you've answered their question by ending your answer with, "Does that answer your question?" In a phone conversation where you can't see the face of the person you are talking to, it's difficult to be sure when they're done talking. That's why it's okay to leave some room for silence and only start answering once you're sure the question is over. Once the telephone interview is complete, thank the interviewer by name and inquire about the next steps of the interview process. This is your opportunity to ask the questions you prepared. You should ask at least two or three questions (more on which questions to ask later, but make sure these questions don't go too deep because the phone screen is more of a topical conversation).

If you forget something, don't call them back. It may be tempting, but it's usually not a good idea. The best thing to do is to make a note of what you forgot so that you can address it in future rounds. Most commonly, the second round of the interview process will be by video, which is what you need to prepare for next.

How to Handle a Video Interview

The video interview commonly follows the phone screen and is the next step in the interview process. In this step, you will be interviewing either with one person or with a panel, but it won't be in person. Instead, it will be through video with both audio and visual. You will be using video call software, such as Microsoft Teams or Zoom, to have your interview.

In this step, you need to consider the technology you will be using, how the interviewers see you, and what you need to do to come across as a professional candidate. One of the biggest keys to executing a video interview successfully is knowing how you look on the other side of the camera. A great way to prepare for this is to ask the company who's going to interview you, how many people will show up, and where the interview is going to be held. This is a normal question to ask before a video interview or a site visit. You need to consider how you're going to look during the interview; assume that you're going to be on a large monitor in a large room. This means that your image and your background will be much larger than what you see on your computer screen and that the microexpressions on your face and the movement of your hands are going to be much more dynamic than you might think. You also need to prepare for the interviewers to have a distracting background. There could be people walking by in the background if they are in a conference room made of glass. There could be several people walking in and out of the interview to ask you questions. You need to consider these things in advance to avoid losing focus during the interview.

Before participating in any video interview, you need to not only do your homework on the organization but also build a video set for yourself. You must test the equipment you will use during the interview and create a well-lit set. You should dress head to toe in the clothes you would wear to a site visit because they might ask you to search for or grab something, and you will have to move. Having a full professional outfit instead of just the top part also gives you more confidence during the interview. You must ensure that you're comfortable and that the interviewers can see you and hear you clearly. The only way you can do this is by testing everything. For both the phone screen and video interview steps, you should do several mock interviews with another person. For video mock interviews, this should be a full dress rehearsal. Wear what you're going to wear and have everything set up the way you're setting it up for the interview to make sure you come across professional. Make sure to check the sound, the visuals, the lighting, and the background ahead of time so that you can make adjustments for the real interview if needed.

Most PhDs forget to ensure they have enough lighting on their face. Ideally, you should turn your desk and computer in a way that allows you to face a window during your interview. If that's not possible, get a lamp and shine it right at your face and eyes. When it comes to audio, make sure that your microphone and speakers are connected to the computer. You don't need a Bluetooth device going in and out, disrupting the conversation. You should avoid huge headsets too. Having something that you can connect to the computer without being too distracting is ideal because it will ensure you have good audio. You will also want to connect the computer you will use for the interview to a hardline internet connection like ethernet or similar.

• •

Try to avoid using Wi-Fi, even if it means buying an ethernet cord and an adapter for your computer. You will not get a second chance for the video interview if your Wi-Fi fails. Poor Wi-Fi is not an excuse. If you can't even manage your own internet connection, why would a company put you in charge of managing anything else?

• •

Finally, you want to add your notes to the computer screen, so the interviewers can't see them. During the interview, you will tend to look at the image of the interviewers on the screen, but you should try to look at your computer camera most of the time as this gives the impression of eye contact. This extra effort will make a big difference, especially if you are projected on a big screen.

Video interviews are often panel interviews because the company wants as many people as possible to see your face and interact with you before committing to bringing you out for a site visit. Once you are told your video interview will be a panel interview, be sure to ask who will be on the panel.

Yes, you can ask this question. You can—and should—ask any question you want about the structure of an industry interview. You should also ask for the job titles of each person on the panel. Your goal is to find out everything you can about all the people who will interview you on the panel. Connect with them on LinkedIn® and scour their profiles. Work to understand their departments and departmental goals. This will give you an idea of the different backgrounds of those on the panel and the questions you can expect from each member.

During the panel interview, make sure you engage with *all* the interviewers, not just the most outgoing participant. Never ignore the quiet person on the panel. Engage with every panelist when answering an individual panelist's question. It's okay if you give special attention to the person who asked the question, but don't leave anyone out of the conversation. Make sure you keep track of each person's name and job title and who asked which question. This is best done by starting your panel interview with a sheet of paper in front of you with each panel member's name listed. Then you can write shorthand notes for each person's question under their name as they ask it.

During a panel interview, you should be prepared for any type of question because there will likely be people from different departments. You might be interviewing for an R&D position, but you'll likely be talking to someone from human resources, R&D, sales, marketing, and perhaps one or two executives. The interests of every panel member will vary, and you need to meet each person's interests individually, as well as the collective interest, to build rapport. Keep in mind that every person on the panel will have a say in whether you move to the next interview round.

To close the panel interview successfully, ask a question like, "Is there any other information you would like to hear from me?" Look directly at the camera when asking this question (or when responding to any question). Try to avoid looking down at the panel members' faces the entire time because this is a very negative posture and comes across as negative or like you're fabricating your answers. Another great question to ask at the end of a video interview is: "Do you still have any doubts that you would like me to address before we move on to the next phase of the interview process?" This question encourages them to address any doubts they may have while you're still present and can help them overcome these doubts or gets them to confirm they have no doubts. Either way, if done properly, your interviewers will now feel a stronger pull to extend a job offer to you to maintain consistency with their acknowledgment that their doubts were resolved or that they didn't have any doubts in the first place.

Additional Early Interview Formats

There are many other types of interviews you may progress through prior to meeting with anyone in person. For many medical, scientific, and technical writing or editing roles, you will be asked to do a take-home test that involves different writing and editing exercises.

For example, you may be asked to write an unstructured abstract to present the research findings at a scientific meeting or edit a two-hundred-word news article down to seventy-two words so it can be published in a magazine read by laypeople. You'll also be asked to submit a portfolio of your work (by the way, saying you don't have a portfolio is not a reasonable response; you must create one). You may also need a portfolio for other types of roles, such as Data Scientist roles.

For most Data Scientist roles, you'll be asked to join a coding call or technical call where you'll be tested on your technical knowledge in the context of the company's business goals. You may be asked questions related to mathematics, statistics, and depending on the role, basic coding or analysis. Although such calls are technical in nature, you still want to use storytelling when you answer to show that you can translate your technical knowledge into business solutions (more on storytelling as way to answer interview questions later). You might be asked about A/B testing, p-values, statistical significance, and linear algebra, but what the employer is most interested in is *how* you answer the questions. What is your problem-solving process, and can you communicate it externally and effectively?

You may also be given a take-home test for which the company will give you a data set and some business context and ask you to answer business-related questions. Many times, you will also have to prepare a presentation of your results and present it during the on-site interview. Likewise, during the Medical Science Liaison interview process, you may be asked to study a clinical trial case study and present the study's findings.

Still other PhD-level industry positions may require you to submit a video in which you answer a list of questions before or after your phone screen. Other companies may simply send you an email with a list of questions before meeting with you again or for the first time.

Regardless of what you are asked to do during the initial stages of the interview process, the purpose of these initial stages is to screen out job candidates who may not be worth inviting to spend a full day with the company's team. If you do get an invite for a site visit, it means the job is yours to lose. You need to prepare for site visits at the absolute highest level to ensure you get a job offer.

Chapter 28

Site Visits, Surveillance Cameras, and Hotel Operatives

· · · · · · · · · · · · · · · · · · · ·

W hen I got on a plane to California for my first site visit, I didn't know that twenty other job candidates were on the 737 headed to the same location as me. When we arrived, there was a large company caravan waiting to pick us up. None of us knew who was applying to which position, so the ride was pretty quiet. I was embarrassed because, unfortunately, I failed to dress professionally for the plane trip. There were two company officials on the caravan welcoming us, and the first impression of how I looked could never be undone.

When we got to the hotel, we were each shown to our room. I found out later that this company sent a dozen or more job candidates to this hotel every single weekday and the hotel staff gave feedback to the company about which candidates were the most polite, kind, and clean. That was a wake-up call.

When we showed up to the company headquarters the next day, we got out of the caravan and walked into the lobby, where we interacted with the front desk administrators and waited to be called for our first interview. After I was hired, I learned that occasionally video surveillance cameras were monitored to see how job candidates interacted with each other and the administrative staff. That day I did four one-on-one interviews, two panel interviews, a behavioral interview, and a presentation.

I also had a lunch interview, which I didn't realize was an interview at the time. After I was on the team, I learned that the two people who sat with me were strategically chosen by the company and given a list of questions to ask me while I was eating and my guard was down.

The Basics of a Site Visit

A site visit is when you go to a company's headquarters or one of their office locations and have meetings with multiple people who work there. A site visit is not just one interview. It's multiple interviews. You could have two or three panel interviews, then lunch with the hiring team, and then three or four more individual interviews.

This is the most important part of the interview process.

If you get invited to a site visit, the job is yours to lose. They want to hire you at this point. Will you give them a reason not to by failing to show up as your best self the entire time you're on site—from leaving your home for the airport to walking back through your front door?

You need to be prepared for several interviews and be prepared to adapt to changes as they happen. Every company will structure their site visits slightly differently, and because it's in real time, the day's plans could change quickly. Perhaps someone who was supposed to interview you took a last-minute personal day and the company has to invent something for you to do for an hour. Roll with it. Or maybe they only have lunch options that you are allergic to. Plan for this and roll with it. When it comes to the actual interviews during your site visit, these are the six common types:

1. One-on-one interviews
2. Panel interviews
3. Group interviews
4. Lunch or dinner interviews
5. Strengths-based interviews
6. Behavioral interviews

One-on-one interviews are between you and just one other person. They focus on highlighting how your skills, experience, and accomplishments prove you are the best candidate for the role. Panel interviews, on the other hand, include multiple interviewers asking a candidate questions. As I discussed earlier, interviewers who are part of a panel will bring viewpoints from different departments within the company. The goal of this interview is to determine how the candidate handles different people's perspectives and cross-functional environments. A group interview is where the hiring team interviews several job candidates at the same time. These are not common for PhD-level positions, but you should still be prepared for them.

. . . .

You may show up to a large company's headquarters only to be met with other job candidates being interviewed for the same or similar positions. Do not overthink this. Focus on yourself. The good news is that you can prepare in advance for this scenario by asking the hiring manager if there will be a group interview of any kind.

. . . .

A lunch or dinner interview is meant to determine how you fit with the rest of the team, not to provide you with a free meal. Don't be fooled by the relaxed setting. This is still an interview, and everything you say will affect your chances of getting the job. Eat something light and avoid messy foods so that you are not distracted. If they offer you a drink, accept it, but don't overindulge; you must be in control of the situation the whole time.

Strengths-based interviews are meant to uncover what you enjoy doing versus what you can do. Companies conducting this type of interview want to be sure that your passions are deeply aligned with the role. You will be asked a lot of Opinion Questions (another one of the four types of interview questions employers will ask you) like "What do you do in your free time?" or "What do you see as your biggest professional success to date?" or "What's your biggest weakness?" or "What's your preferred management style?"

Finally, behavioral interviews test your professional awareness by determining how you behave in detailed scenarios. The interviewer's main objective here is to uncover how you solve problems and how you cope with stress. Behavioral Questions are yet another one of the four interview question types I cover in a later chapter.

How to Prepare for a Site Visit

Regardless of which interview types you will be a part of during your site visit, you should prepare extensively by asking the employer specific questions before the interview, researching the company in detail online, and setting up informational interviews with people currently working at the company. Make sure you find out why they are hiring for this position, what the metrics of success are or likely will be for the role, and what the average salary range is for the position (you'll need this information to comfortably deflect verbal offers and attempts to negotiate on site, but more on that in later chapters). Once you get a confirmation for the site visit, ask about specific details. What is the schedule for the site visit? Who will be interviewing you? What is the goal of the interview? Is a presentation expected?

Overall, your preparation can be broken down into what to do up to one week before the site visit and what to do a day or two before the site visit. If you have a week or more to prepare for your site visit, here is the checklist you should follow:

- Read extensively about the company, including any mergers and acquisitions they are involved in.
- Set up informational interviews with people currently working at the company.
- Make sure you find out why they are hiring for this position.
- Ask yourself how you can help the company achieve their goals for the position at hand. Make a list of your answers.
- Research average and top salaries for this position in the city it is located in.
- Determine your "walk-away number," or the lowest salary you will accept.

As the site visit approaches, you will need to adjust your strategy to focus on the most pressing items to complete before arriving. Here's a checklist to complete a day or two before you arrive on site:

- Contact the company and continue setting up informational interviews to find out how you should dress, who you will be interviewing with, and whether you will be giving a presentation.
- If you will be giving a presentation, ask for specifics on what the presentation should be about and who will be in the audience. Then prepare your presentation.
- Set up and execute at least two thirty-minute mock interviews with friends. Practice giving your site visit presentation, if necessary.
- Review your research notes about the company and why they are hiring.

After you have prepared fully for your site visit, you are ready to show up, impress everyone with your professionalism and knowledge, and get a job offer. The only thing that's left to do is understand the four types of interview questions you will be asked and how to frame your answers for each question, regardless of the type.

Chapter 29

The Four Types of Interview Questions
All PhDs Are Asked

· ·

How you answer different types of interview questions will determine whether you get hired. Employers ask PhDs four key question types to gauge their communication skills as well as their interpersonal skills overall. These question types are used as a framework for the interviewer to determine whether you're a good fit for the position.

Peer-reviewed studies have found that interviewer judgments based on structured interview questions are more predictive of job performance than those from unstructured interviews.[49] Overall, the studies concluded that adding structure to the interview process enhances the reliability and validity of interviewer evaluations. During an industry interview, you will be asked structured questions, and you will be evaluated on how you answer those questions.

In the book, *Promote Yourself: The New Rules For Career Success*, a large-scale survey was reported that asked hundreds of employers about the most important traits they look for when hiring.[50] A surprising 98 percent responded that communication skills were the most important. Another large-scale survey performed by the

Center for Creative Leadership found that poor "interpersonal skills" are the number one reason promising technical careers go off course.[51] Yet another survey by the Workforce Solutions Group, reported in *Time Magazine*, found that 60 percent of all applicants to high-level jobs lack adequate communication and interpersonal skills.[52]

So, like it or not, how you answer interview questions will be the final metric used to determine whether you'll get a job offer.

There are Four Types of Common Interview Questions

As a PhD, there are four different kinds of questions you are likely to face in an industry interview:

- Credibility Questions – e.g., "Can you tell me a little bit about yourself?" or "Can you explain your responsibilities in your previous role?"
- Opinion Questions – e.g., "What type of leader do you prefer to work for?" or "What are your biggest strengths and weaknesses?"
- Behavioral Questions – e.g., "Can you tell me about a conflict you had with your last supervisor and how you handled it?" or "Can you walk me through a time when you had to follow a policy you did not agree with?"
- Competency Questions – e.g., "If you were given XYZ resources, how would you use your skills to achieve ABC result?" or "Do you have any questions for me?"

Respectively, these question types will focus on your experience and credentials, your opinions and how you see the world, the way you handle specific situations, and your technical skills.

Credibility and Opinion Questions

Employers typically start their interviews with the more basic question types, i.e., Credibility Questions and Opinion Questions. According to thousands of post-transition calls I've done with PhDs over the years after they've been hired, these employers will spend about five minutes asking Credibility Questions and five to ten minutes asking Opinion Questions. For interviews early in the interview funnel, such as initial phone screens, employers may spend more of the interview time on these types of questions, as much as 50 to 80 percent. The Behavioral and Competency Questions are leveraged more during the later interview stages, including video, panel, and site visit interviews. For an hour-long interview, twenty minutes or more can be spent on Behavioral Questions and another twenty minutes can be spent on Competency Questions.

Credibility Questions about your experience and credentials are perhaps the easiest to prepare for because they can be anticipated. One credibility question that is almost always asked during an interview, usually at the very beginning, is "Can you tell me a little about yourself?"

Other Credibility Questions might include:

- How long did you work at … ?
- What did you do at … ?
- Can you please explain the results you achieved at … ?

The goal of asking this question type is to get a greater understanding of your breadth of experience (or lack thereof) and what you have been doing to date. Credibility questions can also serve clarify points on your résumé and determine whether you are suitable for the job. As a PhD, these questions will likely focus on your technical skills, prompting you to validate your qualifications and technical experience. Other questions of this type include questions about gaps in your résumé and any career changes you may have made.

Opinion Questions are often future facing and focused on situations. These questions are designed to assess your suitability to work in the company by looking at how you see different difficult situations. Opinion questions are used to determine your fit in the company's organizational culture. They are also used to assess your transferable skills and, more generally, how you see yourself. Some Opinion Questions could be:

- What do you see as your biggest professional success to date?
- What's your preferred management style?
- What would you do if faced with this type of situation?

You should leverage and highlight your transferable skills when answering Opinion Questions. As I mentioned earlier, both Credibility and Opinion Questions are commonly asked early in the interview and are designed to get you talking.

Behavioral and Competency Questions

Behavioral Questions are usually past-facing and the toughest interview questions for PhDs to answer. Here, the interviewer is seeking to find out how you react to different kinds of situations, especially challenging situations. Behavioral Questions are designed to induce stress and determine how you make decisions under pressure, as well as how you communicate. They are also structured to determine if you are the kind of employee who takes personal responsibility for past challenges and focuses on what they can control in situations. Here, employers are looking to sniff out those who jump to playing the blame game or the victim at work. Examples of Behavioral Questions include:

- Can you tell me about a time when you had to deal with a stressful situation and how you coped with it?
- Can you tell me about a time when you had to violate your own ethics to get your work done in a previous role?
- How do you prioritize your work? Can you share an example of when you faced too many tasks and failed to prioritize them effectively?

Competency Questions are those that test whether you have both the required skills and the desired skills to do the job. They are designed to test how you solve problems specifically within the context of the job you will be doing for the company. Here you are being tested on your problem-solving process and how well you communicate that process. Whether your answer is right or wrong is far less important than your process of coming to that answer and whether you were able to communicate the process effectively in its entirety to your interviewers. For example, you may be asked:

- We have a client right now who is struggling to do XYZ. If you were given ABC and DEF, how would you help them solve their problem?
- After an onboarding and training period, you may be asked to do XYZ. What are the first steps you would take to accomplish this task?
- Your department has been working hard on a project in XYZ area, which is why we are hiring for this role. How would you help your new team complete the project?

· ·

There is one final Competency Question that is always asked at the tail end of each interview: "Do you have any questions for us?" You must be well prepared for this final question. This means having a list of at least ten questions to ask each interviewer and adding more questions as needed as the interview progresses. Wrinkling your eyebrow and trying to sound intelligent and thoughtful while you pause strategically before saying, "No, I believe you answered all of them," is not going to fool anyone.

• •

Prepare wisely for each question type by studying the STAR method of answering interview questions, which I cover next, and make sure you have detailed questions of your own to ask too.

Chapter 30

Answering Interview Questions with the STAR Technique

· · · · · · · · · · · · · · · · · · · ·

T he number one purpose of a job interview is to determine whether you are the kind of person others at the company can work next to for eight hours a day, or more, without going crazy.

The second goal of any job interview is to see how you solve problems. Notice I said *how*. Too many PhDs believe their interview is an oral exam for which they can either get the answers right or wrong. They believe if they get enough answers right, they will pass and get a job offer. This is simply not true. *How* you come to the conclusion of each answer you give is far more important than *what* answer you give. As I discuss early in this book, the three skills employers evaluate you on the most are complex problem-solving, critical thinking, and creativity.[53] In other words, they want to see how you find problems, how you determine the right problem to solve at the right time, and how you go about solving the problem.

Human Beings Want to Receive Answers in Story Form

Passing any interview stage requires going beyond "yes," "no," or other one-word answers to telling stories. Human beings learn through stories. Studies using fMRI scans of people's brains during conversations where one person is telling a story and another is listening show that the listener's brain activity mimics the storyteller's almost exactly—just a fraction of a second behind the storyteller's.[54] Similar studies based on fMRI scans show that a person's entire brain "lights up" with activity and increased blood flow in response to listening to a story.[55] Listening to a story also elicits feel-good hormones such as oxytocin.[56] In comparison, only quarter-sized regions light up when the same person is told a fact or statistic.

What does this mean for you as a job candidate?

It means that your interview answers must be framed as very short stories or anecdotes and that you must tell your stories in a simple, easy-to-follow way so the person listening can understand and keep up. The most proven method for answering interview questions in this way is called the Situation-Task-Action-Report, or STAR, method.

How to Answer Using the STAR Technique

The STAR technique is a way to structure an answer to an interviewer's question. It is highly effective and leaves a great impression with interviewers at any organization, whether the organization is a big corporation or small startup, for-profit or nonprofit company, intergovernmental organization (IGO) or nongovernmental organization (NGO).

When answering an interview question with the STAR method, start your response by describing a specific and relevant **situation**. You can use an example from your current job, a previous job, education, personal experience, or any relevant event. Always choose a situation that demonstrates your most impressive results and is relevant to the role for which you are being interviewed. This situation should involve a problem that you had to solve. Give enough detail for the interviewer to understand what was involved in one or two sentences.

Once you've outlined the situation, describe your **tasks** in that situation in one or two sentences. Get specific about the problem. What part of the problem was yours to solve? What were your responsibilities and assignments related to the problem? What had to be done specifically?

Next, you'll need to discuss what **actions** you took to solve the problem. For an interviewer, the action component of the STAR response is the most interesting and important part. It should detail the decisions you made and the steps you took to accomplish the task. Make sure you provide details about each step you took in order, showing your thought processes, how you reached your conclusions, and the important tasks you completed. How did you prioritize your tasks? What sequence did you complete your tasks in? Why? You may feel as if you are being overly descriptive as you explain your actions. However, the detail you provide will showcase your communication skills and prove that you have real-life experience with the skills and actions necessary for your target role.

The **result** component of the STAR method is the second most important part of your answer to an interviewer because it proves that your actions were effective. Talk about what you accomplished, what you delivered in terms of benefit, and what you learned. If appropriate, discuss what you would do differently if you encountered a similar situation in the future. Give evidence to prove your success. This could be in the form of numbers or any positive feedback you received. Finally, discuss the lessons you learned from your experience and, crucially, why those lessons will help you succeed in the role you are interviewing for.

Imagine you are asked the common but dreaded interview question: "What is your biggest weakness?" You might be inclined to answer with a short, meaningless cliché like "I've been told that at times I work too hard," but this will be unmemorable at best and may even tank your chances of moving to the next interview round. Instead, you'll want to follow the STAR method by first providing a situation where you had a weakness that was resolved later through effort. You might say, "Two years ago I was working in the lab and had a series of cloning experiments to perform, but the experiments weren't going well. I really wanted to prove myself, so I kept trying to do the experiments by myself without asking for help." Here, you've set the stage—the **situation**—and have started to move into the **task** at hand. You might then say, "Then we came up against a hard deadline for the cloning data, so I finally got over myself and asked a postdoc in the lab for help understanding the cloning technique I was trying to apply better. Within a week, I had mastered the technique, thanks to their guidance, and now I can execute this technique and many related techniques routinely and near perfectly." Do you see what just happened? You went from the **task** at hand to the **actions** you took to complete the task and provide a **result**.

Now all that's left to do is extend your result by discussing the lessons you learned and why those lessons are relevant to the role you're interviewing for. For example, you could end with, "I realized that not asking for help was a weakness at the time, but like all my weaknesses, I addressed it, learned from it, and overcame it, which is something I would take with me to my role at your company."

You answered a seemingly difficult interview question not through memorization, stock answers, or clichés but by leveraging the right method for answering. Training yourself on the STAR method, rather than guessing which questions you'll be asked and memorizing questions that likely won't be asked, will ensure you can address any question that comes your way with poise.

Mastering an Alternative Answer Framework

Once you've masted the STAR method, you can try your hand at leveraging an even more concise framework for answering interview questions, one that's been used for decades by management consultants and executive advisors. The Situation-Complication-Resolution, or SCR, framework simply refocuses the story arch within the STAR method from the task-and-action-focused story climax to a more central complication, or problem-focused, climax.

The **situation** part of this framework still provides the context and significance of the story you are telling, as well as the task at hand, but instead of moving into a discussion about the actions you took to complete those tasks, you spend a bit more time discussing the problem or **complication**. By describing the problem in depth and using it as the central part of your story, you can make the results more impactful.

In the SCR framework, the **resolution** includes how you solved the problem, the qualitative and quantitative results you achieved, and the lessons you learned from your results and from the problem-solving process as a whole.

While this problem–analysis–solution identification framework might seem more complex at first, it's often simpler to remember and use during an interview. When you get a question, just ask yourself:

- What's a situation I faced that could showcase an answer to this question?
- What was the problem?
- How did I resolve the problem?

Since the focus of this framework is on the problem, you can zero in further on how to best answer any interview question by simply asking yourself, "What problem have I faced that could be used as a good example here?" Now, you're only scanning your memory banks for one answer while simultaneously leveraging your brain's biological negativity bias (i.e., it's often far easier to remember problems you had than solutions).

Once you recall a relevant problem to discuss, the situation you were in when you had that problem and the resolution you achieved will be attached to the memory and easily reiterated to your listeners using the SCR framework.

After you've answered your interviewers' questions using the STAR or SCR method, you will likely be asked if you have any questions of your own to ask, and that's where we are going next.

Chapter 31

Credible Questions to Ask
Industry Employers

· ·

The quality of your candidacy for a position in industry is most clearly reflected in the quality of the questions you ask those interviewing you. You must seize the opportunity in every interview to turn the tables on the interviewer. You must become the interviewer yourself by asking questions that engage the other person and showcase your professionalism, business acumen, and overall understanding of the role, the company, and industry itself.

Asking questions shows you've thought about and are committed to the position at hand. Asking questions also allows you to find out whether the position and company are truly a good fit for you.

Deciding on the Right Questions to Ask

The key here is to ask questions that the interviewer can answer—and wants to answer. As with your informational interviews, play the role of the curious and positive journalist. Do not interrogate the interviewer. Do not ask heavy-handed, rationale-based questions (e.g., "why" questions, such as "Why is the company doing this?"), technical questions, behavioral questions, or any question that may require the interviewer to reveal something proprietary. Instead, ask simple, straightforward "how" questions, "what" questions, and questions about the company's culture. The company's responses to these questions will paint a picture of what working for the company would look like for you to make it easier to decide if you would thrive there.

As you'll see, the questions themselves show that you have mentally moved on from academia and understand how industry operates and what is important to a company's success in industry. When it's your turn to ask the employer questions during an interview, there are eight topics your questions should focus on, including:

1. Hierarchy – Who will I be reporting to?
2. Mergers and Acquisitions – What collaborations are underway?
3. Restructuring – How is the company being restructured?
4. Career Trajectory – Where have others in this position gone?
5. Emerging Markets – Where is the client base expanding?
6. Sales and Marketing – Which products are creating growth?
7. New Products/Projects – What new products are coming out?
8. Corporate Strategy – What are the company's five-year goals?

There are many other quality questions related to the above topics you can ask as well. For example, you might ask, "Who is your ideal candidate?" or "What is the biggest challenge you're facing, and how can I help solve it?" or "Where is this product line going to be in two years?" or "What would I be working on to start?" or "How do you measure success?"

• •

As I mentioned previously, you should always end each interview by asking a question that prompts the interviewer to discuss any objections they might have to hiring you, such as, "Are there any reasons why you wouldn't hire me?"

• •

By planning your questions in advance and asking them during your interview, you will further establish your credibility as the best candidate for the job. Before you get a job offer and can close the deal, however, you may be asked to give an interview presentation. An interview presentation is far different than an academic presentation, and we are going to cover how to prepare this style of presentation next.

STEP #8:

Nail Your Interview Presentation and Close the Deal

"Everything is negotiable. Whether or not the negotiation is easy is another thing."

— Carrie Fisher

Chapter 32

Confession from a Failed
Interview Presentation

· ·

I was told the following story by one of the first PhDs I worked with in the Cheeky Scientist Association. This PhD is now a close friend and a Principal Scientist at a Global 500 company. Yet, his rise in industry was not meteoric. He had to learn the hard way that getting a job in industry requires you to develop an industry mindset and present that mindset. Here is the story he told:

"I walked into my interview presentation confidently. I was interviewing for a Senior Scientist role and had made it to the very end of the interview process. I was asked to give a presentation and was told it could be as long as I wanted but ideally less than an hour and to just talk about myself, my interests, and my work. Fortunately, I had recently prepared a presentation for my postdoc work, so I was able to use those slides and practice a few more times before arriving to present. My presentation went very well. I didn't have to read off the slides, and I built up the story of my talk by showing better and better data until the final slide that showcased my biggest results. It was a wonderful 'Voilà!' moment. I shook hands with everyone and left the site visit that day feeling great. I waited to get my offer by email the next day … only, it never came. A week went by, and I still hadn't heard anything back. Eventually I was sent an email thanking me for my time and telling me that, unfortunately, I did not get the position. I have no idea what happened."

The job search rejection that hits PhDs the hardest is the one after giving an industry interview presentation. To come that far, only to start over, is so painful that many PhDs struggle to restart their job search efforts. But it doesn't have to be this way.

Shifting from Academic to Industry Presentations

By learning from those who came before you, you can ensure your presentation results in a job offer. No matter what position or positions you've decided to target, you should master industry presentations. Sooner or later, you will have to deliver one. You may be asked to give a presentation as part of one of your interviews, and you will also have to present in meetings or other situations on the job once you are in industry. In both cases, a great presentation will go a long way toward helping you achieve your career goals.

The good news is that you already have substantial presentation experience from your PhD journey. However, to fully leverage this valuable experience, you must learn the differences between academic and industry presentations.

Industry presentations frequently differ from academic ones in terms of purpose and audience. There are also industry standards for slide design that you should follow to portray yourself as a professional.

. . . .

Unlike an academic presentation, you want to start with the most important information first. Instead of leaking information or data slide by slide until you get to one climactic slide forty-five minutes later, you'll want to start with that climactic slide. Instead of anticipating a forty-five-minute presentation stuffed with rationale, methods, results, and acknowledgments followed by fifteen minutes of questions, you'll want to anticipate a ten-minute presentation mainly about yourself and how you'll deliver results for the company. And instead of adding multiple figures, boxes of text, keys, p-values and other stats, and conclusions all on one slide, you'll want to limit yourself to one title per slide and one picture or chart per slide with *maybe* one number on the slide too.

. . . .

Creating Effective Industry Presentations

Now that you've started shifting your mindset, it's time to dive into exactly how to devise an effective industry presentation. When it comes to creating effective industry presentations, you must consider what your audience wants to see. In this case, your audience is the company. Most often, the hiring manager you're in contact with will give you a short "brief" to help you prepare for the presentation.

The most common brief is simply, "Talk about yourself, your interests, and your work in ten minutes." Other common industry interview briefs include "Discuss your work on XYZ and how it relates to our business model" or "Review a paper/clinical trial report and summarize the findings the way you would for one of our clients/partners."

Occasionally, depending on the role, you may be specifically asked to give an hour-long presentation about your graduate or postdoc work, but this should not be assumed.

If you are asked to give an interview presentation, make sure you ask:

- How much time will I have for my presentation?
- Who will be sitting in on my presentation?
- Is there anything specific that my presentation should cover?

These questions will not only help you prepare for the presentation but they will also show initiative, which is a very positive transferable skill employers look for at the end of the interview process.

Effectively communicating, during an interview presentation or otherwise, comes down to only two root considerations: your purpose and your audience.

When it comes to communicating your purpose, ask yourself, *What goal do I want my presentation to accomplish? What is the main message I want to convey?* Your purpose should direct every decision you make about your presentation. It should guide what information you include in your slides, in what order you present your slides, and even how you speak. Despite its importance, many PhDs fail to set a purpose for presentations, and the consequences of this are painfully obvious. The result is typically a presentation that explores topics and ideas without offering anything concrete to act on. This is a cardinal sin for any industry role or company. The mantra of industry is "innovate or die." Ideas, conclusions, and the like must be actionable.

Remember, if you don't know what message you're trying to get across as a presenter, your audience won't either, and your presentation will fail. Having multiple purposes is another common presentation mistake PhDs make. Multiple purposes leave the audience confused and unable to follow your train of thought. If you have two messages, you have no message.

In the book *Confessions of a Public Speaker*, Scott Berkun provides evidence that most people who attend a presentation of any kind will only remember one thing about the presentation just days later: the title.[57] Seriously, that's it. Scott goes on to show that those who do remember anything beyond the title will remember a story or story-driven anecdote, not a fact or statistic. With this in mind, what is the one message you want your audience to remember from your presentation? Your answer should be the thread that ties your entire presentation together and should be mentioned repeatedly (at least twice per slide) throughout your talk.

Once you've defined the one message you want to convey in your presentation, it's time to consider your audience.

The best presentation is completely irrelevant if it doesn't resonate with the audience. Unfortunately, many PhD focus only on what works for them when planning their presentations rather than what is best for their audiences. You should account for your audience in every decision you make about your presentation plan, from what time you present to what order you present your slides in. For example, you don't want to present right before lunch, even if the timing would be most convenient for you. Your audience will likely be hungry and unable to focus. You also don't want to cram tons of information into your slides—even if it helps you avoid skipping important details—because it will overwhelm your audience. Instead, make sure every slide makes just one point, includes a single image, and contains as little text as possible. In this way, you will eliminate distractions and add clarity to your presentation.

Gather and consider all the information you have about your audience ahead of time. How many people will be in the audience? Do audience members have a technical or business background? Are audience members mostly Millennials, Zoomers, or Baby Boomers? What is the nationality of your audience? This information will help you decide what data, stories, and speaking styles will most likely connect with your audience.

In addition to considering your audience in the decisions you make beforehand, you should pay attention to audience members' behavior during the presentation. Ignoring nonverbal cues from audience members during a presentation is a mistake. You can use these cues to determine if your plan for engaging your audience is working and adapt accordingly. For example, if people's heads are upright, they are probably not listening, and you will want to adjust your style, pacing, and tone as you speak. However, if audience members' heads have a slight tilt or, more obviously, if people are nodding and laughing at your jokes, your audience is engaged. You need to practice your presentation enough to be able to adapt to your audience's cues without losing track of your message. You can't just ignore the feedback you get from your audience, or your presentation will fail.

There are Three Principles for an Effective Presentation

Beyond the two main considerations of purpose and audience, there are three principles of an effective presentation: energy, clarity, and value. Your presentation plan should address all three.

First, you need to generate and maintain enough energy to hold an audience's attention throughout your presentation. You can control the energy of your presentation by paying attention to pacing, tone, body language, mannerisms, sentence endings, filler words, and silence. Specifically, you should vary the speed of your speech while pausing for silence to give your audience a moment to process what you've said. You should work hard—very hard—to remove filler words (i.e., ums, uhs, ahs, "you know," and "like"). Always speak in complete sentences and finish your sentences firmly and as loudly as you started them. Don't slowly trail off into a rambling mumble at the end of your sentences. Make deliberate use of body language and facial expressions and check to make sure your usage makes sense by doing a mock presentation.

Clarity is the second principle you should pay attention to when presenting. If you're designing your presentation and you wonder if everyone will be able to follow it or have to reassure yourself they will be able to connect the dots, *stop*. They will not be able to follow it, and they will not connect the dots. If you have to convince yourself that others will be able to follow you, they won't be able to follow you. You need to make your presentation so simple an eighth grader can follow it. Seriously. Use the same slide style and theme for all your slides and keep the amount of text on your slides to a minimum. For the content, only include information or data that is relevant for your talk to avoid overwhelming your audience with unnecessary details. Use the rule of three by presenting your concepts or stories in three bullet points, components, or pieces to make them easier to remember. Always be sure to mix facts with stories. Remember, the human brain responds to stories with facts, not facts alone. Stories also help your audience connect with you because they imagine themselves as the protagonists of your stories. Ideally, you will back up every main point of your presentation with a story.

Third, and finally, add as much value for the audience to your presentation as possible. What's in it for them? What are you presenting that will make their lives easier or better in any way? How can you further sell yourself and what you're capable of accomplishing for the company?

Like every other activity in your job search, your industry presentation should strongly communicate the benefits you will bring to the company hiring you. Include ethos, pathos, and logos appeals. Ethos is the credibility appeal. You can leverage ethos in your presentation by incorporating your elevator pitch and making it clear that your training, experience, etc., makes you a reliable person to address your subject. Your unique selling proposition provides another outlet for ethos. Pathos is the emotional appeal, which you should make through your stories, and logos is the logical appeal, which you will address with hard information, data, and facts.

Finally, make sure you conclude your industry presentation with actionable takeaways. These can be actions you already took, actions you plan to take, or actions that might be taken. You must talk about your results in terms of the actionable possibilities they provide if you want the company to see you as someone who will be an action-taker and achiever at the company once hired.

Now that you know how to present to industry employers, you need to learn how to make deals with them. How you negotiate your compensation package will have lasting effects on both your salary and your career trajectory, which is why we are spending the next two chapters on this topic.

Chapter 33

The Fastest You Will Ever Make (or Lose) Money

· ·

The fastest way you will ever make money during your job search is through negotiation. Over the last ten years of working with PhDs on their negotiation skills, I've consistently watched thousands of PhDs instantly increase their salary offers by 5 to 15 percent by asking one simple question.

However, negotiation can also be the fastest way to lose money, and most PhDs lose a lot of money not negotiating—*fast*. According to a study of 2,700 employees in twenty-seven major cities that was done by the recruitment firm Robert Half, only 39 percent of workers attempted to negotiate salary during their last job offer.[58] When you don't negotiate, you automatically accept less than a company is willing to pay you. You might not think that negotiation makes much of a difference. However, your starting salary sets your salary trajectory, and those who negotiate can earn millions of dollars more than those who don't over the course of their careers.

. . . .

Consider the following example: Aditya is offered a $45,000 salary and accepts the offer without negotiating while Sarah is offered the same amount but negotiates just 10 percent higher for $50,000. Both receive the industry standard 1 percent raise year over year, but Sarah negotiates a 4 percent raise every three years, which is a very nonaggressive promotion schedule. In just five years, Sarah is making $6,816 more than Aditya per year, and at retirement forty-five years later, Sarah is making $43,616 more per year. This results in Sarah making $1,037,773 more than Aditya over the course of her lifetime.

. . . .

Why You Must Negotiate

Failing to negotiate your salary offer is devastating to both your income and to your career.

The good news is that industry employers expect you to negotiate.

In fact, if you don't negotiate, your employer might second-guess your value in industry. They might start to see you as unqualified, desperate, and easy to replace. They might also think less of your character and credibility, and you will have to work harder to prove yourself after getting hired—if you get hired—than someone who negotiates. All of this is because making deals is a key transferable skill in industry. Those at the top of any company have mastered this skill better than those below them. On a long enough timeline, the only two skills that will matter in terms of being promoted in industry are networking and making deals.

These points should empower you to follow the first rule of negotiation: do it.

That said, there are right and wrong approaches to salary negotiation, and each stage of the hiring process requires a different approach; therefore, you should learn to negotiate well before you receive your first job offer.

Most PhDs erroneously believe that negotiation only comes into play when the company extends a formal job offer. While it's true that you should never bring up salary and concrete numbers until you've received a written offer, you should know that the entire hiring process involves negotiation. In every interaction with the company, you should be building the case for why you are the best person for their open position. By doing so, you increase your perceived value and build leverage for later salary discussions.

When to Negotiate and How to Deflect

Be aware that the company will try to negotiate salary with you before giving you a written offer. Any number you provide in this context will only hurt you; therefore, you should prepare to deflect these attempts. You may have to deflect these attempts dozens of times with the same person.

Yes, dozens.

If you get too uncomfortable during this process to continue deflecting, you will not be paid what you are worth.

If you allow your brain to convince you that you did everything you could and agree verbally to an offer or a salary range, you will not be paid what you are worth.

Only discuss salary once the company has decided they want to hire you enough to make you an offer on paper. You only have leverage in a negotiation once you have such an offer on paper.

No written offer, no leverage.

No leverage, you lose.

You can only come to a win-win deal if you deflect their attempts to negotiate until they give you an offer on paper. I'm stressing this because most PhDs have no experience negotiating, and they get extremely uncomfortable the first time the employer pushes back by saying "We have a salary cap," "No, we can't negotiate," "I need a number from you before we can proceed," or something similar.

Don't let those statements derail your efforts or make you tense. They're just negotiating.

The key to deflecting early negotiation attempts is to keep the discussion relaxed and conversational. If you find yourself getting uptight, take a step back mentally and remind yourself, *Take it easy. This is fun.*

Practice deflecting by answering a question with another question. Approach any question with curiosity and add more curiosity to it. You can lean into any ignorance or lack of experience you have when it comes to negotiating or working in industry. Don't try to be the smartest person in the room. For example, if you're asked about your salary expectations, you can deflect with, "Oh wow, I haven't thought much about this yet. I'm more concerned with learning about who I'll be working with and what I'll be doing. Any reasonable offer will be considered."

Likely, the conversation won't stop there, so don't expect it to. The employer may come back with, "I appreciate that, but I really need a number to take to my boss."

Don't freeze here or get tense. Instead, just say, "Ah, I see what you're saying. Well, I defer to whatever you think is reasonable. What do you think I'm worth to the company based on what you know right now?"

Maybe they'll back off, maybe they'll give you a number, or maybe they'll say, "Okay, but seriously, I need to know from you what a reasonable salary is." If they get tense, it might be on purpose. Either way, it's good for you if they're getting tense early, as long as you have a walk-away number and haven't put all your hopes into one company's offer (more on this later). Here you could simply reply by asking, "Well, what's possible?"

Very often, after several attempts to get a number and several deflections, the conversation may move to salary ranges. The employer might say, "You'll have to at least give me a range before we can move forward."

Here, still, it's important to remember to stay calm, be curious, play dumb, and keep things conversational. It also helps to add extra transparency by calling out what is going on by saying, "Of course. I just thought I'd ask if it would be possible for us to move forward without setting a range in stone now. I'm asking because I've heard that committing to a range now can be used to offer me a lower salary than I'm worth. Is this the case here?"

Hopefully you can see that most PhDs fail in such a discussion by not having the stomach to deflect the employer's attempts multiple times. Deflecting requires staying calm and sitting in uncertainty and uncomfortableness, but it's worth it.

You are worth it.

Securing Your Leverage

There are two things you should do prior to interviewing with any employer.

First, do whatever you can to secure an interview with another employer so that you have more than one option.

Second, establish your walk-away number, or the lowest salary you're willing to accept from the company given your needs and the position at hand.

In any negotiation, options are levers. Whoever has more options, and therefore is less reliant on any one option, has more leverage. It may seem that the employer has all the power in most hiring situations because they have many options in the form of candidates to choose from; however, if you are talking to an employer directly, especially past the phone screen stage, the employer has invested substantial time, money, and human resources into your candidacy. They want to hire you. They do not want to start over. On average, an employer spends as much to hire you as they pay you in salary during your first year of employment. That's right. If your starting salary is $90,000, they will have spent $90,000 in resources to hire you.

Imagine all the human hours it takes just to review your résumé in person, coordinate interview times, meet with you, and so on. There's rarely just one person in charge of this. Multiple people complete various tasks, not to mention the administrative and technical costs associated with every aspect of interviewing you. ATS software is not free. LinkedIn® Recruiter is not free. Background checks are not free. Plane tickets are not free. The salaries for the three people in your panel interview are not free.

You have leverage—and you need more leverage. Here the best way to increase your leverage is by pursuing multiple jobs at once.

Ideally, you should never go to an interview unless you have other interviews lined up. When you can tell potential employers that other companies are interested in you, it provides social proof of your value as an employee. The goal is not to brag about all the other employers interested in you or name the companies interested (never do this, by the way); the goal is to put yourself in a position of power. You will feel more confident if you know you have other options, and prospective employers will notice. Conversely, you may come across as desperate if you think the job you are interviewing for is your only option, and employers will take advantage of your desperation when determining how much salary to offer you.

The most potent lever you have at your disposal during a negotiation—if you set it—is your walk-away number. Years ago, when Cheeky Scientist was much smaller, my team was hiring a Transition Support Specialist, and because the candidate didn't have any experience, we offered her a salary at the lower end of the range for this position. To everyone's surprise, the candidate immediately thanked us and rejected the offer. She was kind, polite, professional—and bold. The candidate knew her worth.

The first question we found ourselves asking was, *Why? What does this person know about their value that we don't?* The second question we asked was, *How can we turn this around?* We even asked, *How can we win this person back?*

Her bold move, commitment to self, and strength of character—perceived or otherwise—inspired us. By shutting down our low offer, she made us want to hire her more.

This is the power of having a walk-away number.

Before interviewing—no, before even applying to a position at a company—decide on a walk-away number and commit to it in advance. Otherwise you will talk yourself into accepting less than you should. You'll think, *I've already invested so much time in my job search and have spent weeks following up with this company and interviewing for this position. I don't want to start over. Lowering my expectations a bit will compensate for how much time and energy I've invested.*

If you don't set a walk-away number, you will make concessions. You will get emotional and be influenced by the relationships you've started to build with the company during the hiring process or the time you've invested in that company or your overall job search or even how much you like the company's facilities and other minor benefits. Understand that your salary dictates your salary trajectory, which, in large part, dictates your career trajectory.

You must set a walk-away number, and you must be willing to walk away.

If you're not willing to walk away, you're not negotiating—you're begging.

Once your walk-away number is established, you can start mapping out a clear negotiation strategy, which involves eight core tenets.

CASE STUDY 6
Sonali Pandhe, PhD

I so happy to share my transition story as a case study for this book because I want every PhD to remember their value and stop being afraid to take risks. You are worth so much more than you are asking for right now! I hope my story helps convince you of this once and for all. In my job search, I worked with the Cheeky Scientist Association to get into a very competitive role. In one instance, I applied for an industry job without hearing back … for two months. Despite this, I kept setting up informational interviews with people at the company, and after hearing that they were still hiring, I picked up the phone and asked to be interviewed. Yes, you can do this. You can call employers and ask to be interviewed. They love this kind of initiative in industry!

After requesting to be interviewed, I was flown out for a site visit. During the site visit, I met with so many people and had to give a presentation on a peer-reviewed journal article. The presentation was in front of various employees at the company, including hiring managers, vice presidents, and cross-functional team members. After I presented, everyone asked me behavioral and situational questions. After my presentation, the site visit ended, and I got into a taxi to go back to the airport. As I was writing emails on my phone to thank everyone, the main hiring manager called me and said, "Congratulations! I am offering you the position!"

I literally received a verbal offer ten minutes after my site visit with this first company. Just then, only minutes later, another hiring manager from a second company called me and offered me a job too! Unreal! I couldn't believe it! The only problem was the second company played hardball and refused to give me a written offer unless I accepted their verbal offer. I listened to the advice I received in the Association and deflected their attempts to get me to commit verbally. I told them that I had another offer on the table. This was my chance to leverage both offers against each other to get the best offer possible. After all, this was going to be my first industry job and this first salary would establish my salary trajectory in industry for years to come. I told both companies that I had another offer and asked if there was anything they could do to bump up their offers. I had worked too hard in my job search not to seize this moment. This was my moment!

After years and years of working for next to nothing as a PhD in academia. After moving countries and leaving my old life behind. After countless rejections, disappointments, and failures—I was not going to let anyone else set limits on my worth. This was my chance to be courageous and confidently ask for what I was worth. I did it! I negotiated for

5 percent more despite both companies telling me it wasn't possible multiple times and that they had salary caps. Everything is negotiable! If I can do it, you can do it too. Remember your value as a PhD!

***

If you're ready to transition into your dream industry position, you can apply to book a free Transition Call with me or one of my trained Transition Specialists at: https://cheekyscientist.com/transition-book.

Chapter 34

The Eight Tenets of Salary Negotiation
· ·

"Wow! Yikes, really? You made that much?" This is what the hiring manager said to me when I told him how much I was making at my current job. His reaction really threw me off. I was making good money but not great money. That's what I thought anyway.

But, after hearing his reaction, I started thinking that maybe I was making great money and maybe I shouldn't ask for any more money. The hiring manager was with a big company that was trying to hire me. They'd flown me out for an interview and had the hiring manager talk to me several times, but they hadn't sent me an offer yet. I figured that once the hiring manager sent me an offer, I would start negotiating.

Little did I know that the negotiations had already begun.

After acting shocked about how much I was making, the hiring manager asked if I was considering any other positions. I foolishly said no. Then he started telling me about all the great benefits I would be getting. He told me about the healthcare package, the 401K, and the company car. *Wow*, I thought, *I can't believe I'll get all this*. The benefits seemed so great that I felt bad about asking for anything else. But I was able to muster up just enough nerve to ask for an extra week of vacation. The manager said he didn't think the company allowed it, but he would check with human resources and get back to me if anything could be done. The next day human resources sent me a contract with a salary offer that was the same as my current salary, with no signing bonus or relocation allowance but with three extra days of vacation. I gratefully signed it.

Without realizing it, I had allowed the hiring manager to use all eight tenets of salary negotiation against me while violating all eight tenets on my end. Those eight tenets are:

1. Don't be impressed with the first offer.
2. Ask open-ended questions.
3. Appeal to a higher authority to buy time.
4. Ask for double the increase you expect to get back and back it up with research.
5. Be overly positive and polite during the entirety of your negotiations.
6. Always bring the conversation back to the value you will add to the company.
7. Secure your salary first before negotiating other benefits.
8. Leave the other side feeling like they won something.

Learning the Flinching Technique

To start, you must understand the "flinching technique" of negotiation. This simply means that you don't act impressed with whatever offer you are given initially. In fact, you should "flinch" at it, which might be a subtle shift in your body language to show some displeasure, a long pause on the phone, or writing in an email, "The numbers don't look quite right here." Don't say, "Wow—I've never seen so many zeros before!" or "I can't believe you're going to pay me *this* much money!"

Don't even think it, especially if you're on the phone or in person, because it will weaken your negotiation position. Even a temporary moment of visibly flying high ruins your rationale for needing more money.

No matter how high the salary is in the first offer you receive, do *not* act impressed. Instead, stay neutral. Or better, act unimpressed. Simply say, "I appreciate the offer" or "Thank you for the details." The less impressed you act while still maintaining a polite and positive demeanor, the stronger your negotiating position becomes.

The Two Questions That Have Helped Thousands of PhDs

After reviewing the initial offer and staying grateful for the opportunity but neutral (at most) toward the salary amount, you should get curious about what else is possible. This is best done by asking the employer open-ended questions such as, "What can we do to increase the salary a bit?" or, if they say "nothing" to this first question, "What can we increase instead of the salary?"

These two questions are the questions I refer to in the previous chapter that have helped thousands of PhDs swiftly get a 5 to 15 percent increase in salary and a 20 to 40 percent increase in their signing bonuses.

Very often, the employer responds by saying, "Sure, let me ask the department head" and then "Okay, we can increase the salary by $5,000—good?" The key is to avoid including any specifics in your open-ended questions or in your responses to any counterquestions the employer asks. When you give specifics, you risk capping your salary offer lower than what the employer is willing to pay you. For example, you want to avoid saying, "I'm really excited about this opportunity, but I was wondering if we could go $5,000 higher in terms of the starting salary?"

In response, the employer might quickly agree (which probably means they were willing to pay you much more), or they might take the opportunity to meet you in the middle by saying, "How about we settle halfway at $2,500 more?"

Instead, say, "I'm really excited about this offer, but I was wondering what more we could do in terms of salary?" This phrasing puts the impetus for proposing a higher offer on the employer.

Whenever possible, have these open-ended discussions in person or over the phone instead of email. Try to get as many people on the phone as possible. Push to do a quick conference call with the hiring manager and whoever else is part of the decision-making process. The more you engage the other party in real time, the better your chances of getting the salary offer increased. Sure, you might be more uncomfortable negotiating over the phone than over email, but the employer will feel more uncomfortable saying "no" too. Some additional questions you could ask during this discussion include:

- What is the most you offered anyone in this role previously, and what is the difference between that person and me?
- I really had in mind more than that, but I'm really excited about this opportunity. What can we do?
- I'd like to move these numbers up a bit if we could. How much room is there to move these numbers?

As I cover in the previous chapter, always keep your negotiations conversational. Using open-ended questions is a great way to do this. Carefully consider each of the below prompts from an interviewer. How would you respond? You will see my suggested responses in bold.

- "What do you think is a reasonable salary?" **What's possible?**
- "We might be able to increase the salary. What did you have in mind?" **What's possible?**
- "We can't increase the salary, unfortunately." **When have you increased the salary in the past?**
- "We have a salary cap for this position. No increase is possible." **When have you increased the salary in the past?**
- "We are considering several other candidates who would accept this salary." **How does my candidacy stand out from the other candidates?**
- "If we offer you $100,000 per year right now, would you take it?" **When might I be able to see an offer on paper?**
- "We can increase the salary to $110,000. Agreed?" **Can we increase that number a little more?**
- "Due to budget cuts, we can't negotiate salary." **What exceptions have you made for this in the past when hiring other candidates?**

Remember, the interviewer is maneuvering to make you feel just uncomfortable enough to settle on their terms. Your goal is to calmly and professionally maneuver in a way that keeps the conversation open.

What to Do Once You Have an Offer on Paper

Once you get an offer on paper, the best course of action is to ask for time to discuss the offer at home. This negotiating tactic is called "appealing to a higher authority." You can—and should—use it whether you live with nothing more than a plant or are married with ten kids. The hiring manager is not going to ask who you are going to discuss it with. That question would be far too personal. By keeping the higher authority vague (in this case, simply someone or something at home), you make it nearly impossible for the other person to pinpoint who is making the salary decision on your behalf.

More importantly, you buy yourself time to think about the offer and decide how you want to respond. You also buy time to follow up with other job leads and tell them that you have an offer in hand and you would like them to interview you or, if you've already been interviewed, extend you an offer before the deadline.

I remember getting a call from Yuri, a PhD I worked with to get hired into his first industry position. He had been unemployed twice after doing two three-year postdocs. It was not a good situation, but by following the methodology you've read about in this book, we got him his first offer for a huge, brand-name company.

When Yuri called me, he had already been made full-time at his current company and had another company pursuing him with a very, very generous offer and a senior-level title. Yuri had followed my training, so as soon as he got this first offer, he reached out to another company he had interviewed with but had yet to receive an offer from and told them this was their last chance to make a deal. As a result, this second company gave Yuri an offer too.

He asked me, "How can I further leverage these offers against each other?" I told him to keep things conversational by asking more open-ended questions about what was possible in terms of elevating the compensation package and by always "selling into the close" by reminding both companies how excited he was to work with them and the value he could add as soon as he started. After a few meetings with both companies, one company's offer started to pull ahead of the other company's offer so much that Yuri couldn't refuse. He accepted the offer and has since been further promoted to director at this company.

I've helped many other PhDs get promoted into senior-level and director-level roles in industry, including Jeannette and Elisa who were hired at Biogen and Janssen (a Johnson & Johnson company), respectively. You can watch them tell their stories of how they first transitioned into industry at: https://cheekyscientist.com/transition-book.

Always use any offer you get to get as many other offers as possible. Keep the conversation going until you have multiple offers on paper, and after you've bumped the offer up as much as you can through open-ended questioning, you can give your counteroffer.

Giving Your Counteroffer

For your counteroffer, you want to ask for double the increase you expect to get and back it up with research after you've reviewed your offer at home.

Once you've encouraged the employer to make a first offer (and hopefully a second, higher offer), it's your turn to suggest specifics. The key is to ask for more than you're willing to accept. The biggest reason to ask is simple: you just might get what you ask for. However, it's not the only reason to ask for more than you expect. By asking for more than you're willing to settle for, you give yourself space to make concessions.

Let's say a company offers you $80,000 per year when you were really hoping for $90,000. In this circumstance, you should ask for $100,000. In doing so, you make room for the other side to meet you in the middle by lowering your proposed amount to $90,000. This negotiation technique is called "bracketing." Humans love to split the difference when negotiating because it seems fair. Just make sure you're the one creating the anchor for the split and backing it up with salary data on paper. By presenting information about the cost of living and the highest salaries paid for the position you're seeking, whether in a PDF attached to an email or a hard copy faxed to the employer, you will motivate the employer to take you seriously and get closer to meeting your terms. This negotiation strategy is called the "briefcase technique," and the research can easily be done on various pay data websites.[59] Links to some of those websites can be found at: https://cheekyscientist.com/book-resources.

How to Sell into the Close

While negotiating, you should consistently "sell into the close," which is negotiation language for being overly positive and polite and always bringing the conversation back to what you will do for the company. Too many PhDs mistakenly take a win-lose approach to negotiation. They think either they win, or the employer does. As a result, they get angry and tense. They may try to get their way by acting firm, condescending, or annoying. These foolish tactics will only either make the other side fight harder to get what they want or rescind your employment offer.

Instead, take a win-win approach to negotiation. It will strengthen your position. It is also realistic. You will win by securing a higher salary, and the employer will win by securing a valuable employee with a good offer.

This should go without saying, but always stay positive and polite when discussing salary. You never know who else is on the call or if your emails are being forwarded.

Also, continue to express enthusiasm for the role because it will show the employer that you would be a valuable employee worth a higher salary offer. There's one cold, hard truth that you should always keep in your mind when negotiating a salary contract: the other side doesn't care about you more than you care about you.

In fact, they don't care about you personally much at all. How could they? They don't even know you yet.

What they do care about, though, is the work you're going to do for them; therefore, always bring the conversation back to your professional strengths and the value you offer the company. Make everything you say about what you can do for them. Constantly remind them of what they are buying: your professional value.

What to Do in Muddy Waters

For many industry companies, offering a benefits package is standard because most components in those packages are tax write-offs. The company is incentivized to provide certain perks like company cars, relocation allowances, corporate housing, retirement plans, and healthcare. Other benefits may be required by law, such as vacation or healthcare packages. Giving you a bigger monthly paycheck, on the other hand, gets the employer nothing. Because of this, employers may try to negotiate your salary and benefits package at the same time. In this way, they treat salary and benefits as equally valuable to encourage you to accept extra benefits in exchange for a lower base salary.

This is called "muddying the waters" because it forces you to compare apples to oranges, so to speak. These exchanges actually reduce the value of your compensation package because, over time, salary will make a much bigger difference to your net worth than benefits. Don't let employers mix and match job offer items in your compensation package. Instead, ask them to "set aside" the benefits package until you come to an agreement on the salary package.

Once you've secured your salary, you can start negotiating for a better benefits package, and you should tackle each benefit individually in the order listed below:

- Salary
- Signing bonus
- Stocks or equity
- Relocation allowance
- Vacation
- Special circumstances (e.g., a week off to attend a wedding right after being hired)

Don't be surprised if the employer pushes back on each and every benefit listed above as you negotiate them. This is normal, and you should be prepared for it. You should also be prepared to drive the conversation forward after each benefit has been agreed upon. For example, don't come to an agreement on salary and assume you'll be given a signing bonus. Don't ask *if* there is a signing bonus either. Instead, you casually pivot by asking, "And *what* will my signing bonus be?"

Here are a few scripts you can use to direct the conversation about your compensation package:

- To bring the conversation back to your base salary when benefits are brought up: "Oh, that's great. I really appreciate it. Is there anything we can do to make the base salary higher?"
- To address your signing bonus: "I'm glad we established that the base would be $xx. That's great. What will my signing bonus be?"
- If the employer says that they don't give signing bonuses: "That's a real surprise! New truck drivers are getting $5,000 signing bonuses right now. I'm sure I'm worth more than a truck driver, so I just assumed there would be a signing bonus. What's possible?"
- To address options for equity in the company and investment benefits: "Can you help me understand the options for equity participation, profit sharing, stock options, grants, and retirement matching?"
- To address your relocation (if applicable): "I'd like to discuss a relocation allowance. Can you tell me what the company usually offers in terms of relocation packages? And can you get me [xx days/months] in a corporate apartment? That way I don't have to be distracted by trying to find a place to live and can focus on the job for those first xx days/months?"
- To negotiate special circumstances: "I need a week off in the middle of the year, and I need that to be written into the offer because it is that important to me. My family and I have been renting a houseboat for over ten years. We're going to keep doing it, and I need to know up front if this is going to be a problem." or "I already had two weeks accrued at my last job, so I'm not really excited about starting over. Can we at least match what I had at my last job?"

When you're negotiating for a new job, time is always on your side. It might not seem like it, but it is. This is especially true if you've created leverage by going into the negotiation with more than one option. Your goal should be to get the other side to invest in you as much as possible.

There are many ways to encourage prospective employers to invest in you prior to negotiation. Get them to send you as many emails as possible. Get them to talk with you on the phone as much as possible. Get as many people from the company involved as possible. Request a second tour of the office or to see one of their satellite facilities. When you engage in these activities, the employer will feel like they won when they finally do get you to sign—even if they had to increase their salary offer.

You will also help the employer feel like they are winning in your negotiations by taking a win-win approach, asking open-ended questions to let them increase your compensation options, and always reminding them of the value you will add to the company.

Resist the temptation to try to squeeze every last drop out of them. This approach may cause the employer to resent you when you start the job or, worse, during the final stages of the negotiation before you've been given the job. If you're down to negotiating for an extra three paid days off for a wedding in June, let it go. You will leave the employer feeling better about your candidacy and your professionalism, and as a result, you will secure the job and finally transition out of academia into industry. Your first few months at your new job will be more positive, productive, and rewarding as well.

Once you've signed your agreement and locked arms with your new employer, it's time to celebrate (yes, even PhDs should celebrate here!) and prepare for onboarding. You'll want to set yourself up for your first promotion as soon as possible and make sure you make it through any probationary periods without a hitch.

Conclusion

What to Do Once You're Hired
· ·

"Carefully watch your thoughts, for they become your words. Manage and watch your words, for they will become your actions. Consider and judge your actions, for they have become your habits. Acknowledge and watch your habits, for they shall become your values. Understand and embrace your values, for they become your destiny."

— Mahatma Gandhi

O nce you've transitioned into industry, you must work to become valuable to the organization.

Before being hired, and for several months after being hired, your value to the company is effectively zero. In fact, it may be less than zero. Your potential, however, is limitless. It is your job and the employer's job to work together to help you realize your potential.

The process by which you start to realize your potential is called onboarding, and the goal of the onboarding process is to help you start adding value in your new

218

role. The better and faster a company can train you, the sooner they can increase your economic value and make your hiring process worth the investment.

Doing so is beneficial for you, the employee, as well. You want to assimilate into the company's culture—the way things get done, the processes, and the people—so you can start progressing in your career. You want to start completing your projects, hitting your individual milestones, hitting the goals for your position, and working toward your next promotion.

There Are Two Zones for Becoming Valuable to a Company

There is a process to becoming valuable to a company, and not everything is about speed. This can be divided into two zones: the "investment zone" and the "return zone." The "investment zone" is where the organization is investing in you as a new employee. This is where you are costing them even more money in training time, equipment, space, and many other resources. The "return zone," on the other hand, is where the organization finally starts benefiting from your work and the value you're adding in your role.

There are four stages across the investment and return zones of onboarding that help clarify when and how you become valuable to the company:

1. New hire
2. Onboarding
3. Training
4. New assignment

Each of these phases has a different focus and comes with a different set of expectations.

The new hire stage covers your first days on a new job. It's okay for you not to know how to do things during this stage. To get to the point where you are producing in your new role, you also need to go through the onboarding stage. Onboarding is a period of deep observation, and you should focus your mindset accordingly. You'll want to study the culture, teams, power structures, and processes of your new company.

• •

Remember, while you're in the new hire and onboarding phases, you're not expected to have a positive return on investment. The more you learn during these phases, though, the better you will perform in the later phases of your employment.

• •

Once your onboarding is complete, you are past the investment zone and bring your economic value to the company into the positive. The first phase you'll go through once you enter this return zone is called training. In the training phase, you're starting to do projects yourself and work with the other members of your team. The company will be watching you closely during this phase to see how you work compared to the average employee. If the company sees that your engagement is higher than average, you can end up in a position where you don't have to be micromanaged. You can be allowed to work more autonomously because management knows you can make decisions. Employers want to see their new employees reach this level of autonomy in their work, often referred to as the "new assignment phase." It is easier for employees to achieve this goal if they have been trained and onboarded well, which is why onboarding is so important.

Technically, onboarding begins at job acceptance, not the first day of employment. There should be mechanisms in place for you to begin onboarding right after you sign a contract, even if there is a two-month period between your signing date and your official start date. If you're not regularly hearing from your new employer during this time, you should reach out every week and ask them what you should be doing to prepare for your new role. You should expect organized support, advice, and feedback from your employer during this time.

Types of Onboarding

That being said, the type of support and the level of onboarding an organization provides will vary from company to company and can be influenced by a variety of factors, including the sector of industry, company size, seasonality, current market position, staffing changes, and much more. According to Donald Asher, PhD, author of *Cracking the Hidden Job Market*, companies use one of three approaches when onboarding their new hires:

1. Foundational onboarding
2. Optimal onboarding
3. Strategic onboarding[60]

Foundational onboarding is used by roughly one-third of industry organizations. This type of onboarding involves basic compliance activities, such as filling out your tax forms. You'll also get some clarification about your role and expectations. There will also be (uncoordinated) attempts to provide culture and connection guidance, which may cover company practices such as dressing more casually on Friday, clocking in for your position, or other basics you need to know to function in your new job. Companies that use the foundational onboarding approach generally view onboarding as a simple checklist of actions every new employee must complete.

A second third of companies will use optimal onboarding to train their new employees. In optimal onboarding, compliance and job role clarification are done very well. Culture and connection mechanisms, such as a team day with new hires on the first day of the job or other practices that encourage team members to meet you, are in place. These practices encourage and facilitate your integration into your new team. However, systematic processes for helping new employees assimilate into the entire organization are still lacking.

The final third of industry employers will use a strategic onboarding process to train their new hires. These companies do onboarding well across the entire company and formally address compliance, clarification, culture, and connection. In most cases, human resources departments will take charge of this process, which will likely begin with an entire week of training on the company processes. You're not expected to do anything during this time except learn how everything works at that company.

Ensuring a Successful First Ninety Days

Once you start your new job, you'll want to work with your employer to make sure you're doing things right during your first thirty, sixty, and ninety days. Remember, it is as much your responsibility as the employer's responsibility to ensure that you onboard into your new role appropriately. These first ninety days are critical because they can set you on a trajectory for career success—or not.

To help ensure your first ninety days are successful, both you and your employer should have thirty-, sixty-, and ninety-day plans. The company will have a different set of expectations for you for each of these time periods. You should make sure your plan aligns with those expectations so that you can successfully work through your ninety-day probation period, the company will know that hiring you was the right decision, and you can stay with the company long term.

In general, the number one thing you want to do in your first thirty days is learn the tools and systems of the company. You need to be able to answer questions such as: Where are things? How can you access them? And how can you use them? In this way, you will learn how things operate.

Your next priority is to get comfortable with the culture. Remember, culture is how things are done, how you feel, and how other people feel. You want to get to know the culture. You want to understand the product or service, the treatment, or whatever it is that you're supporting. You might also take on a small project during this time.

In your first sixty days, you'll start working with your team or teams. You'll communicate with teams in your first thirty days, but it won't be until after that first month that you will really start working with them. Your goal is to start being seen as an asset to the team. You'll want to take on a big project during this time, and you should still have some mentorship from your manager and other employees as you do so. During this phase, companies expect you to start understanding the unwritten rules at the company. For example, the person who is in charge on paper might not really be in charge. You'll want to figure out the actual power structure of the company during this time. You'll also want to figure out what practices you need to follow, which may differ from the practices the company says it uses. For example, some companies will tell you that you can start your workday at any time, but the unwritten rule might be that everybody starts at 9 a.m. The company expects you to learn the unwritten rules, the shared beliefs about the company, and the shared practices by the end of this onboarding phase.

Finally, by day ninety, you'll want to start juggling bigger responsibilities and taking on big projects independently. Around day ninety, you need to demonstrate your real value to the company by showing that you can take on a big project related to your role independently with minimal supervision. Doing so ensures that the company values you and shows that you've integrated yourself into the company and you're succeeding in your role.

By the end of the first ninety days, you'll want to make sure you've connected with a number of key people, including your manager (the person you're directly reporting to), your team (the people you work with on a daily basis), and your peers (people on your level, both on your team and in other departments). You'll also want to connect with your superiors in higher levels of the organization. You may not be directly reporting to these people, but they can be seen as mentors who may advocate for you if you build relationships with them.

Out of all those relationships, the one with your direct supervisor or manager is the most important. You want to make sure they feel comfortable having you come to them at any time and vice versa, since this will set you and the company up for success in the long term.

The expectation of the company is that at the end of onboarding you will have achieved full acculturation. To achieve acculturation, you must be deeply integrated into the company's culture. You should start seeing your team members as your companions, not just as other employees. There should be a certain level of comradery in your relationship with your fellow team members. By internalizing the culture, your team, and the overall company, you will secure your position at that company.

The company views onboarding as a process, and you should too. It takes time and effort for a new employee to integrate into the culture of the company and be seen as part of the team. Depending on the company, this process can take up to six months. Keep this in mind when you start your new role. Be patient, learn, be open to receiving feedback, and ask questions to make sure you're setting yourself up for success during this time.

***

Now that you've transitioned into industry and have established yourself fully into your company's culture, you are ready to take on all the exciting challenges that come with being an industry PhD. You now have the resources to make the impact you've always wanted to on the world. You now have a platform for living the purpose-driven career and life you imagined when you first entered graduate school.

But there is much work to be done still.

Fortunately, you now have the respect, direction, compensation, and team support you earned while getting your PhD that will allow you to achieve your biggest goals in life.

Now that you are in industry, keep climbing to greater and greater heights. The world needs you at the top of industry. Never let anyone else limit your career or individual success again—certainly not yourself.

And always, always remember your value as a PhD.

Next Steps

· · · · · · · · · · · · · · · · · · ·

This book has armed you with the knowledge you need to get hired into your dream industry job. Now it's time for action. To help you get started, I've created a reference page that includes links to resources mentioned in this book:

https://cheekyscientist.com/book-resources.

If you're ready to start your transition into industry, you can apply to book a free Transition Call with me or one of my trained Transition Specialists at:

https://cheekyscientist.com/transition-book.

Finally, if you would like to speak with me about your industry transition or about anything in this book, you can email me at: powerofaphd@cheekyscientist.com.

Your dream career is waiting, and I would be honored to help you transition into it.

About the Author

· ·

Dr. Isaiah Hankel is the Founder and CEO of the largest career training platform for PhDs in the world: Cheeky Scientist. His articles, podcasts, and trainings are consumed by three million PhDs annually in over 150 different countries. He has helped PhDs transition into top companies like Amazon, Google, Apple, Intel, Dow Chemical, BASF, Merck, Genentech, Home Depot, Nestle, Hilton, SpaceX, Tesla, Syngenta, the CDC, United Nations, and Ford Foundation.

Dr. Hankel's work has been featured in the *Harvard Business Review, Nature, Forbes, The Guardian, Fast Company, Entrepreneur Magazine,* and *Success Magazine.* His books have been translated into multiple languages and have hit number one on bestseller lists worldwide, including number one in business nonfiction in the UK and number one in multiple Amazon categories. Dr. Hankel has delivered presentations to over one hundred thousand people, including over one thousand workshops and keynotes to over fifty countries worldwide.

Isaiah grew up working on a sheep farm in the Pacific Northwest of the United States before getting his PhD. He went on to have successful industry career in the United States, Germany, the UK, and Australia. He currently runs Cheeky Scientist at the company's headquarters in the US and lives with his wife and daughters.

Industry Job Title Examples

· ·

Account Manager

Actuarial Manager

Advanced Analytics, Big Data & AI
Analyst

Advanced Application Engineer &
Bioinformatics Lead

Advanced Imaging Specialist

Advanced Materials Engineer

Advisor to the CEO

Air Resources Engineer

Analyst

Analyst II

Analyst III

Analytical Consultant

Analytics and Marketing Head

Application Engineering Associate

Application Scientist

Applications Support Engineer II

Area Sales Manager

Assay Automation Engineer

Assay Development Scientist

Assistant Consultant

Assistant CRA

Assistant Engineer

Assistant Project Manager

Associate Scientist & Project Manager

Associate Clinical Account Specialist

Associate Clinical Operations Associate

Associate Consultant

Associate Data Team Lead

Associate Director

Associate Director of Bioinformatics

Associate Director of Scientific
Communications

Associate Drug Safety Administrator

Associate Manager of Medical Writing

Associate Medical Director

Associate Product Manager

Associate Program Development
Associate Project Manager
Associate Proposal Development
    Consultant
Associate Research Scientist
Associate Scientific Director
Associate Scientist
Associate Scientist II
Associate Scientist III
Associate Director
Battery Reliability Engineer
Bioinformatics Review Editor
Bioinformatics Scientist
Biological Scientist
Biotech & Sequencing Specialist
Business Analyst
Business Analytics Manager
Business Developer
Business Development & Marketing
    Associate
Business Development Manager
Business Development Specialist
Business Intelligence Developer
Capital Equipment & In Vivo Imaging
    Sales Specialist
Cell Culture Researcher
Chemical Engineer
Chemist
Chief Editor
Chief Scientific Officer
Client Portfolio Manager
Client Support Specialist
Clinical Affairs Consultant
Clinical Analyst
Clinical Biomarker Scientist
Clinical Director

Clinical Evaluation Researcher
Clinical Instrumentation Specialist
Clinical Manager
Clinical Operations Leader
Clinical Product Risk Specialist
Clinical Project Manager
Clinical Quality Assurance Project
    Manager
Clinical Research Administrator
Clinical Research Associate
Clinical Research Compliance &
    Regulatory Officer
Clinical Research Coordinator
Clinical Research Program Coordinator
Clinical Research Project Manager
Clinical Research Scientist
Clinical Research Supervisor
Clinical Scientist
Clinical Site Manager
Clinical Specialist
Clinical Trials Associate
Clinical Trials Coordinator
Clinical Trials Manager
Clinical Validation Specialist
Clinical Writer
CNS Research Scientist
Coatings Chemist
Commercial Associate
Commercial Innovation Manager
Commissioning Editor
Communications Officer
Communications Associate
Community Medical Liaison
Competitive Intelligence Analyst
Compound Lead
Computational Biologist

Confocal Applications Specialist

Consultant

Consultant of Defense

Consultant Engagement Manager

Consultant in Data Science

Customer Success Scientist

Data Analyst

Data Analytics Consultant

Data Assurance Associate

Data Engineer

Data Privacy Analyst

Data Scientist

Data Scientist & External Project Lead

Data Scientist Consultant

Deep Learning Application Scientist

Defect Metrology & Yield Engineer

Development Engineer

Development Operations Manager

Development Scientist

Diagnostic Scientist

Digital Acceleration Manager

Digital Biomarker Technology and Study Manager

Director of Admissions and Recruitment

Director of Business & Sales

Director of Client Engagement

Director of Compliance and Regulatory Affairs

Director of Development in Philanthropy Communication

Director of Healthcare and Life Sciences

Director of Laboratory Operations

Director of Neuromuscular Restoration

Director of Production

Director of Quality and Compliance

Director of Research & Evaluation

Director of Scientific Research Services

Director of Strategic Analytics

Director of Strategy & Franchise Communication Lead

Director R&D

Downstream Processing R&D Scientist

Drug Safety Associate

EDG Heme Lead

Editor

Editorial Advisor

Embedded Software Engineer

Energy Analyst

Engineer

Engines Structural Analyst II

Entrepreneur

Environmental Scientist

Environmental Toxicologist & Project Manager

Epidemiological Specialist

Epidemiologist

ESI Application Scientist

Evidence Evaluation Specialist

Executive Director of Research

Executive Director

Executive Search and Assessment Professional

Experience Design Researcher

Feasibility Research Fellow

Fermentation Scientist

Field Application Scientist

Field Applications Specialist

Field Clinical Specialist

Field Medical Director

Field Medical Senior Manager

Field Service Engineer

Field Technical Support Specialist

Flow Sorting Global Training Leader

Food Additives & Contaminants Regulator

Formulation Scientist

Founder & CEO

Founder and Principal Scientist

Freelance Medical Writer

Freelance Writer

Full-Stack JavaScript Developer

Gaming Developer & Programmer

Global Analytical Technical Support Scientist

Global Clinical Research Manager

Global Food Scientist

Global Medical Affairs & Scientific Director

Global Study Manager

Head of Medical Affairs

Head of Open Data

Head of R&D

Health & Human Services Leadership Development Lead

Health Science Policy Analyst

Healthcare Consultant

Health Services Research Group Consultant

Imaging Expert

Imaging Field Applications Scientist

Implementation Lead

Independent AI & Analytics Consultant

Independent Development Analyst

Industrial Consultant

Informatics & Business Technical Researcher

Innovation Consultant & Business Analyst, Life Sciences and Digital Health

Inside Sales & Marketing Representative

Institutional Effectiveness Senior Research Associate

Institutional Review Board Management Associate

Instructional Design Lead

International Editor

International Project Manager of Quality IT Systems

Invention Associate

IT Consultant

IT Project Manager & Laboratory Specialist

Junior Consultant

Key Account Manager

Knowledge Broker

Lab Manager

Lab Testing Manager

Laboratory Animal Nutritionist

Lead Engineer

Lead Experimentalist & Biologist

Lead R&D Chemical Engineer

Lead Scientist

Learning and Development Specialist

Licensing Associate

Life Science Consultant

Life Science Sales Specialist

Local Collaboration Coordinator

LSAH Project Lead for NASA

Machine Learning Data Scientist

Management Consultant

Manager of Pharmacokinetics & Exploratory Development

Managing Principal Consultant

Market and Competitor Insights Analyst

Market Research Analyst

Marketing Analytics Specialist

Marketing Associate & Patent Agent

Materials and Process Engineer

Materials Scientist

Medical Affairs Specialist

Medical Communication Lead

Medical Communication Manager

Medical Communications Associate

Medical Device Analyst

Medical Device Investigator

Medical Director

Medical Education Manager

Medical Field Director

Medical Manager Liver Disease

Medical Science Expert

Medical Science Liaison

Medical Technologist

Medical Writer

Medical Writer & Consultant

Medical Writer & Pharmaceutical Sales Trainer

Medical Writer I

Medical Writing Associate

Medicinal Chemistry

Melting Technology Engineer

Microbiologist

Microbiology Laboratory Leader

Microscopy Specialist

Model Design Consultant

Modelling & Analytical Management Consultant

Molecular Biologist & Pharmaceutical Product Development Manager

Neuroscience Product Specialist

NMR Systems Engineer

Nuclear Chemical Engineer

Nutrition Innovation Coordinator

Oceanographer

Operations Research and Data Scientist

Optical & Electrical Engineer

Optical Scientist

Optics Engineer

Owner and Lead Medical Writer

Patent Agent

Patent Analyst

Patent Associate

Patent Lawyer

Pediatric Blood & Marrow Transplant Program Manager

Pharmaceutical Affairs Executive

Pharmaceutical Consultant

Pharmacology & Toxicology Reviewer

Pharmacovigilance & Drug Safety Specialist

Pharmacovigilance Consultant

Physical Scientist

Pilot Plant Engineer

Plant and Soil Process Modeling Scientist

Plant Breeder

Policy Analyst and Scientist Reviewer

Presales Engineer

Pricing & Market Access Consultant

Principal Engineer

Principal Formulation Scientist

Principal Measurement Scientist

Principal Medical Writer

Principal Statistician

Process Development Scientist

Process Engineer

Process Integration Engineer
Process Scientist
Product Application Scientist
Product Development Associate
Product Manufacturing Engineer
Program Applications Manager
Program Coordinator
Program Manager
Project Architect
Project Coordinator
Project Engineer
Project Leader of Innovation &
  Business Development
Project Manager
Project Officer Research Integrity
Protein Engineer and Data Scientist
Protein Engineering Scientist &
  Crystallographer
Protocol Project Manager
Protocol Specialist II
PTD Module & Integration Device
  Yield Engineer
Public Health Analyst
Publications Manager in Medical
  Affairs
QC Analyst
QC Analytical Scientist
QC/QA Chemist
Quality & Reliability Engineer
Quality Associate, III
Quality Control Scientist
Quality Control Supervisor
Quality Engineer
Quality Manager
Quality Manager and Cosmetic Chemist
Quantitative Finance Analyst

Quantitative Analyst
R&D Analytical Chemist
R&D Chemist
R&D Development Chemist
R&D Engineer
R&D Manager
R&D Professional
R&D Project Manager
R&D Scientist
Realtor
Recruitment Specialist
Regional Medical Manager
Regional Medical Director
Regional Medical Liaison
Regional Technical Director of Chemistry
Regulatory Affairs
Regulatory Affairs Associate
Regulatory Affairs Coordinator
Regulatory Affairs Officer
Regulatory Affairs Specialist
Regulatory Associate
Regulatory Medical Writer
Regulatory Scientist
Regulatory Submission Coordinator
Regulatory Toxicologist
Regulatory Writer
Remote Site Monitor
Remote Technical Application Scientist
Research & Evaluation Specialist
Research & Innovation Technical
  Manager
Research Agent
Research Assistant
Research Biologist
Research Chemist
Research Development/Grant Writing

Research Engineer

Research Entomologist

Research Funding Specialist

Research Hydrologist

Research Imaging Specialist

Research Lab Manager

Research Product Development

Research Project Manager

Research Scientist

Research Scientist in Molecular Biology
& Virology

Research Services Coordinator

Research Software Engineering

Research Specialist

Research Support Scientist

Researcher, Linguistic Insights

Risk Analyst

Sales & Marketing & Applications

Sales Biotech Manager

Sales Genomics Manager

Sales Representative

School Advocate/Mathematics Specialist

Science Communication Officer

Science Curator

Science Editor

Science Officer

Science Policy Fellowship

Science Services Manager

Science Writer

Scientific Advisor

Scientific and Technical Officer

Scientific Assistant

Scientific Communications Executive

Scientific Communications Manager

Scientific Consultant

Scientific Director

Scientific Editor

Scientific Innovation Officer

Scientific Manager

Scientific Officer Consultant

Scientific Project Manager

Scientific Researcher

Scientific Reviewer in Publication Support Services

Scientific Sales Representative

Scientific Solutions Consultant

Scientific Strategist

Scientist & Analytical Team Lead

Scientist & Manager of Business Operations

Scientist in Virology & Analytical Development

Scientist of Assay Development

Scientist of Platform Development

Senior AI Engineer

Senior Analyst Human Health Toxicologist

Senior Application Specialist Advanced Staining

Senior Associate Business Analyst

Senior Associate Scientist

Senior Chemical Engineer

Senior Chemist

Senior Consultant

Senior Content Research Associate

Senior Data Scientist

Senior Developer Software

Senior Development Scientist

Senior Engineer

Senior Environmental Engineer

Senior Knowledge Partner

Senior Manager

Senior Manager of Business Operations

Senior Manager of Spinal Muscular
Atrophy

Senior Marketing Specialist

Senior Medical Science Liaison

Senior Packaging R&D Engineer

Senior Physicist

Senior Planetary Scientist

Senior Principal Scientist Manager

Senior Process Engineer

Senior Program Evaluator

Senior Project Associate

Senior Research Scientist

Senior Specialist in Regulatory
Submissions

Senior Systems Performance Engineer

Senior Technical Specialist

Senior Venture Manager

Simulation Engineer

Site Reliability Lead

Social Media Analyst

Software Application Engineer

Software Engineer

Solution Architect

Solution Sales Manager

Solutions Architect

Staff Engineer

Staff Regulatory Specialist

Staff Scientist

Study Design Lead

Study Director

Submission Writer

Support Scientist

Surgical Study Director

Synthetic Organic Chemist

Systems Verification Scientist

Talent Assessment and Analytics
Consultant

Technical & Marketing Writer

Technical Advisor

Technical Business Manager

Technical Marketing Engineer

Technical Project Leader

Technical Sales

Technical Sales Engineer

Technical Sales Manager

Technical Sales Specialist

Technical Service Manager

Technical Support Scientist

Technology Specialist

Technology Transfer Officer

Territory Manager

Toxicologist

Training Experience Manager

Translational Research Project
Administrator

Translational Scientist Liaison

User Experience Researcher

User Experience Scientist

UX Associate

UX Designer

UX Research & Development Associate

Vaccine Lab Scientist

Vaccine Specialist Consultant

Validation Engineer

Validation Scientist

Variant Scientist

Vice President Research

Virology Scientist

Transferable Skills List

. . . .

Flexible and versatile researcher

Superior product and market knowledge

Expertise in performance management

Expertise in change management

Experience in product development

Virtual training expertise

Mentorship expertise

Cross-functional collaborator

Project management expertise

Ability to delegate tasks

Documentation and reporting skills

Budgeting skills

Risk management expertise

Risk mitigation experience

Systemization expert

Knowledge of current industry trends

Financial acumen

Regulatory acumen

Technical literacy

Strong work ethic and initiative

Self-motivated with an ability to work
autonomously

Technical communication skills

Ability to manage stress

Strongly driven to succeed

Dynamic and motivated team member

Fast-paced, dynamic innovator

Ability to work in a collaborative
team-oriented environment

Ability to identify process pain points

Ability to resolve the underlying problems

Ability to assess process challenges

Interpersonal skills

Communication skills

Problem-solving skills

Organizational skills

Talented project manager

Sales and support experience

Ability to work cross-departmentally

Ability to work with external vendors

Ability to assist in project installation

Ability to manage team relationships

Ability to manage client relationships

Talented client relationship manager

Administrative support skills

Administrative experience

Ability to manage project details and tasks

Experience in managing project details and tasks

Research and analysis expertise

Growth-oriented researcher

Ability to work independently and within a team

Ability to exceed expectations

Highly motivated

Process optimization expert

Ability to create new methods and technologies

Ability to enhance productivities and process efficiencies

Time management skills

Ability to manage project timelines

Technical transfer skills

Ability to improve efficiencies

Research and development experience

Experience in platform processes and workflows

Ability to develop new methods

Ability to deepen scientific understanding

Troubleshooting expertise

Ability to work collaboratively and cross-functionally

Ability to manage multiple projects

Ability to work with colleagues in other functional areas

Ability to meet team and company goals

Ability to present scientific data and concepts

Experience reviewing technical reports, protocols, and other key documents

Ability to adhere to corporate standards regarding code of conduct

Knowledgeable in documentation, safety, and the appropriate handling of materials

Strong communication skills

Ability to manage projects and priorities

Experience working with multidisciplinary teams

Ability to manage existing projects

Ability to self-teach

Ability to contribute to a team

Ability to interface with a team virtually or in person

Development and fulfillment leader

Strong communication skills

Ability to prioritize and change priorities

Ability to conduct experiments

Ability to work collaboratively with a team

Ability to build a robust testing plan

Ability to complete reports with a high level of detail

Experience guiding junior team members

Strong understanding of regulatory expectations

Ability to resolve technical issues

Ability to write, edit, and review internal technical reports and SOPs

Strategic planner

Ability to troubleshoot and resolve technical issues

Ability to solve problems in a timely manner

Expert innovator

Curious, imaginative, and dedicated researcher

Strategic visionary

Ability to design and conduct experiments

Expertise in strategic initiatives

Ability to formulate industry-leading solutions

Ability to manage projects internally

Ability to work with clients worldwide

Ability to build solutions proactively

Ability to work professionally with leading minds in the industry

Proactive problem-solver

Ability to drive innovation

Ability to ensure compliance with company and regulatory policies

Multidisciplinary team collaborator

Expertise in systemization and standard operating procedures

Ability to write standard operating procedures

Ability to develop and write procedures

Ability to work with key stakeholders

Energized researcher

Ability to write clinical-study related documents

Technical writing expertise

Scientific and technical writing expert

Understanding of interdependencies of various contributing functions

Ability to quickly assess complex situations

Ability to make key organizational process improvements

Expertise in regulatory submissions

Ability to write clinical regulatory documents

Ability to meet regulatory requirements

Expertise in implementing effective plans for solutions

High-level technical, statistical, and computer skills

Expertise in expediting document preparation

Ability to review tools and automation

Experience reviewing reporting and analysis plans

Strong oral and written communications

Ability to adjust behaviors and priorities based on a changing environment

Appendix C:

Technical Skills List

· ·

In-depth knowledge of XYZ research technique

Expertise in XYZ research technique

Experience in innovative lab technologies such as XYZ technology

Experience with XYZ research platforms, including XYZ platform

Experience in XYZ instruments, including XYZ instrument

Experience in high-throughput systems, including XYZ system

Ability to maintain XYZ instrumentation

Expertise in automated technologies, including XYZ technology

Expertise in XYZ technical processes

Expertise in designing novel processes such as XYZ process

Expertise in XYZ-related data analysis skills

Varying ranges of research knowledge, including knowledge in XYZ technique

With # years professional research experience in XYZ technical field

With strong proficiency and experience in XYZ technical field

Ability to work with and interpret data from XYZ instruments

With expertise in quantitative statistical software packages, including XYZ software package

Experience with qualitative data collection and analysis, including XYZ qualitative method

Experience with multivariate statistical techniques

Ability to complete research projects in XYZ field

Experience with data visualization tools and techniques related to XYZ field

Experience presenting statistical analysis results related to XYZ field

Ability to present data from XYZ experiments

With # years' experience in XYZ research field

With wide-ranging expertise in XYZ discipline

Expertise in XYZ study protocols

Ability to design XYZ experiments

Ability to develop and test questionnaires related to XYZ field

Ability to create XYZ data analysis plans

Expertise in ensuring quality control across XYZ experiments

Ability to interpret study results related to XYX field

Ability to interpret XYZ study results

Expertise in identifying patterns in XYZ study data

Expertise in identifying patterns in XYZ study results

Experience in XYZ high-throughput, automation-based approaches

Ability to develop and characterize XYZ processes

Expertise in programming and implementing XYZ methodologies

Expertise in XYZ automation-based approaches

Ability to investigate, evaluate, and propose solutions in XYZ field

Expertise in the integration and characterization of XYZ devices and systems

Experience in high-throughput data management, including XYZ data visualizations

Ability to assess current state of existing technology in XYZ space

Expertise in handing off XYZ technical information to technical team members

Ability to keep an inventory of XYZ research equipment

Ability to produce time-dependent deliverables for XYZ project deliverables

Ability to evaluate, characterize, and improve on XYZ methodologies

Ability to evaluate, characterize, and improve on XYZ designs

Ability to perform in-depth characterizations of XYZ

Experience in fabrication and assembly of XYZ

Experience with XYZ instrumentation

Expertise in the practical application of XYZ

Ability to develop XYZ-based analytical methods

With an ability to perform XYZ assay optimization

With process development expertise

With process characterization expertise

With in-depth knowledge and advanced experience in XYZ field

Expertise in XYZ and ABC technologies

Ability to perform analytical experiments

Ability to develop and implement XYZ an ABC-based assays

Ability to perform quantification analyses of XYZ-related products

Expertise in platform optimization

Ability to perform XYZ assay validation

Ability to identify and develop XYZ-based analytical methods

Ability to write, edit, and review internal technical reports and SOPs

Ability to conduct XYZ experiments

Ability to characterize XYZ

Ability to perform release and stability testing for XYZ-related products

Experience troubleshooting and resolving XYZ technical issues

Ability to design, code, and test XYZ

With software development expertise in XYZ

Ability to build XYZ software systems

Ability to prototype, test, and release new technologies

Ability to maintain XYZ architecture documentation

Ability to design indexing strategies for XYZ

Expertise in keeping company databases secure

Ability to develop scripts to automate frequent tasks in XYZ field

Ability to support the writing of selected regulatory documents

Ability to work with scientific and clinical project data

Ability to work with licensing authorities

Expertise in matrix organization

Ability to design and deliver high-quality, fit-for-purpose clinical regulatory documents

Ability to design effective protocols for XYZ

Ability to write and submit XYZ reports

Ability to write and maintain XYZ submission documents

Expertise in writing investigator brochures

Ability to write briefing documents

Ability to answer regulatory authority questions

Ability to support documents in XYZ area

Ability to interpret complex clinical data

Expertise in assessing trends and patterns in XYZ data

Appendix D:

Quantified Results List

· ·

- … resulting in # ABC reports.
- … resulting in # poster presentations on ABC topic.
- … resulting in # publications, including a publication in ABC journal.
- … as evidenced by # collaborations, including a collaboration with ABC research group.
- … as evidenced by mentoring # professionals on ABC topic.
- … as evidenced by # ABC documents.
- … as evidenced by # optimized methodologies, including ABC methodology.
- … as demonstrated by # SOPs on ABC topic.
- … resulting in # experiments that led to # discoveries in ABC field.
- … resulting in # discoveries, including ABC discovery.
- … as evidenced by teaching # professionals on ABC topic.
- … as evidenced by teaching # professionals on ABC topic with a #% completion rate.
- … as evidenced by the creation of # methodologies, including ABC methodology.
- … as demonstrated by # SOPs on ABC topic.

- … as evidenced by teaching # professionals on ABC topic with a #% success rate.
- … as evidenced by the innovation of # methodologies, including ABC methodology.
- … as evidenced by the development of # systems in ABC field.
- … resulting in # in grant funding on ABC topic.
- … as demonstrated by the development of # ABC processes.
- … as evidenced by the innovation of # high-throughput experimental procedures in ABC field.
- … as evidenced by the optimization of # ABC systems.
- … as demonstrated by teaching # students, resulting in their completion of the course.
- … as evidenced by volunteering with # organizations in ABC field.
- … leading to the development of # new ABC documentation processes.
- … leading to the design of # new ABC platforms.
- … as evidenced by a cross-functional collaboration with # different labs.
- … leading to # ABC-based discoveries published in # peer-review figures.
- … resulting in # poster presentations at # international conferences.
- … resulting in # cross-departmental seminar presentations, including a well-received presentation on ABC topic.
- … as evidenced by findings in # research presentations.
- … resulting in the completion of # e-courses on ABC topic.
- … as demonstrated by teaching ABC to DEF over the course of # months.
- … leading to the development of ABC system that resulted in # funding.
- … as evidenced by # courses taught on ABC topic to # professionals.
- … as evidenced by ABC technical experience with DEF group to achieve # result.
- … as evidenced by # technical experiences with ABC group.
- … resulting in spearheading # successful scientific projects related to the ABC research techniques.
- … as evidenced by # peer-reviewed publications and # book chapters on ABC topic.
- … leading to the completion of # ABC-related technical documents and # DEF-related presentations.
- … as evidenced by a #% success rate of mentored professionals in ABC field.
- … as demonstrated by # analyses of ABC to answer question DEF.

- … leading to the completion of a PhD in ABC with a focus on DEF in # years.
- … leading to the publication of # scholarly documents.
- … leading to the #% success rate of # mentored students in ABC class.
- … leading to # discoveries presented at # conferences.
- … leading to the presentation of a research talk on ABC to an international community at DEF conference attended by # researchers.
- … leading to the production of # figures on ABC topic.
- … as evidenced by giving # lectures to # students on ABC topic.
- … as evidenced by the design and grading of # tests given to # students in ABC class.
- … leading to the publication of # papers, including # first-author papers.
- … as evidenced by giving # lectures to # students over the course of # months.
- … as demonstrated by the design and use of # ABC programs for # DEF research projects.
- … as demonstrated by the design and use of # programs in ABC software system.
- … as evidenced by # meetings with research advisers for # different research groups.
- … as demonstrated by teaching ABC to # people in DEF location.
- … resulting in # successful collaborations from research groups in ABC field.
- … leading to # simulations for ABC system using software package DEF.
- … as evidenced by the analysis of # experimental data sets using ABC software system.
- … as evidenced by the installation of ABC on DEF operating system in # time.
- … as evidenced by the analysis of a #-year complex data set for ABC study.
- … leading to the completion of # research projects on ABC and DEF topics.
- … leading to the completion of # ABC regulatory documents in # time.
- … leading to the execution of # projects funded by ABC institution.
- … leading to the completion of a #-month project at ABC organization.
- … as evidenced by volunteering with ABC organization to raise # in funds.
- … as evidenced by volunteering with ABC organization to achieve # results.
- … resulting in # poster presentations, including a presentation at ABC conference on DEF topic.
- … resulting in the completion of # technical reports and the publication of # research papers.
- … as evidenced by the review of # research articles for ABC and DEF journals.

- ... as demonstrated by reviewing and editing # research articles for ABC journal.
- ... as evidenced by the review of # student research synopses as ABC member of DEF group.
- ... leading to the discovery of # new ABCs.
- ... as evidenced by the design and presentation of # charts on ABC topic.
- ... as demonstrated by obtaining # scientific grants ranging from # to # amount in ABC currency for progress on # projects on the topic of DEF.
- ... as evidenced by obtaining # travel grants and # awards for ABC.
- ... resulting in # travel grants for ABC.
- ... as evidenced by the completion of # collaborative research projects, including one with ABC organization.
- ... as evidenced by the supervision of # professionals for ABC organization.
- ... as demonstrated by work with teams of # professionals.

LinkedIn® Headline Examples

· ·

R&D Scientist | Molecular Biologist | Environmental Sciences | Cross-Functional Collaborator | Functional Genomics | Sustainable Agriculture| Scientific Writing | Yoga Enthusiast

Data Scientist | Leader | Computational | Chemical | Physicist | Taekwondo Black Belt

Experience Design Researcher | UX | CX | XD | Art Enthusiast

Medical Science Liaison | Science Communicator | Key Opinion Leader Relationship Builder | Oncology | Neurology | Hiking

Product Manager | Poet | Interdisciplinary PhD | Clinical Research Associate | Oncology | Clinical Trials | Disease Strategy Development | Cricket Enthusiast

Management Consultant | Project Management | Materials Scientist | Nanotechnology | Scuba & Skydiver | Gardening

245

Field Applications Scientist | Dynamic Communicator | Accomplished Researcher | Relationship Builder | Travel Enthusiast

Clinical Research Scientist | Neuroscientist | Proteomics | Microscopist | Avid Reader

Informatics Specialist | Patient-Friendly Trials | Clinical Studies | Futurist ENFP

Research Scientist | Cancer Biologist | Molecular Target Discovery | 3D Cancer Organoids | CRISPR | Project Management | Creative Problem-SSolver | Willing to Relocate | Fitness Enthusiast

Program Coordinator | IGO | NGO | Government | Humanities | Leader | Philanthropist | Community Organizer

Data Scientist | Atmospheric Scientist | Python | SQL | Soccer

Translational Research Scientist | Biomedical Sciences | Project Manager | Regulatory Affairs | Yogi

Chemist | Nanomaterials Expert | Process Development | Creative Problem-Solver | Cross-Functional Collaborator | Bookworm

Entrepreneur | Scientist | Leader | Speaker | Philanthropist | Health Enthusiast

Clinical Outcomes Research Scientist | Psychologist | Sociology | Effective Collaborator

Endnotes

1   https://www.nature.com/articles/30831
2   https://www.theguardian.com/higher-education-network/blog/2014/oct/24/
    bullying-academia-universities-stress-support
3   https://www.chronicle.com/article/the-future-of-tenure
4   https://royalsociety.org/~/media/Royal_Society_Content/policy/publica-
    tions/2010/4294970126.pdf
5   https://www.cbsnews.com/news/12-reasons-not-to-get-a-phd
6   https://www.theatlantic.com/business/archive/2013/02/the-phd-bust-americas-
    awful-market-for-young-scientists-in-7-charts/273339/
7   https://www.nature.com/articles/d41586-020-03381-3
8   https://www.nytimes.com/2020/03/05/upshot/academic-job-crisis-phd.html
9   https://www.bostonglobe.com/metro/2014/10/04/glut-postdoc-research-
    ers-stirs-quiet-crisis-science/HWxyErx9RNIW17khv0MWTN/story.html
10 https://policyoptions.irpp.org/magazines/july-2019/the-phd-employment-
    crisis-is-systemic/
11 https://www.nature.com/articles/nature.2016.21084
12 https://www.weforum.org/agenda/2016/01/the-10-skills-you-need-to-thrive-in-
    the-fourth-industrial-revolution
13 https://www.census.gov/library/stories/2019/02/number-of-people-with-
    masters-and-phd-degrees-double-since-2000.html

14 https://www.glassdoor.com/employers/blog/50-hr-recruiting-stats-make-think

15 https://sidsavara.com/wp-content/uploads/2008/09/researchsummary2.pdf

16 https://ncses.nsf.gov/pubs/nsb20202

17 https://www.investopedia.com/terms/s/sp500.asp

18 https://www.jobscan.co/blog/fortune-500-use-applicant-tracking-systems/; https://www.jobscan.co/blog/8-things-you-need-to-know-about-applicant-tracking-systems/; https://www.forbes.com/sites/jacquelynsmith/2013/04/17/7-things-you-probably-didnt-know-about-your-job-search/?sh=387e03be3811

19 https://www.pewresearch.org/fact-tank/2021/09/21/who-doesnt-read-books-in-america

20 https://business.linkedin.com/talent-solutions/recruiter

21 https://www.hrdive.com/news/it-managers-say-wrong-skills-interpersonal-issues-are-signs-of-bad-hires/530309

22 https://www.talent-works.com/; https://blog.careerbeacon.com/sorry-team-players-need-not-apply

23 https://www.shrm.org/ResourcesAndTools/hr-topics/technology/Pages/Study-Most-Job-Seekers-Abandon-Online-Job-Applications.aspx; https://www.prweb.com/releases/2015/03/prweb12603990.htm

24 https://comfyliving.net/reading-statistics/

25 https://theundercoverrecruiter.com/infographic-recruiters-spend-5-7-seconds-reading-your-cv

26 https://www.glassdoor.com/employers/blog/50-hr-recruiting-stats-make-think

27 https://www.hrdive.com/news/eye-tracking-study-shows-recruiters-look-at-resumes-for-7-seconds/541582

28 https://www.theladders.com/static/images/basicSite/pdfs/TheLadders-EyeTracking-StudyC2.pdf

29 https://www.theladders.com/static/images/basicSite/pdfs/TheLadders-EyeTracking-StudyC2.pdf

30 https://www.freewordcloudgenerator.com/

31 https://money.usnews.com/money/blogs/outside-voices-careers/articles/2017-05-05/how-headhunters-use-linkedin-to-find-talented-candidates/

32 https://www.wsj.com/articles/microsoft-to-acquire-linkedin-in-deal-valued-at-26-2-billion-1465821523

33 https://www.linkedin.com/sales/ssi

34 https://www.statista.com/chart/17535/linkedin-profile-boosts-job-chances

35 https://pixabay.com; https://www.pexels.com/royalty-free-images

36 https://www.ncbi.nlm.nih.gov/books/NBK84226

37 https://www.bizjournals.com/news/technology/startups

38 https://aom.org/research/journals/journal

39 https://www.nytimes.com/2013/01/28/business/employers-increasingly-rely-on-internal-referrals-in-hiring.html

40 https://www.ere.net/10-compelling-numbers-that-reveal-the-power-of-employee-referrals

41 https://www.thebalancecareers.com/what-are-employee-referral-bonuses-2062988

42 https://www.scientificamerican.com/article/the-neuroscience-of-everybody-favorite-topic-themselves

43 https://www.nature.com/articles/nj7435-137a

44 https://www.wsj.com/articles/SB10001424127887323386960457836873343736 46820

45 https://www.icims.com/en-gb/solutions/hire-talent/

46 https://theundercoverrecruiter.com/infographic-recruiters-spend-5-7-seconds-reading-your-cv

47 https://theundercoverrecruiter.com/infographic-how-interviewers-know-when-hire-you-90-seconds

48 https://www.theladders.com/career-advice/how-are-you-today-top-7-interview-answers

49 https://www.sciencedirect.com/science/article/abs/pii/S1053482209000382

50 https://danschawbel.com/promote-yourself/

51 https://www.ccl.org/

52 http://workforcesolutionsgroup.com/; https://business.time.com/2013/11/10/the-real-reason-new-college-grads-cant-get-hired

53 https://www.weforum.org/agenda/2016/01/the-10-skills-you-need-to-thrive-in-the-fourth-industrial-revolution

54 https://www.pnas.org/content/107/32/14425

55 https://www.medicalnewstoday.com/articles/326140

56 https://www.ncbi.nlm.nih.gov/pmc/articles/PMC4445577/

57 https://scottberkun.com/the-books/confessions-of-a-public-speake/

58 https://rh-us.mediaroom.com/2018-02-05-Starting-Salary-Negotiable-or-Not

59 Salary.com; PayScale.com; Glassdoor.com

60 https://www.amazon.com/Cracking-Hidden-Job-Market-Opportunity/dp/158008494X

A free ebook edition is available with the purchase of this book.

To claim your free ebook edition:

1. Visit MorganJamesBOGO.com
2. Sign your name CLEARLY in the space
3. Complete the form and submit a photo of the entire copyright page
4. You or your friend can download the ebook to your preferred device

Print & Digital Together Forever.

Snap a photo

Free ebook

Read anywhere